The Norman Geras

MANCHESTER
1824

Manchester University Press

The Norman Geras Reader

'What's there is there'

Edited by
BEN COHEN and **EVE GARRARD**

Manchester University Press

The right of Ben Cohen and Eve Garrard to be identified as the editors of this work has
been asserted by them in accordance with the Copyright, Designs and Patents Act 1988.

Published by Manchester University Press
Altrincham Street, Manchester M1 7JA
www.manchesteruniversitypress.co.uk

British Library Cataloguing-in-Publication Data
A catalogue record for this book is available from the British Library

ISBN   978 1 5261 0385 7 *hardback*
ISBN   978 1 5261 0386 4 *paperback*

First published 2017

The publisher has no responsibility for the persistence or accuracy of URLs for any
external or third-party internet websites referred to in this book, and does not guarantee
that any content on such websites is, or will remain, accurate or appropriate.

Typeset in Minion with Rotis display by
Koinonia, Manchester
Printed in Great Britain by
CPI Group (UK) Ltd, Croydon CR0 4YY

Contents

Notes on contributors

Ben Cohen is a writer and media strategist based in New York City. His essays and articles on politics and international affairs have been published by *The Wall Street Journal, Commentary, Haaretz, Tablet Magazine, The Tower Magazine, Fathom* and many other outlets. Cohen also writes a weekly syndicated column on Jewish affairs. During his undergraduate degree at the University of Manchester, he studied with Norman Geras.

Eve Garrard is an Honorary Research Fellow in the Department of Philosophy at the University of Manchester. Her main research interests are in moral theory and bioethics, and in philosophical issues related to the Holocaust. Before joining Manchester she lectured at Keele University, and worked for several years for the Open University. She has a special interest in teaching philosophy to beginning students. She has published various papers on the nature of evil and of forgiveness, and co-edited *Moral Philosophy and the Holocaust* (Ashgate, 2002) with Geoffrey Scarre. She co-authored, with David McNaughton, *Forgiveness* (Acumen, 2010). She also co-edited, with Stephen de Wijze, the festschrift for Norman Geras, *Thinking Towards Humanity* (Manchester University Press, 2012). She has published on antisemitism in the online journal *Fathom* (see 'The Pleasures of Antisemitism', *Fathom*, Summer 2013, and 'Anti-Zionism, Anti-Judaism, Anti-Semitism' in *Fathom*, Winter 2015). She is currently working on further papers on forgiveness and evil.

Terry Glavin has worked as a reporter, columnist and editor for a variety of newspapers and is presently a columnist with the *National Post* and the *Ottawa Citizen*. His assignments in recent years have taken him to Afghanistan, Israel, the Russian Far East, the Eastern Himalayas, Iraq, Syria, Turkey, Jordan, Geneva, China and Central America. He is the author of seven books and the co-author of three. His books have been published in Canada, Germany, the United States and the United Kingdom. He has won more than a dozen literary and journalism awards. Glavin's most recent book is *Come from the Shadows: The Long and Lonely Struggle for Peace in Afghanistan*.

Alan Johnson is the editor of the journal *Fathom: for a Deeper Understanding of Israel and the Region.* He was a professor of democratic theory and prac-tice at Edge Hill University before joining the Britain Israel Communica-tions and Research Centre (BICOM), an independent research centre, in 2011 as Senior Research Fellow. He founded and edited *Democratiya*, a free online journal of international politics from 2005 until its incorporation in 2009 into *Dissent* magazine, where he served on the editorial board. He was a co-author of the 2006 'Euston Manifesto', a modern statement of social demo-cratic anti-totalitarianism, and in 2007 he edited *Global Politics after 9/11: The Democratiya Interviews.* His essays on Rosa Luxemburg, Hal Draper, Etienne Balibar, Richard Rorty, Slavoj Žižek, and other left-wing thinkers have appeared in *Radical Philosophy, Historical Materialism, Dissent, New Politics, Jacobin* and many other academic and non-academic journals.

Introduction:
'What's there is there'

Ben Cohen and Eve Garrard

A first word about the title of this anthology. The phrase 'what's there is there' is taken from a 13 May 2009 blogpost by Norman Geras on the subject of Karl Marx's antisemitism. Many Marxists have been, at best, unwilling to deal with these less savoury aspects of Marx's thought and character. But, as Geras noted, 'The only reason for not facing up to these things is to protect Marx's reputation as a thinker. But this is not a good reason, because it's no protection; what's there is there.'

That observation might be said to encapsulate the approach of Norman Geras as a general rule. Much of his work involved significant dissent from the Marxist tradition in which he located himself, precisely because unvarnished honesty prevented him from glossing over the many troubling ideas and notions that, simply, are there. This openness, in our view, is one of the key reasons why Geras's extensive writings should be introduced to a wider audience seeking to understand not just past evolutions of political thought but their relevance to the extraordinary shifts now taking place in the twenty-first century.

Indeed, Geras's acute awareness of where these shifts were headed on the political left – the moral relativism that brooked no difference between the Ba'athist tyranny in Iraq and the democratic republic that is the United States, an increasing stench of antisemitism, a growing tendency to turn to conspiracy theories as a means of explanation – led him, during the last decade of his life, to dedicate more of his time and energy to blogging, alongside his academic endeavours.

When Normblog launched, on 28 July 2003, it did so with a bang: posts on Iraq, on other bloggers, quotations from Christopher Hitchens, lists of favourite movies – all prefiguring the steady flow of political, philosophical, literary, argumentative, meditative, satirical, and just plain funny posts that would go on to define its output. But ten years later, after thousands of posts, and with hundreds of thousands of readers, Normblog was abruptly shuttered. The very final entry, dated 18 October 2013, was a single paragraph posted by Geras's daughter, Jenny. 'I am very sad to announce that Norm died in Addenbrooke's hospital in Cambridge in the early hours of this morning,' Jenny Geras wrote. 'Writing this blog, and communicating with all his readers, has brought him an enormous amount of pleasure in the last ten years. I know that since writing here about his illness earlier in the year he received a lot of support from many of you, and that has meant a great deal to him, and to us, his family.'

The news was not unexpected. As his close friends and colleagues were painfully aware, Geras's cancer had recently taken a turn for the worse. As the internet lit up with homages to Geras and his writings, the sense of grief was palpable. Above all, there was widespread regret, even a kind of anger, at the realisation that Norman Geras, a writer and thinker with so much more to say, had been abruptly silenced.

For a good fortnight after Geras passed away, tributes appeared in all sorts of publications, from the small blogs that venerated Normblog as a model of the blogging medium to the major newspapers like *The Guardian* and *The Times*. One group of writers announced themselves on Twitter with the handle 'The Gerasites'. Another group carefully assembled the tributes paid to Geras on a website entitled 'Normfest'. It was heartening, especially for his family, to observe that the camaraderie and warmth that accompanied Geras during his life was also present at his premature death at the age of seventy.

It was during this period that the idea for this anthology first crystallised. From different vantage points – Eve Garrard had worked closely with Geras, including several guest contributions on Normblog, while Ben Cohen had studied with him at Manchester University during the late 1980s – we both came to the same conclusion: there was room for, and indeed a need for, a volume which illustrated the continuity between his academic writings, begun in earnest during the 1970s, and his later contributions on politics and culture that were shared principally on Normblog. The presentation of that continuity by way of a selection of some of Geras's best work, in all the fields that interested him, is what we have set out to achieve in this anthology.

Geras was a prolific writer from the outset of his career. Much of his work in the 1970s concerned itself with debates within Marxism, ranging from original insights into the Marxian economic concept of 'fetishism' through to the relationship between socialism and democracy as carried through the revolutionary activism of the German Jewish Marxist Rosa Luxemburg. His later work, which occupies the main focus of this anthology, turned to the common threads between Marxism and liberalism, and the ways in which Marxism might be enriched by an endorsement of core liberal values. (A special introduction to the Marxism section in this anthology, by Geras's co-author on the 2006 Euston Manifesto, Alan Johnson, explains and explores the complicated evolutions in Geras's attitude to Marxism.)

In a trenchant critique of political theorists Ernesto Laclau and Chantal Mouffe published in 1987 in the *New Left Review*, on whose editorial board he served for several years, Geras pronounced, 'If Marxist thought now stands against rather than for a necessary grasp of social complexity, that is more easily put across by presenting as Marxism what is less than Marxism, nothing but a wretched travesty in fact' (emphasis added). At the same time, and in keeping with his understanding of Marxism as a rich tradition more than capable of interpreting social complexity, Geras began engaging with the broader themes that were to inform his later work: human nature, specifically Marx's conception of it; justice, examined both historically and philosophically in the context of the Holocaust; the duty to bring aid to those suffering terrible oppression, particularly at the hands of the state; and perhaps most importantly of all, the common ground between Marxism and liberalism.

In the introduction to 'Solidarity in the Conversation of Humankind', his imagined dialogue with the American philosopher Richard Rorty, Geras addressed this last point simply and explicitly. '[I]t is the values Rorty espouses that engage me and which have encouraged this effort of response,' he wrote. 'That may surprise some people, since he describes himself as a liberal or, on occasion, a social democrat, whereas I have been my adult life, and remain, some kind of Marxist. But I mean here Rorty's values, and not his overall political outlook.'

This willingness to draw out the good in liberalism from a Marxist standpoint was one key reason for the distinctiveness of Geras's approach to modern political theory. By the time that he started writing seriously about the philosophical and moral issues undergirding the themes that would later define Normblog – such as the idea of universal human rights, or the imperative to prevent authoritarian regimes from behaving with extreme cruelty – his readers could clearly sense the outlines of an anti-authoritarian version of Marxist thought.

The end of the Cold War was quickly followed by spasms of genocidal violence from the Balkans to central Africa, along with the rise of Islamism as a political and military force in the Middle East. In the light of these developments, Geras turned to the topic of humanitarian intervention: the delivery of aid, up to and including the use, if necessary, of military force, to prevent serial evils like the ethnic and religiously targeted massacres that have defined the gruesome civil war in Syria. He saw this duty to help as a moral requirement, writing, 'there is a moral basis for such duties of human solidarity, and that one principal reason why we should acknowledge the duty to help those in need is that the alternative is to recognise that when we ourselves are suffering or in need, others owe us nothing'.

It was that commitment to the moral basis of human solidarity that defined Geras's work in the latter part of his life, and which therefore occupies the greatest part of this anthology. Developed through a sustained engagement with the febrile political debates at the turn of the twenty-first century, during

which the bulk of the left remained wedded to the morally blind anti-imperialist politics that first took shape in the late 1960s, Geras again sounded a
unique tone, giving critical support to the wars against the Taliban in Afghanistan and Saddam Hussein's Ba'athist regime in Iraq, calling out the antisemitism that stained a disturbingly large volume of leftist interventions on the
conflict between the Palestinians and Israel, and helping to chart an alternative
course for that part of the left that understood the grave danger to human
security presented by the survival of corrupt and authoritarian rulers in the
post-colonial world.

The most definitive statement of this intellectual and political current in his
thought took the form of the 2006 'Euston Manifesto', included in this volume.
Drafted by Geras and a number of co-thinkers, the manifesto was named in
honour of the area of London where Geras and his colleagues gathered. In
keeping with the tradition of a left that does not shy away from comradely
disagreement on critical issues, not all the Eustonites were in complete agreement with each other. As Stephen De Wijze, a colleague and close friend of
Geras's, observed in a conversation with the editors, those who composed the
Manifesto 'strongly disagreed among themselves about the wisdom of going to
war against Saddam. However, what they did agree upon was the urgent need
to confront a warped "progressive" moral landscape employed by significant
parts of the anti-imperialist left to support tyranny in the name of fighting
imperialism.'

In some ways, Normblog was an extension of this viewpoint, a day-to-day
record of the arguments and disputes that rocked the left during and immediately after the era of George W. Bush and Tony Blair. It also demonstrated,
in concise and conversational language, how Geras, as a Marxist, took on the
shibboleths of the postmodern left, and in particular the relativism whose
malign influence he had noted when writing his book on Marx's conception
of human nature.

But Normblog was also much more. There were regular features that were
more tangentially related to politics, which his readers loved, such as the
weekly interviews with other bloggers, in which his subjects were asked to list
their influences, their favourite songs, their purpose for writing and much else.
The blog was also a platform for Geras's love of literature, and especially the
novels of Jane Austen. Highlights of these writings are included here, chosen
by an impromptu committee which pored over a decade of Normblog entries
to come up with this selection. Doubtless, there will be readers unhappy that
their own favourite Normblog entries are not featured here. That, it can be said,
is a testament to the depth and diversity of Normblog (which remains online
at normblog.typepad.com.)

The years since Geras's passing in 2013 have offered little of encouragement
to his manner of interpreting the world. Human solidarity as a motivational

principle in international affairs has been shunted aside by a realist aversion to the project of 'nation-building'. Antisemitism has continued to rise in Europe, symbolised most grotesquely by the Islamist terror attacks against institutions and people belonging to a community, the European Jews, that makes just 10 per cent of the global Jewish population of 15 million. In the democratic world, classically liberal approaches to government have been seriously challenged by protectionist and nativist forces on both sides of the Atlantic.

On the level of emotion, that perhaps explains why the loss of Norman Geras was taken so personally by his admirers: simply put, we need his distinctive voice and he is no longer there.

This century has already been buffeted by powerful reactionary tendencies that have consumed politics on a global scale, with a very notable lack of the kind of human solidarity and protection of human rights for which Geras steadfastly argued. Hence the opportunity to present Geras's humane and closely argued views on the critical subjects which organise this volume is one which, we feel, can only do good.

Our profound thanks are due to a number of individuals without whom this anthology would not have been possible. First and foremost, we wish to record our gratitude to Adèle Geras, Norm's wife, as well as his daughter Jenny. We are also grateful to Terry Glavin and Alan Johnson for their introductions and commentary to the various sections of this anthology, and to Stephen De Wijze and Nick Cohen for their support and insights. The selections from Normblog were made by the editors along with Adèle and Jenny Geras, Eamonn MacDonagh, Damien Counsell and Norm's old friend and companion at the home games of Manchester United, Morris Sheftel. We are indebted to all of them. We extend our warmest thanks as well to Aaron Wilson for preparing the index to this volume. We are especially grateful to John Garrard and Aline, Jonah and Samuel Cohen for their love and support as we assembled this volume. Geras disliked editorial interference with his work, and we have not sought to impose consistent styles on the notes, or on the bibliography, which was compiled by him.

The true reward of this anthology, we emphasise, lies in Geras's own writings. Readers who wish to consult his works in full will find them listed in a comprehensive bibliography at the end of this anthology.

PART I

Marxism and liberalism

On Geras's Marxism

Alan Johnson

an unwavering commitment to the goal of anti-capitalist social transformation, a transparent sense of humanity and a conception of democracy informed by vital liberal assumptions. This is a combination still to be commended, I believe, today.

Norman Geras, 2002[1]

In a body of work marked by the meticulous exegesis, scrupulous critique and creative development of the classical Marxist tradition, Norman Geras established himself as the twentieth-century Marxist theoretician we need most in the twenty-first century. Why? Three reasons: few understood better that the core of classical Marxism was its theory of human self-emancipation; few were better able or more willing, none the less, to critique the obstacles to self-emancipation, the footholds for authoritarianism within the very same tradition; and fewer still understood that Marxism needed to negotiate articles of conciliation (not surrender) with liberalism if all those obstacles were to be overcome.

A popular and democratic Marxism

'The principle of self-emancipation', wrote Geras in 1971, 'is central, not incidental, to historical materialism.' Armed with that insight, he proceeded to excavate from the Marxist tradition some precious theoretical resources to serve a democratic and self-emancipatory socialism, resources that had been buried by Stalinism and scorned by social democratic reformism: foremost among these was an appreciation of the creative power of mass popular struggle. That appreciation could hardly be more relevant today when things are once again 'kicking off all over', to use the title of a book by the broadcaster and writer (and former Trotskyist) Paul Mason. There are few better accounts of the intimate relation between 'the widest and deepest mobilization of the masses' on the one hand, and the achievement of social progress and human self-emancipation on the other, than the writings of Norman Geras, two supreme examples being 'The Mass Strike' and 'The Literature of Revolution', his reflections on the thought of Rosa Luxemburg and Leon Trotsky respectively.

Marx's principle of human self-emancipation is simple enough: the muck of ages – poverty and exploitation, violence and oppression – will be sloughed off not from above by an elite but from below by 'the self-conscious, independent movement of the immense majority, in the interest of the immense majority'. However, the immense majority can only become 'fit to rule' through a practical education punctuated by popular struggles. Many of Geras's writings are concerned with fidelity not merely to Marx's principle but to the critical investigation of its theoretical status and the practical conditions of its realisation, from questions of political organisation and socialist strategy to the ethics of revolutionary violence.

Geras returned again and again to the theme of untrammelled democracy as the only possible political form in which that practical education could take place and human self-emancipation be secured. One of the essential strands of the legacy of Rosa Luxemburg, he insisted, was precisely her appreciation of 'the vital importance of elementary democratic rights as instruments for the self-emancipation of the working class', and her understanding that if people really are to work out their own liberation then they need 'the most extensive, thoroughgoing, "unlimited" democratic rights and liberties'.

An anti-authoritarian Marxism

But Geras was no mere celebrant of classical Marxism. He tracked down to their theoretical lairs a series of disabling anti-democratic and illiberal tendencies that lurked within Marxism itself and undermined the principle of self-emancipation: among them, an elitist conception of the relation between party and class, a tendency to insouciance about 'bourgeois' democratic rights, a failure to properly think through the ethics of revolutionary violence and a dogmatic rejection of the very idea of a biological human nature. In each case, Geras tried to separate the disabling tendency or reactionary impulse from what he believed were deeper, truer impulses to human emancipation within the tradition, and to trace the historical conditions and political consequences of the error. (He was willing to deal in notions of truth and error, not able to see how either the pursuit of knowledge or the pursuit of justice could proceed without those notions.)

For example, he showed why those Marxists, such as Althusser and Marcuse, who treated people as mere dupes, 'the total objects of their circumstances', stood at odds to the principle of self-emancipation, for each had to rest their strategy for the transition on what Marx called 'the old crap': the need for an authoritarian Legislator to liberate from above the poor befuddled masses down below. And Geras knew where forcing people to be free ended up.

Geras even showed how the conceptions of democracy and political representation in the thought of his heroes, Trotsky and Luxemburg, were deficient in some important senses. In his essays 'Classical Marxism and Prole-tarian Representation' (1981) and 'Democracy and the Ends of Marxism' (1994) he moved from highlighting the huge strengths of both thinkers to alerting us to those lacunae and errors in their thought that inadvertently offered points of support to authoritarianism. In the case of Trotsky, Geras pointed out that the error was not always inadvertent. He argued that the Old Man had badly lost his way from 1919 to 1921 when he defended the Communist Party's right to 'assert its dictatorship even if that dictatorship temporarily clashed with the passing moods of the workers' democracy'. Geras, then himself a militant in the British section of Trotsky's Fourth International, insisted that that 'amounted to an explicit violation of the principles of socialist democracy'.

And, famously, Geras showed us there was explanatory and normative significance for a self-emancipatory politics in the fact that 'Marx did not reject the idea of human nature', adding that 'he was right not to do so'. It is not easy to convey to people what a brave (and liberating) move this was at the time in Marxist circles where the dismissal of any kind of human nature, and crucially, therefore, any serious notion of human limit, was routine.

A liberal Marxism

Later, and in relative solitude, Geras did much to work out the shape of arti-cles of conciliation (not surrender) between Marxism and liberalism. I believe he came to see that the immanent critique of Marxism of the kind he had mounted himself, drawing on the resources of Marxism, while still vital, was not enough. Not all the resources needed were there, not all the gaps could be filled. Marxism had 'elements that are wanted', i.e. lacking, and liberalism possessed some resources that were needed. So we Marxists, he thought, must be willing to put ourselves into 'liberalism's more advanced school', when it is more advanced, and study its 'rich and impressive philosophical literature on the subject of justice'. More: while the name of his desire, human self-eman-cipation, did not change, he framed it now as – this happy phrase is his – a 'minimum utopia'. We had to settle for that given the nature of 'that most complex being'. 'Any feasible conception of progress today', he wrote, 'needs to come to terms with the likely persistence of some of the less pleasant tenden-cies and potentialities that are lodged within the characteristic make-up of human beings.' He remained committed to self-emancipation, but he had a more critical and realistic understanding of what made up the self, and what the self was capable of, for good and ill.

However, he never allowed his sharper awareness of our 'less pleasant tendencies and potentialities' to form part of what he lambasted as the Great Moving Right Show. His 'minimum utopia' may no longer have been the world revolution envisaged by the first four congresses of the Third International, but it was still nothing less than a new civilisation: a revolutionary rupture with the entire culture of dog-eat-dog possessive individualism he despised – a culture for which we might use the term neoliberalism. His book *The Contract of Mutual Indifference: Political Philosophy after the Holocaust* (1998) included a stinging indictment of liberalism as a culture which *underwrote* that contract, licensing possessive individualism and bystanding.

Even as Geras opened up new lines of traffic with liberalism, he was scrupulous in his defence of Marxism against criticisms that he saw as careless or ignorant ploys to reduce and traduce the tradition and its thinkers. He famously assailed seven types of obloquy in a brilliant essay in *The Socialist Register*. And in a coruscating series of exchanges in the *New Left Review* with the political theorists Ernesto Laclau and Chantal Mouffe, Geras comprehensively criticised their reduction of the Marxist tradition to a crude economic necessitarianism – 'ex-Marxism without substance', he called it.

A Gerasian Marxism?

In his careful survey 'The Marxism of Norman Geras', Professor David McLellan thinks that late Geras sometimes sounded 'more like Bernstein than Luxemburg'.[2] And indeed he did. We moved from proletarian self-emancipation to human emancipation, and from class interest towards ethical universalism as defining the socialist goal; the idea of socialism as being historically guaranteed, never significant to him at any time, had long gone, and a crop of 'vital liberal assumptions' were now firmly ensconced somewhere near the centre of his Marxism.

But if Geras sometimes sounded like Eduard Bernstein, he also still sounded much of the time like Rosa Luxemburg. Am I reading into Norman what I want to find there if I say that part of his legacy is precisely to suggest to us what it would be to mediate between those two great social democrats? Perhaps. But then, perhaps not. Geras refused to let go of two profound insights he drew from the democratic revolutionary socialist Rosa Luxemburg: that, simply put, and in her words, 'the masses are the decisive factor' when it comes to social change, and that the historic choice we face is still what she said it was: 'socialism or barbarism'. I think it was while holding fast to those truths that Geras opened up new lines of communication with a liberal socialism that many identify with Eduard Bernstein. And Norman could have led us to many worse places than that. From there we can set out again.

By way of a final word, this good news: those willing to really study the essays of Norman Geras will secure for themselves a genuine, old-fashioned, honest-to-goodness *education*! In a field routinely disfigured by needlessly recondite writing, Geras's essays on Marxism are models of clarity and intelligence; reading them, one is given every opportunity not just to grasp his argument but to grasp what argument *is*, not just to see his reasoning but to learn *how* to reason. I was lucky enough to be Norman's student in the early 1980s and a few of us read his book *Marx and Human Nature* in draft form. He shared it with us because we were all Trotskyist militants in those days, and he was genuinely interested in what we thought of it. (To be taken that seriously at that age is quite something. Three decades later, when the two of us co-wrote, with others, the Euston Manifesto, reproduced in this volume, I was still in awe of him.) I recall now my feeling about *Marx and Human Nature*. I have felt it often after reading Norman Geras's writing. It was the joy one feels when the clouds part, the sun shines and the meaning and importance of theory becomes not just clear but part of one's own flourishing. For those who have not yet read Geras-as-Marxist, that joy awaits.

Notes

1 From 'Marxism, the Holocaust and September 11: An Interview with Norman Geras', *Imprints*, Vol. 6, No. 3, 2002–3.
2 David McLellan, 'The Marxism of Norman Geras', in Stephen De Wijze and Eve Garrard (eds), *Thinking Towards Humanity* (Manchester University Press, 2012); pp. 27–43.

1

Human nature and historical materialism

(Chapter 3 of *Marx and Human Nature: Refutation of a Legend*, Verso/NLB, London, 1983)

It is surely remarkable that so many have discerned, with the emergency of the materialist conception of history, a dismissal by Marx of the idea of human nature. *The German Ideology*, after all, setting down that celebrated conception for the first time, expressly criticizes the mistake of those who, ignoring what it terms the 'real basis of history', thereby exclude from the historical process 'the relation of man to nature', create an 'antithesis of nature and history'.[1] It might be thought that, for Marx, this antithesis is mistaken only with respect to external nature, and not also with respect to nature as something inherent in humanity. But it is easy to show that this is not the case. Marx includes such an inner, human nature squarely within the 'real basis of history'.

In fact, *The German Ideology* at one point echoes a passage from *The Holy Family* just in emphasizing nature's internal as well as external dimensions. In both works, the intent behind the emphasis is a materialist one, a 'double' natural constraint being insisted upon in opposition to themes which are manifestly idealist. In *The Holy Family*, Marx accuses Bruno Bauer of †sublimating 'all that affirms a *finite* material existence *outside infinite self-consciousness*' and, hence, of combating nature – 'nature both as it exists *outside* man and as man's nature'. Bauer, Marx also says, does not recognize 'any *power of human nature* distinct from *reason*'.[2] In the passage from *The German Ideology*, it is Christianity, rather, that is the object of criticism:

> The only reason why Christianity wanted to free us from the domination of the flesh and 'desires as a driving force' was because it regarded our flesh, our desires as something foreign to us; it wanted to free us from determination by nature only because it regarded our own nature as not belonging to us. For if I myself am not nature, if my natural desires, my whole natural character, do not belong to myself – and this is the doctrine of Christianity – then all determination by nature – whether due to my own natural character or to what is known as external nature – seems to me a determination by something foreign, a fetter, compulsion

used against me, *heteronomy as opposed to autonomy of the spirit* ... Christianity
has indeed never succeeded in freeing us from the domination of desires ...'[3]

The resemblance between the passages is striking enough not to have to
be laboured. Affirming certain natural determinants, both exploit the same
linguistic device, separating nature as a whole into what is external to man
and man's own. Both thereby refer to a 'nature' human beings possess in virtue
precisely of nature, not of the 'particular form of society'; thus to a make-up
that, relative to particular social forms, is enduring and general, a human
nature in our sense. As we shall see, this sort of materialist usage of it – of
'power(s) of human nature', 'natural desires' (more often: 'needs'), 'natural
character' – plays an important, *explanatory* role in the formulation of Marx's
theory of history.

However, *The Holy Family* is also echoed by *The German Ideology* in a second,
normative usage of the same idea. In some familiar lines from the former of
these works, Marx had spoken of the proletariat's indignation at its abasement,
'an indignation to which it is necessarily driven by the contradiction between
its human *nature* and its condition of life'.[4] *The German Ideology* describes the
proletarian similarly: as one 'who is not in a position to satisfy even the needs
that he has in common with all human beings'; one whose 'position does not
even allow him to satisfy the needs arising directly from his human nature'.[5]
For the way in which they conflict with the needs of a common human nature,
the social relations responsible for the proletarian position and condition are
here implicitly condemned.

These similarities in the two works may serve to give us our bearings. In the
sequence of Marx's writings, the *Theses on Feuerbach* come between *The Holy
Family*, composed in late 1844, and *The German Ideology*, begun during the
autumn of 1845 and discontinued the following summer. *The Holy Family* is an
'early' work; in other words, it antedates historical materialism. That it makes
reference to human nature will surprise no one, since it is well-known that the
concept is to be found in Marx's early writings. *The German Ideology*, on the
other hand, itself proposes the theory of historical materialism. Whether or
not the virtually identical references that it makes to human nature surprise
anyone, they are *prima facie* testimony to a continuity of thought exactly where
the sixth thesis is alleged to mark a rupture.*

The German Ideology, like the *Theses*, remained unpublished during Marx's
lifetime, but too much should not be made of this. For two years he and Engels
tried hard to get it published, and failed.[6] Although in the event not completed,
then depleted by the criticism of the mice and other vicissitudes, it is the most

---

* Editors' note: Geras is discussing the sixth of Marx's eleven *Theses* on the German philosopher
  Ludwig Feuerbach, in which Marx describes 'the essense of man' as 'the ensemble of the social
  relations'.

reliable guide we have to the ideas its authors at this time wished to put forth.*

If a clue is needed to difficulties in the *Theses*, it is as likely as anything is to provide one since, written only shortly after them, it manifestly shares and enlarges upon their preoccupations, its most interesting and important section being given over partly to critical remarks about Feuerbach. Of course, this work is only an initial, hence somewhat rough, statement of historical materialism. But it is more relevant than anything written later to deciphering the meaning of the sixth thesis, and we shall be able to see in any case how things stand with Marx's subsequent works.

In *The German Ideology*, as well as the similarities with *The Holy Family* just observed, we find indeed the crux of the present question. Let us examine one passage, the best known amongst several like it and occurring, be it noted, not just in the same work as, but right in the thick of, the presentation of Marx's new conception of history. There is a formulation in it that is nearly identical in character to the central formulation of the sixth thesis. Where this one differs from that, however, is in being implanted within a context better indicative of what it might, and also of what it cannot, mean.

> This mode of production must not be considered simply as being the reproduction of the physical existence of the individuals. Rather it is a definite form of activity of these individuals, a definite form of expressing their life, a definite *mode of life* on their part. As individuals express their life, so they are. What they are, therefore, coincides with their production, both with *what* they produce and with *how* they produce. Hence what individuals are depends on the material conditions of their production.[7]

The mode of production is said here to be the form in which individuals express their life, which form is said in turn to bear intimately on what they are. What individuals are is declared, in consequence, to coincide with their mode of production, and it is this, the penultimate statement of the passage, that is the crucial one. Despite the terminological variation, its tendency is substantially the same as that of the third sentence of the thesis. Obviously, 'what individuals are' is quite near, in the entity it denotes, of their 'nature', and that it is stated in this case to coincide with, rather than just be, the mode of production is itself a difference of little significance. Whether we have that what individuals are *coincides with*[8] their mode of production or that man's 'nature' is the ensemble of social relations, either way we have a relationship that is very close but whose content is otherwise somewhat vague, in need of clearer definition. In fact these are only two of a whole family of similar formulations that Marx was disposed to use at about this time. I shall introduce further of its members in due course.

---

* Editors' note: Geras is referring here to Marx's acerbic remark, in the introduction to 'A Contribution to the Critique of Political Economy', that he and Engels had abandoned a manuscript to the 'gnawing criticism of the mice'.

In the present instance, we find clues to what the formulation might mean in its immediate context. Just before it, there is the idea that in the mode of production individuals express their life in a certain way and, according as they do so, what they are. Perhaps the penultimate sentence here is meant only to round off what has gone before, affirming such a relation of expression between mode of production and what individuals are. It would then resemble (2) above,* that man's 'nature' is manifested in the ensemble of social relations. Alternatively, perhaps its meaning is explicated in what directly follows it, the assertion of a relation of dependence. On that assumption, if we take the dependence – of what individuals are upon the conditions of production – as being anything short of a total and exclusive one, then we have an idea similar to (1) above, that the nature of man is conditioned by the social relations. With neither suggestion would the formulation under scrutiny evidence any rejection of a human nature. However, *could* Marx plausibly be thought to have intended it as a rejection? Whether because he meant by it to reduce what individuals are to their mode of production, or because he did indeed have in mind a relation of total dependence, or whatever? Could he, *here*, be taken as having meant something like (3)? No, he could not. He could not, because in the very same place in this work, as direct preamble to the quoted passage, use is made of precisely a concept of human nature. Not only that; this use shows it to be fundamental rather than incidental to the historical conception being proposed. It is fundamental to historical materialism in the exact sense of being a part of its theoretical foundation.

What precedes the excerpt I have already quoted is this:

> The first premise of all human history is, of course, the existence of living human individuals. Thus the first fact to be established is *the physical organization of these individuals* and their consequent relation to the rest of nature. Of course, we cannot here go either into *the actual physical nature of man*, or into the natural conditions in which man finds himself – geological, oro-hydrographical, climatic and so on. *All historical writing must set out from these natural bases* and their modification in the course of history through the action of men.[9]

Italics in this passage are mine but notice the emphasis that is original to it: the 'first' fact to be established; again, one of the natural 'bases' from which historical research must 'set out' – man's physical constitution. Then, lest anyone should think to dissipate what is so plainly given here as a point of departure,

---

* Editors' note: Earlier in *Marx and Human Nature*, Geras summarises three variations of Marx's conception of human nature: '(1) In its reality the nature of man is conditioned by the ensemble of social relations. (2) In its reality human nature, or the nature of man, is manifested in the ensemble of social relations. (3) In its reality the nature of man is determined by, or human nature is dissolved in, the ensemble of social relations.' The numbers (1), (2), (3) above refer to these definitions. Geras adds that 'the idea behind each is similar enough to justify considering them together'. See p. 46 of *Marx and Human Nature*.

by leaning on the last phrase about its 'modification', the text at once goes on to associate with this basic physical make-up a quite general human attribute, an attribute indeed, cited by Marx as specifically, distinctively human: 'Men can be distinguished from animals by consciousness, by religion or anything else you like. They themselves begin to distinguish themselves from animals as soon as they begin to *produce* their means of subsistence, a step which is conditioned by their physical organization.'[10] Only after this – a notion of human nature if such there be – do we come to the congruence we have just now seen asserted between what individuals are and a particular *mode* of production.

The identical pattern of thought is found in more compressed form at other points in *The German Ideology*. Also right in the midst of the exposition of historical materialism, there is Marx's observation, 'Men have history because they must *produce* their life, and because they must produce it moreover in a *certain* way: this is determined by their physical organization; their consciousness is determined in just the same way.' I shall digress for a moment to comment that since, hard by in the text, consciousness is identified thus with language: 'Language is as old as consciousness, language *is* practical, real consciousness that exists for other men as well, and only therefore does it also exist for me';[11] we have confirmation of the hypothesis, formulated earlier apropos of language, that Marx could perfectly well have recognized certain capacities as inherent in the natural constitution of the individual whilst urging in the strongest terms the social dimension of them. Now, let us articulate the pattern of thought ascertained. It may be put as follows: if diversity in the character of human beings is in large measure set down by Marx to historical variation in their social relations of production, the very fact that they produce and that they have a history, he explains in turn by some of their general and constant, intrinsic, constitutional characteristics; in short by their human nature. This concept is therefore indispensable to his historical theory. It contributes to founding what he gives out in the theory as the material basis of society and history. To reformulate the point in the terms that have been used throughout this essay: if the nature of man depends upon the ensemble of social relations, it does not depend wholly on them, it is conditioned but not determined by them, because they themselves depend on, that is, are partly explained by human nature, which is a component of the nature of man.

One further example of this train of thought before we proceed. Elsewhere Marx again alludes to those powers of human beings that are distinctively human, in saying that 'the production, as well as the satisfaction, of [their] needs is an historical process, which is not found in the case of a sheep or a dog'. At the same place, in the sequel to this, he goes on in a vein now surely familiar:

> The conditions under which individuals have intercourse with each other... are conditions appertaining to their individuality, in no way external to them; conditions under which alone these definite individuals, living under definite

relations, can produce their material life and what is connected with it, are thus the conditions of their self-activity and are produced by this self-activity. The definite condition under which they produce thus corresponds… to the reality of their conditioned nature, their one-sided existence…'[12]

Observe the form of the last assertion. Before we had coincidence, now we have correspondence, between the actuality of individuals and the conditions of their production. Here as there, the context licenses the interpretation that the character of individuals is conditioned by the latter; it might, perhaps, license the interpretation that in the conditions of production – these being for their part 'produced by this self-activity' of the individuals – their character is in some sort manifested. However, here as there, there can be no excuse for reading the formula as a reductionist one, dismissive of human nature.

In the way of an anthropology implicated in Marx's materialist conception, we have so far encountered the idea of general human capacities or powers: in the first place that of production, but also language, as embodying human consciousness. *The German Ideology* also contains much about individuals' needs. These it explicitly assimilates at one point to their 'nature', when it states that 'their *needs, consequently their nature*, and the method of satisfying their needs' have always bound them into relations with one another.[13] It would be consistent with the argument of this essay concerning an innate human nature if Marx, then, had something to say about universal or permanent human needs, and so he does. Once more the foundational character of it is as clear as can be. Beyond those needs implicit in the statement just mentioned, namely, sexual, under the rubric 'relations between the sexes', and the social one itself – as it is expressed elsewhere, 'the need, the necessity, of intercourse with other men', 'that men need and *always have needed* each other'[14] – there is also this, in a recurring phrase 'first premise … of all history':

> Men must be in a position to live in order to be able to 'make history'. But life involves before everything else eating and drinking, housing, clothing and various other things. The first historical act is thus the production of the means to satisfy these needs, the production of material life itself. And indeed this is an historical act, a fundamental condition of all history, which today, as thousands of years ago, must daily and hourly be fulfilled merely in order to sustain human life … Therefore in any conception of history one has first of all to observe this funda-mental fact in all its significance and all its implications and to accord it its due importance.

The Germans, so we are told, have not done this but the French and the English have begun to, to give historiography 'a materialistic basis' in the first histories of civil society and industry.[15]

So we see what putting the study of history on a 'materialistic basis' here connotes: not 'anthropology's theoretical pretensions … shattered'[16] and so forth, but taking fully into account the enduring imperative of essential human needs. As if the point were still wanting in emphasis, Marx afterwards reiterates that responding to this imperative is, together with the creation of new needs and the propagation of the species, one of 'three aspects of social activity … which have existed simultaneously since the dawn of history today'.[17] Much the same idea is encompassed also in the reference, at another place, to 'desires which exist under all relations, and only change their form and direction under different social relations', the sex instinct and need to eat being cited in this connection; as contrasted with 'those originating solely in a particular society, under particular conditions of [production] and intercourse'.[18]

Essential human needs fulfil not just a theoretical function in the argument of *The German Ideology*, explanatory along with man's general powers of the productive infrastructure of human society. As befits Marx's revolutionary standpoint, they possess an overtly practical implication too, serving as a norm of judgment and of action. Thus, for example, the same needs as figure in elaborating the aforesaid first premise of all history figure equally as preconditions of human liberation. Dismissing speculative notions of this, Marx writes, '… it is possible to achieve real liberation only in the real world and by real means … in general, people cannot be liberated as long as they are unable to obtain food and drink, housing and clothing in adequate quality and quantity'.[19] Similarly, the necessity of social revolution is justified in the light of basic human needs in the following stricture which is directed specifically at Feuerbach:

> He gives no criticism of the present conditions of life. Thus he never manages to conceive the sensuous world as the total living sensuous *activity* of the individuals composing it; therefore when, for example, he sees instead of healthy men a crowd of scrofulous, over-worked and consumptive starvelings, he is compelled to take refuge in the 'higher perception' and in the 'ideal compensation in the species', and thus to relapse into idealism at the very point where the communist materialist sees the necessity, and at the same time the condition, of a transformation both of industry and of the social structure.[20]

Instead of healthy men … people whose need for rest and need for food are insufficiently met, their health wanting. This is in line with the normative usage of human nature already attested, adverse judgment upon social conditions which fail the very needs common and intrinsic to humankind, adverse because they fail them. Noticeable in the excerpt, moreover, is a certain kinship with the *Theses on Feuerbach*. Its second assertion descends directly from both the first and the fifth of them, whilst the initial sentence is a clear echo of something in the sixth thesis itself. But the relationship is closer still than that and more relevant to our present concern. For, just prior to the lines quoted, Feuerbach is criticized in these terms, cognate beyond all possible doubt or cavil with the matter of the sixth and the seventh theses: '… because he still remains in the realm of theory and conceives of men not in their given social connection, not under their existing conditions of life, which have made them *what* they are, he never arrives at the actually existing, active men, but stops at the abstraction "man"...'.[21] As it is their social conditions, according to this, that make men what they are, it too might have been seen perhaps as evidence of a denial of human nature. Only, we know from the sequel that what they have made them in the particular case is sick, and also overworked and hungry, all of which evokes needs that human beings do not owe to 'their given social connection' but merely to their natural constitution as human beings, even if they do owe it to the former that these needs are not more amply satisfied.

We must conclude that the 'making' in question here is conditioning, in our sense, of the nature of man; that the above criticism of Feuerbach is the mild one and not the stern, qualification not rejection of the postulate of an inherent human make-up; that it is criticism only for treating this in isolation from the effects worked on man by the given historical milieu (hence: he *stops at* the abstraction 'man'). We may take note also of the conception: the sensuous world *as* the sensuous activity of the individuals composing it; which may be suggested to resemble at least somewhat that of man's 'nature' as manifested in the ensemble of social relations. And as such are Marx's meanings in this passage on Feuerbach, it seems probable that such too was his intent in the sixth thesis, so obviously related to it. I submit in any case that this is getting to look ever more probable than interpretations (3). If, out of everything either stated or implied by Marx in this connection, we now make a schedule of general human needs, then so far we have these: for other human beings, for sexual relations, for food, water, clothing, shelter, rest and, more generally, for circumstances that are conducive to physical health rather than disease. There is another one to be added to them before we leave *The German Ideology*, the need of people for a breadth and diversity of pursuit and hence of personal development, as Marx himself expresses these, 'all-round activity', 'all-round development of individuals', 'free development of individuals', 'the means of cultivating [one's] gifts in all directions', and so on.[22] Some will doubtless want to contest the generality of such a need. However, it is there in the work irrespective of anyone's assessment of it and my purpose for the moment is only exegesis. Marx does not, of course, take it to be a need of survival, as for example nourishment is. But then, besides considering the survival needs common to all human existence, he is sensible also, as we have already seen, of the requirements of 'healthy' human beings and of what is 'adequate' for 'liberated' ones; he speaks too of conditions that will allow a 'normal' satisfaction of needs.[23] These epithets plainly show that, for all his well-known emphasis on the historical variability of human needs, he still conceives the variation as falling within some limits and those not just the limits of a bare subsistence. Even above subsistence level, too meagre provision for, equally repression of, certain common needs will be the cause of one kind and degree of *suffering* or another: illness or disability, malnutrition, physical pain, relentless monotony and exhaustion, unhappiness, despair. The requirement, as Marx sees it, for variety of activity has to be understood in this sense, precondition not of existence as such but of a fulfilled or satisfying, a joyful, one.

Just see how he talks about neglect of the need in question. He talks of 'subjection of the individual under the division of labour' and of an exclusive sphere of activity as 'forced upon him';[24] of labour as 'unbearable' for the worker, deprived of 'all semblance of self-activity' and, again, 'forced upon him';[25] of the worker himself as 'sacrificed from youth onwards'.[26] Labour is said only to sustain the life of individuals 'by stunting it' and the existing social relations to be responsible for 'crippling' them[27] – a 'physical, intellectual and social crippling and enslavement' this, one of whose aspects is the 'suppression' of artistic talent in most people as a consequence of the division of labour.[28] Throughout history hitherto, according to Marx, 'some persons satisfied their needs at the expense of others, and therefore some – the minority – obtained the monopoly of development, while others – the majority – owing to the constant struggle to satisfy their most essential needs, were for the time being (i.e., until the creation of new revolutionary productive forces) excluded from any development'.[29] This is not the language of a belief that the nature of man depends simply upon the historically given form of society but a language of some tension between them, and its premise, manifestly, the frustration of enduring human needs.

That ends my argument from *The German Ideology*. We have seen there: explicit references to a human nature; usage of the concept that is integral to Marx's new theory of history, being of a fundamental explanatory kind; usage equally of a normative kind; and some part of the substance of his idea of human nature, certain general human characteristics, both capacities and needs. We have seen moreover, passages bearing a resemblance to the sixth thesis, and I have tried to show that they support my interpretation (1) and maybe also (2) but nowise the contested interpretation (3). Having begun thus by going forward in time from the *Theses on Feuerbach*, I want next to go back from them, to things written just the year before. This may sound at first to be a rather pointless exercise, since those who contend Marx broke with all idea of a human nature generally locate the break from 1845 onwards. In the circumstances, what could writings of 1844 possibly disclose? They disclose in fact matter of the greatest relevance: a veritable *reductio ad absurdum* of the tradition that the concise central formula of the sixth thesis – of all things, Marx's formula associating man's 'nature' with the ensemble of social relations – is proof and expression of that conceptual break.

For the truth is that the passages which are closest to this laconic affirmation, which most resemble it in form, inflection, emphasis, these passages actually predate it. They belong precisely to Marx's early writings. We encountered in *The German Ideology* assertions to the effect that what individuals are, their reality, *coincides* or *corresponds* with their mode, or with their conditions, of production, or else is what their conditions have *made* them; and I proposed a substantial similarity between this sort of assertion and the third sentence of the thesis. In earlier texts, however, the similarity of substance is complemented by an identify of form as Marx puts forward, exactly in the manner of the sixth thesis, that now man, now man's 'nature', now the individual simply *is* society or the community or the social whole. To claim of the passages in which he does this that *they* are denials of human nature would be absurdity indeed. For one thing, they wear it upon their face that they are not. For another, which is explanation of the first, they coexist with the entire conception of human nature known to pervade the early writings, sitting cheek by jowl with ideas of alienation and human emancipation that depend on it. In exhibiting these several passages, I call attention yet again to the support that is provided for (1) and (2) as ways of construing the sixth thesis.

The first of them is from the *Contribution to the Critique of Hegel's Philosophy of Right. Introduction:* 'Man makes religion, religion does not make man. Religion is the self-consciousness and self-esteem of man who has either not yet found himself or has already lost himself again. But *man* is no abstract being encamped outside the world. Man is *the world of man*, the state, society. This state, this society, produce religion, an *inverted world-consciousness*, because they are an *inverted world*.'[30] The point of departure, as in the sixth thesis, is religion and it is stated, as in the seventh, to be a social product. One and the same context therefore, and lo and behold: *But man is no abstract being* (Wesen) … *Man is the world of man … society* – one and the same thought as well beyond any question. The reminder is perhaps appropriate that it is in this *Introduction* that Marx makes the following, somewhat 'humanist' declaration: 'To be radical is to grasp the root of the matter. But for the man the root is man himself … The criticism of religion ends … with the *categorical imperative to overthrow all relations* in which man is a debased, enslaved, forsaken, despicable being.'[31]

Now here is an extract from Marx's Paris notebooks, from his *Comments on James Mill*: 'Since *human* nature is the *true community* of men, by manifesting their *nature* men *create*, produce, the *human community*, the social entity, which is no abstract universal power opposed to the single individual, but is the essential nature of each individual, his own activity, his own life, his own spirit, his own wealth.'

A few lines further on, it is said again of this community: 'Men, not as an abstraction, but as real, living, particular individuals, *are* this entity. Hence, *as they are, so is this entity itself*.'

And shortly after that, there is reference to: 'The *community of men*, or the manifestation of the nature of *men*, their mutual complementing the result of which is species-life …'.[32] Thus, man's 'nature' and the social entity are identified repeatedly, with the former, quite explicitly here, held to be manifested in the latter.

The themes of these excerpts from Marx's notebooks then recur in the *Economic and Philosophical Manuscripts*. One passage there distinctly echoes the first excerpt: 'Above all we must avoid postulating "society" again as an abstraction *vis-à-vis* the individual. The individual *is the social being*. His manifestations of life – even if they may not appear in the direct form of *communal* manifestations of life carried out in association with others – *are* therefore an expression and confirmation of *social life*.'

What follows recalls, in turn, the second one: 'Man much as he may therefore be a *particular* individual (and it is precisely his particularity which makes him an individual, and a real *individual* social being), is just as much the *totality*.'[33]

It so happens, in other words, that this type of formulation comes very freely from Marx's pen before 1845 and evidently without signifying renunciation of the idea of human nature. What reason, then, is there for thinking that exactly the same type of formulation suddenly becomes in the *Theses on Feuerbach*, the expression of just such a renunciation? There is an argument due to (the late French philosopher Louis) Althusser which might be offered in response to the question but it fails here. It is that every theoretical element – formula, assertion or concept – takes its significance only from the wider conceptual field which it inhabits. Within two different 'problematics', elements that are ostensibly similar may diverge in meaning. However, for this reasoning to be applicable in the present case, it is not enough that, as is demonstrable, a new theory emerges in Marx's work from 1845. In addition we must already know the theory to contain material permitting the inference that he now dispenses with assumptions of human nature. But as things stand, we do not *already* know this. It is what is in question.

Marx's characterization of man's 'nature' in the sixth thesis is itself supposed to be the evidence for it, remember. Once we have shown what poor evidence that is by displaying its continuity with a group of similar formulations in the early writings, mere gesturing towards the notion of the 'problematic' cannot restore its credentials. It would require something rather more cogent, substantive evidence *from* the wider conceptual context, to establish that this apparent continuity is actually a discontinuity and a species of assertion hitherto perfectly compatible with the assumption of a human nature now contradicts it flatly. The wider context of Marx's famous characterization of man's 'nature' is formed, in the first instance, only by a few brief notes, the rest of the *Theses on Feuerbach*. There is nothing in them that could prove there has been this abrupt change of meaning. And we have already seen what happens when we look further afield to the work that directly follows. We are left, therefore, with a nice irony, in the circumstances of this discussion: the formula cited with such facility and frequency as revealing Marx's repudiation of his youthful belief in the existence of a human nature has the clearest possible pedigree precisely in the writings of his youth.

I have no quarrel, incidentally, with the view that the developments which do occur in Marx's thought around 1845 are of a decisive importance. The theoretical ensemble that begins to take shape then, by tradition 'historical materialism', outweighs in intellectual fertility and power, as well as in its political consequence, the content of the early writings. Althusser's proposal of the *epistemological break* had the merit of focusing upon this when it needed emphasis, in face of a widespread tendency to promote the early at the expense of the later writings, a Marxist ethic at the expense of Marx's theory, his humanism at the expense of his scientific and political achievement. However, nobody is obliged by the alternative simplicities, 'One Marx or two?' The real picture is of a theoretical development marked in places by genuine novelty and change, but marked equally by some stability of conception, by definite continuities and strong ones. Its details are amenable to careful study. Besides rendering a worthwhile service, the epistemological break also carried with it a lot of excess doctrinal baggage and some bad intellectual habits. A whole obscurantism of the 'problematic' enabled the discovery in Marx of concepts, novelties – the latest Parisian fashions – positions, discontinuities, that simply are not there. Amongst such 'absent presences' is his alleged break with every general anthropology. In truth, there is a continuity here: he subscribed to the supposition of a common human nature from beginning to end. I finish the demonstration of this by moving now beyond the immediate textual environment of the *Theses* to works of a later period.

The products of Marx's maturity, in particular *Capital* and the writings most closely related to it, provide ample reinforcement of virtually everything that has been set out above. It would be tedious and is unnecessary to go through at length. My case is in essence already made, the rebuttal of (3) as an interpretation of the sixth thesis having deprived the standpoint which I contest of its only presentable support. At this stage, it will be sufficient if we just confirm that the broad lines of what has been established run on into Marx's subsequent works.

To begin with, there is still the overt talk of a human nature in our sense. One instance of it, part of some unfavourable comment on Jeremy Bentham, is the following:

> To know what is useful for a dog, one must investigate the nature of dogs. This nature is not itself deducible from the principle of utility. Applying this to man, he that would judge all human acts, movements, relations, etc. according to the principle of utility would first have to deal with human nature in general, and then with human nature as historically modified in each epoch. Bentham does not trouble himself with this. With the driest naiveté he assumes that the modern petty bourgeois, especially the English petty bourgeois, is the normal man.[34]

It could be no clearer surely, a distinction pretty well matching the one used here throughout and Bentham accused in the light of it, but of generalizing arbitrarily and not for the idea itself of a general human nature; accused indeed of failure to explore what human nature is in a serious way. A second instance – the normative usage this time – concerns Marx's distinction between the realm of necessity and the realm of freedom. Referring to the former, the sphere of material production, he writes: 'Freedom in this field can only consist in socialized man, the associated producers, rationally regulating their interchange with nature, bringing it under their common control, instead of being ruled by it as by the blind forces of nature; and achieving this with the least expenditure of energy and under conditions most favourable to, and worthy of, their human nature.'[35]

Another instance involves the division within nature that we encountered earlier. Marx speaks of wealth, stripped of its bourgeois form, as the 'full development of human mastery over the forces of nature, those of so-called nature as well as of humanity's own nature'; and he links this to something else we have already encountered, namely the 'absolute working-out of [man's] creative potentialities', with 'the development of all human powers as such the end in itself'.[36] The same idea recurs in a defence of Ricardo: 'production for its own sake means nothing but the development of human productive forces, in other words the *development of the richness of human nature as an end in itself*.[37] And by contrast there is repeated allusion to this 'nature', seat of potentialities and powers, as setting also certain natural *limits* – on the productivity of labour, on the length of the working day, at the lower end of the value of labour-power.[38]

Besides references to human nature of a direct kind, all the complementary theoretical matter gathered from *The German Ideology* also persists. If there is no longer any exact counterpart of the type of formulation exemplified by the third sentence of the sixth thesis and with which the writings close to the *Theses* are replete, there is still, time and again, the assertion of at least a part of its central point. The human being is a social being, 'not merely a gregarious animal, but an animal which can individuate itself only in the midst of society'.[39] It is not uncommon, of course, to treat this very insistence upon man's sociality, in historicist fashion, as repelling any assumption of a human uniformity. But that is the simplest of logical errors. Whatever degree of historical variation the thought may imply, it is itself a *generalization about human nature*. As a caution against historicist responses to it, it is worth drawing attention to a visibly naturalist, some will doubtless say even 'vulgar materialist', dimension of this thought. In the chapter on 'Co-operation' in *Capital*, Marx puts forward the view: 'Apart from the new power that arises from the fusion of so many forces into a single force, mere social contact begets in most industries a rivalry and a stimulation of the "animal spirits", which heightens the efficiency of each individual worker … This originates from the fact that man, if not as Aristotle thought a political animal, is at all events a social animal.'[40] A little further on, he repeats this – that the combination of individuals 'raises their animal spirits'

– as one amongst several aspects of 'the productive power of social labour', of the fact that the worker, cooperating with others, 'strips off the fetters of his individuality, and develops the capabilities of his species.'[41]

Amongst such capabilities of the human species, the first place in Marx's interest continues to be occupied by production. It is a human universal, its universality expressed in terms both of possibility and of necessity. As possibility, it is labour-power, 'the labour-power possessed in his bodily organism by every ordinary man', 'the aggregate of those mental and physical capabilities existing in the physical form, the living personality, of a human being.'[42] These, 'the natural forces which belong to his own body, his arms, legs, head and hands',[43] man sets in motion in the labour process and the labour process is itself a necessity. It is 'a condition of human existence which is independent of all forms of society; it is an eternal natural necessity which mediates the metabolism between man and nature, and therefore human life itself.'[44] It is, again, 'the universal condition for the metabolic interaction between man and nature … common to all forms of society in which human beings live.'[45] And it distinguishes the species. 'We presuppose labour', Marx writes, 'in a form in which it is an exclusively human characteristic' and, contrasting it with 'those first instinctive forms of labour which remain on the animal level', he emphasizes, in the famous comparison of the architect and the bee, its purposiveness or intentionality, the conscious regulation of the mode of activity according to ends that are conceived in advance.[46] Equally, the 'use and construction of instruments of labour, although present in germ among certain species of animals, is characteristic of the specifically human labour process.'[47] The elements of this process, materials, instruments and the worker's activity, Marx describes as 'immutable natural conditions' and 'absolute determinations of *human* labour as such, as soon as it has evolved beyond the purely animal.'[48]

What we find in the later writings with respect to this human power, the faculty of production, we find also with respect to man's needs – confirmation of the position previously expounded. There is the same conceptual conjunction that was noted in *The German Ideology*, in the form now, 'my needs … my own nature, this totality of needs and drives',[49] and consonant with our case that for Marx the individual's 'nature' incorporates a constant, a human nature as defined, there are needs once more of a permanent and general kind. They appear under various headings, 'natural needs', 'physically indispensable means of subsistence', 'physical needs', on the one hand; but also 'social requirements', on the other.[50] To be sure, the first sort are said to vary with climatic and other circumstances and the second to be conditioned by the 'level of civilization'. Yet a certain generality of needs remains intact for all that, and as before we may make a schedule of them, this one a little more elaborate than the first: food, clothing, shelter, fuel, rest and sleep; hygiene, 'healthy maintenance of the body', fresh air and sunlight; intellectual requirements, social intercourse, sexual needs in so far as they are presupposed by 'relations between the sexes'; the needs of support specific to infancy, old age and incapacity, and the need for a safe and healthy working environment ('space, light, air and protection against the dangerous or the unhealthy concomitants of the production process' – otherwise the 'five senses ... pay the penalty').[51]

Such needs determine the universal 'metabolism' between man and nature and constitute an element in the value of labour-power; they establish the upper limit on the length of the working day and account for the portion of surplus labour which must always be performed on behalf of those incapable of working. In addition, however, to what they are called upon by Marx to explain, their normative function in his mature work is as prominent as ever. Whatever else it is, theory and socio-historical explanation, and scientific as it may be, that work is a moral indictment resting on a conception of essential human needs, an ethical standpoint, in other words, in which a view of human nature is involved. Is it really possible to doubt or overlook this in face of the clear, persistent, passionate discourse of *Capital*? We read there of the 'horrors' and the 'torture' and the 'brutality' of overwork;[52] of capital's 'robbery' and 'theft', within the labour process, of the most elementary prerequisites of the worker's health, 'the absence of all provisions to render the production process human, agreeable or at least bearable';[53] that the search for economy here is 'murderous' – hence of industrial 'horrors' surpassing those in Dante's Inferno – and that capital also 'usurps' and 'steals' the time for meeting other vital needs,[54] and of 'necessities of life' insufficient to satisfy the mass of the people 'decently and humanely', 'overcrowded habitations, absolutely unfit for human beings', 'vile housing conditions', 'accumulation of misery', 'physical and mental degradation'.[55] We read of capital's lack of concern for the 'normal maintenance' of labour-power, of concern solely for its maximum expenditure, 'no matter how diseased, compulsory and painful it may be';[56] of a 'shameless squandering', a 'reckless squandering', a 'laying waste and debilitating' of labour-power, a laying waste thereby of 'the natural force of human beings';[57] and of 'the prodigious dissipation of the labourer's life and health' by a mode of production 'altogether too prodigal with its human material'.[58] Marx describes the lot of the workers as requiring 'ceaseless human sacrifices' and as a 'martyrology'.[59] The increase of wealth under capitalism he describes as being brought about 'at the expense of the individual human being'.[60]

Extant amongst his preoccupations, finally, is 'the worker's own need for development': therefore the time available for 'the free play of the vital forces of his body and his mind'; '*scope* for the development of man's faculties'; and a variety of pursuits – for 'a man's vital forces ... find recreation and delight,' Marx says, in 'change of activity'.[61] Of course, time, scope and variety do not necessarily mean the absence of all effort and are not in fact proposed by him in that sense. The expenditure of labour-power, he contends, is 'man's normal life-activity', some work and 'suspension of tranquillity' a need, the 'overcoming of obstacles … a liberating activity'. Genuinely free work can require 'the most intense exertion'.[62] However, this is self-determining exertion and conceived as part of a breadth of individual development. From the *Communist Manifesto*, with its well-known phrase concerning 'the free development of each' and 'the free development of all', to the *Critique of the Gotha Programme*, which canvasses 'the all-round development of the individual',[63] that preoccupation of Marx's is manifested in writings of directly programmatic import and, as for his theoretical writings, they are fairly strewn with the signs of it: 'artistic, scientific etc. development' and 'full development' and 'free intellectual and social activity' of the individual;[64] 'free activity … not dominated by the pressure of an extraneous purpose' and 'that development of human energy which is an end in itself',[65] 'a society in which the full and free development of every individual forms the ruling principle' and an education, correspondingly, of 'fully developed human beings'.[66] In these expressions and others like them, Marx envisages a better life for human beings. Simultaneously, in a language and imagery of suffering, oppression, incompletion and impairment, he seeks to depict a long and ongoing experience of deficiency, one more category of unfulfilled human need. Thus, exploited and externally imposed, labour is 'repulsive', a 'torment', 'slavery'.[67] In the capitalist division of labour, 'hideous' or 'monstrous' in its forms,[68] the worker is 'annexed for life by a limited function' – a single faculty developed 'at the expense of all others' – 'crippled … through the suppression of a whole world of productive drives and inclinations', crippled in 'body and mind' and attacked 'at the very roots of his life', 'bound hand and foot for life to a single specialized operation', 'riveted to the most simple manipulations'.[69] There is a 'suppression of his individual vitality, freedom and autonomy' and of 'the many-sided play of the muscles'.[70] Transformed from an early age into a 'mere machine for the production of surplus-value', or having to be 'a part of a specialized machine', a 'living appendage' of it, the worker is distorted – into 'a fragment of a man'.[71]

Notes

1 Karl Marx and Fredrick Engels, *Collected Works* (CW) London, 1975, Vol. 5, p. 55.
2 CW, Vol. 4, p. 141.
3 CW, Vol. 5, p. 254
4 CW, Vol. 4, p. 36.
5 CW, Vol. 5, p. 289.
6 See David McLellan, *Karl Marx: His Life and Thought*, London, 1973, p. 151.
7 Ibid.
8 The German is 'fallt zusammen mit'.
9 CW, Vol. 5, p. 31.
10 Ibid.

11 CW, Vol. 5, pp. 43–44.
12 CW, Vol. 5, p. 82; 'the reality of their conditioned nature' translates 'ihrer wirkli-
    chen Bedingtheit'.
13 CW, Vol. 5, p. 437; 'needs' is italicized in the original – the remaining emphasis is
    mine.
14 CW, Vol. 5, pp. 44, 57.
15 CW, Vol. 5, pp. 41–42.
16 See n. 13 above.
17 CW, Vol. 5, p. 43.
18 CW, Vol. 5, p. 256. This is from a passage crossed out in the manuscript; but it is
    legitimate to draw on it in so far as it only confirms what can be established inde-
    pendently.
19 CW, Vol. 5, p. 38.
20 CW, Vol. 5, p. 41.
21 Ibid.
22 CW, Vol. 5, pp. 255, 439, 78.
23 CW, Vol. 5, pp. 255, 256.
24 CW, Vol. 5, pp. 64, 47.
25 CW, Vol. 5, pp. 74, 87, 79.
26 CW, Vol. 5, p. 79.
27 CW, Vol. 5, pp. 87, 425.
28 CW, Vol. 5, pp. 432, 394.
29 CW, Vol. 5, pp. 431–432.
30 CW, Vol. 3, p. 289.
31 Ibid.
32 Ibid.
33 Ibid.
34 Karl Marx, *Capital*, Vol. I (Penguin edition), Harmondsworth, 1976, pp. 758–759.
35 Karl Marx, *Capital*, Vol. III, Moscow, 1962, p. 800.
36 Karl Marx, *Grundrisse*, Harmondsworth, 1973, p. 488.
37 Karl Marx, *Theories of Surplus Value*, Moscow, 1968–72, Vol. II, pp. 117–118.
38 *Capital*, Vol. I, pp. 647, 664, 526–527; *Capital*, Vol. III, p. 837.
39 *Grundrisse*, p. 84; and cf. *Capital*, Vol. I, p. 144 n.
40 *Capital*, Vol. I, pp. 443–444.
41 *Capital*, Vol. I, p. 447.
42 *Capital*, Vol. I, pp. 135, 270.
43 *Capital*, Vol. I, p. 283.
44 *Capital*, Vol. I, p. 133.
45 *Capital*, Vol. I, p. 290; and cf. 'Results of the Immediate Process of Production',
    printed as an Appendix to this volume, p. 998 [Editors' note: 'this volume' – i.e.
    Capital, Vol. I].
46 *Capital*, Vol. I, pp. 283–284, 287, 290; cf. here, incidentally, CW, Vol. 1, pp. 166–167.
47 *Capital*, Vol. I, p. 286.
48 'Results of the Immediate Process of Production', pp. 1021–1022.
49 *Grundrisse*, p. 245.
50 *Capital*, Vol. I, pp. 275, 277, 341; cf *Capital*, Vol. III, p. 837.

51 Except for the last item, this list is constructed from *Capital*, Vol. I, pp. 275, 341, 375–376, 621; *Capital, Vol.* III, pp. 826, 854. For the last item, see: *Capital*, Vol. I, pp. 552–553, 586, 591; *Capital*, Vol. III p. 86.
52 *Capital*, Vol. I, pp. 345, 381, 599.
53 *Capital*, Vol. I, pp. 553, 591, 599; *Capital*, Vol. III, p. 86.
54 *Capital*, Vol I, pp. 592, 356, 375–376.
55 *Capital*, Vol. III, p. 252; *Capital*, Vol. I, pp. 813, 799, 381.
56 *Capital*, Vol. I, p. 376.
57 *Capital*, Vol. I, pp. 517, 591, 618, 638; *Capital*, Vol. III, p. 793.
58 *Capital*, Vol. III, p. 86.
59 *Capital*, Vol. I, pp. 618, 638.
60 'Results of the Immediate Process of Production', p. 1037.
61 *Capital*, Vol. I, pp. 772, 375, 460; *Theories of Surplus Value*, Moscow, 1968, Vol. III, p. 256.
62 *Capital*, Vol. I, p. 138; *Grundrisse*, p. 611.
63 CW, Vol. 6, p. 506; *Selected Works*, Moscow, 1969, Vol. 3, p. 19.
64 *Grundrisse*, pp. 706, 711; *Capital*, Vol. I, p. 667. And cf. *Grundrisse*, pp. 158, 708; *Capital*, Vol. I, p. 618; *Capital*, Vol. I, p. 618 ; *Capital*, Vol. III, p. 854
65 *Theories of Surplus Value*, Vol. III, p. 257; *Capital*, Vol. III, p. 800.
66 *Capital*, Vol. I, pp. 739, 614; and cf. p. 638
67 *Grundisse*, p. 611; *Capital*, Vol. I, p. 799; 'Results of the Immediate Process of Production', p. 989; *Theories of Surplus Value*, Vol. III, p. 257.
68 *Capital*, Vol. I, pp. 547, 614.
69 *Capital*, Vol. I, pp. 469, 474, 481, 484, 614, 615.
70 *Capital*, Vol. I, pp. 638, 548.
71 *Capital*, Vol. I, pp. 523, 547, 614, 799.

2

'That most complex being'

(Chapter 2 of *Solidarity in the Conversation of Humankind: The Ungroundable Liberalism of Richard Rorty*, Verso, London, 1995)

The centrality of arguments about human nature to social and political theories is a familiar theme to students of the subject. Such arguments may be of an affirmative kind, asserting some given characteristic or behaviour pattern as generally or typically human. Nearly as often perhaps they will be self-consciously negative, denying there is anything of substance to be brought usefully under the heading of 'human nature'. In addition to explicit assertion and counter-assertion of this kind, there are usually also, informing any theoretically elaborated view about politics or society, some less overt, less considered assumptions in the matter.

One philosopher who expresses himself emphatically about human nature, and whose works have attracted wide interest, is Richard Rorty.[*] Rorty is, on the face of it, attached to the second of the two generic standpoints just described: he denies any intrinsic or universal human nature. The denial is part of a broader commitment, to what he commends at one point as 'a generalized anti-essentialism'.[1] But that is on the face of it. Closer analysis reveals a more complicated picture. In what follows I explore Rorty's various usages on the question of human nature and the tensions and anomalies as I shall argue they display.

Rorty is an astute and provocative as well as influential thinker. Detailed attention to his work may need no greater justification than that. All the same, the sort of conceptions to be explored here are of a more general interest. They are to be found not only, as they have long been, amongst political radicals of one kind and another, but are popular also with the enthusiasts of post-modernism. These are currently many. Though Rorty's own relationship to post-modernism is not an altogether enthusiastic one,[2] the aforesaid anti-essentialism is a trope he has in common with it. An analysis of what he says about the idea of human nature, then, may serve a wider effort of clarification and exchange.

---

[*] Editors' note: Richard Rorty (1931–2007) was an influential American philosopher who published widely on politics, philosophy and literary theory.

After some preliminary remarks, I examine six recurrent types of usage on this issue in Rorty's work. I go on to offer a few reflections on the story they conjointly tell.

I

One or more of a number of things can be involved in arguments about human nature. Three such things are these:

(1) claims about characteristics held to be shared by human beings cross-culturally and transhistorically;
(2) attempts to focus on some putative *differentia specifica*, on a shared characteristic or set of characteristics that distinguishes humankind from other species;
(3) the identification of traits thought to be of normative importance, guiding us towards better ways to live or constraining how we should treat one another.

(3) is often linked to (2) and/or (1) – judgements of normative importance to qualities held to be universal, whether humanly specific or not – via notions of potentiality and limitation.

It will be my contention here that in each of three meanings indicated by these three sorts of concern Rorty clearly relies on a conception of human nature. And yet his books are replete with dismissals of the idea. How does this come about? It comes about, I shall argue, in two ways. The first is by a kind of continual shifting of ground, so that in now one, now another meaning, a human nature is denied by Rorty, even while in one or other of the meanings not currently being denied a human nature is also implicitly affirmed by him. J.L. Austin, as Rorty himself tells us, once put this so: 'There's the bit where you say it and the bit where you take it back.'[3] The second way is through a tendency on Rorty's part to suggest that in order to subscribe to a notion of human nature you must be committed to something so excessively narrow and specific as to have to overlook differences, historical, cultural or simply inter-individual, that are manifest and impossible to deny.

I shall support these claims by reviewing the major critical uses and rhetorical emphases of Rorty's omnipresent rejection of the idea of a human nature. Each of the five sub-sections to follow carries a brief opening paraphrase of the Rortian theme it documents and discusses.

(a) *There is nothing to people other than what is the result of their socialization (such as the capacity to communicate with one another through language).* Rorty sometimes writes as though people were simply what their society and culture make of them. They have no inherent nature. We may begin by noting the relation of this discursive figure to the broader anti-essentialist viewpoint of which it is a part. What is needed, according to Rorty, is 'a repudiation of the very idea of anything – mind or matter, self or world – having an intrinsic nature to be expressed or represented'. Such an idea, 'that the world or the self has an intrinsic nature ... is a remnant of the idea that the world is a divine creation'.[4] 'The absence of an intrinsic human nature',[5] then, belongs for him to a more general existential situation.

We are not to think, in any case, that '"the human sciences" have a nature, any more than we think that man does'; or that 'there is something which stands to my community as my community stands to me, some larger community called "humanity" which has an intrinsic nature'; or that '"humanity" ha[s] a nature over and above the various forms of life which history has thrown up so far'.[6] Rorty suggests that (the French philosopher Michel) Foucault did not perhaps accept without all reservation 'that the self, the human subject, is simply whatever acculturation makes of it'. Putting the same point otherwise, he says that 'Socialization ... goes all the way down'.[7]

If there is nothing intrinsic in human beings, are there any universal traits? It does not follow as a matter of strict entailment that there could not be, since by a large transhistorical accident globally common and continuous forms of socialization might have occurred – although the probability of that may seem low. Rorty appears to reject the notion of any such universal. The job of the novelist, he says, 'can only be undertaken with a whole heart by someone untroubled by dreams of an ahistorical framework within which human history is enacted, a universal human nature by reference to which history can be explained ...'. He speaks, similarly, of a need to 'avoid the embarrassments of the universalist claim that the term "human being" ... names an unchanging essence, an ahistorical natural kind with a permanent set of intrinsic features'.[8]

It may seem, therefore, that Rorty rejects the idea of a human nature in the first of the three meanings flagged above. According to this – (1) – our human nature would be just those characteristics which are an intrinsic part of our make-up and as such universally shared. But in *this* meaning Rorty does not in fact reject the idea of a human nature, however things may seem. By principles of ordinary interpretative charity we can take every appearance of such a rejection as being merely an incomplete statement of his view. For there are places where he makes plain the awareness of something that is inherent and common to all human beings.

(b) *The only thing we share with other human beings we also share with other animals: susceptibility to pain.* Rorty here and there puts a qualifier on his denial of intrinsic and universal traits. It is not that there are no such traits at all, only that there are none that are distinctively human. Rorty is with the 'historicist thinkers ... [who] have denied that there is such a thing as "human nature" ... [who] insist that socialization, and thus historical circumstance, goes all the way down – that there is nothing "beneath" socialization or prior to history which is definatory of the human'. Or again, he is with those who 'have given up the Enlightenment assumption that religion, myth, and tradition can be opposed to something ahistorical, something common to all human beings qua human.'[9] The inherent qualities people have in common they also have in common with other species: 'the only intrinsic features of human beings are those they share with the brutes – for example, the ability to suffer and inflict pain.'[10]

Now, one might think it a pedantic quibble to suggest, in light of this specification, that some amendment of the usages exemplified in (a) above would be more appropriate. For, in the light of it, people are then more than simply what socialization or acculturation makes of them; permanent features, hence some kinds of universalist claim, should not be so embarrassing; and so on. In some ways, perhaps this is a quibble. But two questions are to the point nevertheless. First, is there any good reason for the regular use of discursive forms that tend to obscure the existence of characteristics human beings do indeed have in common – albeit that these are not distinctively human characteristics? Granted, no novelist will get very far with her eyes fixed only on them. Should they be held on that account as unimportant from every point of view? Rorty, as we shall see, does not think so. Second, even if what is thus common to human beings is not a specifically *human* nature – because like pain, it 'is what we human beings have that ties us to the nonlanguage-using beasts'[11] – why is it not still a nature, the sort of intrinsic entity repudiated by Rorty for 'anything'? And how would the idea of *this* sort of intrinsic entity willy-nilly implicate the person entertaining it in a belief in divine creation?[12] In other words, even if, on an adjusted definition, the denial of a human nature still stands, 'generalized anti-essentialism' would already seem to be more precarious.

I shall return to the issue raised by the first of these questions, regarding the importance of intrinsic features like the ability to suffer pain, in section II below. The questions about anti-essentialism are the subject of Chapter 4. I now formalize the situation reached so far with the hypothesis that it might then be rather in the second of the three meanings flagged earlier that Rorty dismisses the idea of a human nature. According to this meaning – (2) – our human nature would be those common traits people share that are, in addition, distinctively human. In the usages illustrated here at (b), Rorty suggests there are no such traits. But this way of understanding his repudiation of human nature is equally problematic. For he also affirms categorically that there are some such traits.

(c) *Human beings, however they have been socialized, do share a susceptibility other animals lack: to a particular sort of pain. They can be humiliated by the violent disruption of their patterns of belief and cherished values.* Rorty knows as well as anyone that we have species-specific qualities. Amongst them is 'that special sort of pain which the brutes do not share with the human – humiliation'. We have 'a common susceptibility to humiliation'.[13] We are vulnerable to it by virtue of the beliefs and attachments that can be belittled and exposed to ridicule; and because a person can be coerced into doing or saying and sometimes even thinking things 'which later she will be unable to cope with having done or thought'.[14] As Rorty also says, '... the best way to cause people long-lasting pain is to humiliate them by making the things that seemed most important to them look futile, obsolete, and powerless'.[15]

It will be readily evident that, involving as it does our structures of value and belief, this capacity we have and other animals lack, to be subjected to a particular kind of pain, is predicated on further capacities that we have and they lack. One is the capacity for language; another the more general capacity it yields for symbolic inventiveness and individuality. Rorty refers to the human specificity of these capacities. He speaks, for instance, of 'the sort of pain which the torturer hopes to create in his victim by depriving him of language and thereby of a connection with human institutions'. He writes with regard to Freud: 'By seeing every human being as consciously or unconsciously acting out an idiosyncratic fantasy, we can see the distinctively human, as opposed to animal, portion of each human life as the use for symbolic purposes of every particular person, object, situation, event, and word encountered in later life.' He quotes with approval Lionel Trilling's view of Freud – who 'showed us that poetry is indigenous to the very constitution of the mind'.[16]

A question arising now is whether and how history can be explained *without* reference to such human abilities as these.[17] But the question I shall instead pursue is why Rorty should sometimes, as we have seen at (b) above, deny that people share a common nature composed of characteristics specific to them as humans, when he also affirms precisely such common human characteristics. One suggestion, which I consider briefly only to set aside, might be this. Though there are some humanly specific traits, they are not a nature because they are not intrinsic. We only acquire them by being socialized. Well, in a way they are not intrinsic, but in a way they also are. Language and the rest does not come 'naturally' to an altogether isolated human being. But that it comes only to a human being when not isolated, when socialized, is a consequence of capacities that are intrinsic to that being. Another way of putting this is to say that it is not because they have not been socialized, or socialized properly, that animals do not read Heidegger.

These are banal points. Rorty knows and uses the concept of 'human potentiality'.[18] And he is as emphatic about its natural basis as it is possible to be without calling it a natural basis. 'Language', he has told an interviewer, '... [is] an ability which distinguishes us from other intelligent animals and enables us to perform actions which are not accessible to them ... [P]ragmatism considers language as the ability to attain higher purposes, outside the scope of and even inconceivable for the animals, who are deprived of it.'[19]

Let us therefore consider another suggestion. If Rorty relies on a notion of human nature on the second as well as on the first of the three meanings I have distinguished, but just not under the heading 'human nature', perhaps the reason for his denials really lies elsewhere than it so often appears to lie: with some concern other than what traits there are common to human beings, or what traits there are both common to and distinctive of them.

(d) *There is nothing within all of us, no common human nature, no inherent fellow feeling or unity of interest, to use as a moral reference point.* Rorty often writes in this vein: 'Habermas and Derrida ... disagree about whether there is something universally human to serve as a foundation for ethics'; and he is with Derrida in finding Habermas's sort of universalism 'pointlessly "metaphysical"'.[20] He (Rorty) is one of those 'people who say that "humanity" is a biological rather than a moral notion'. Again: 'The absence of an intrinsic human nature, and thus of built-in moral obligations, seems to us pragmatists compatible with any and every decision about what sort of life to lead, or what sort of politics to pursue'.[21]

Rorty proposes that we might think of ourselves as being machines, artefacts: 'If humanity is a natural kind, then perhaps we can find our centre and so learn how to live well. But if we are machines, then it is up to us to invest a use for ourselves.' And if we are machines, we can see ourselves as requiring 'much tinkering, rather than as a substance with a precious essence to be discovered and cherished'.[22] To put the point in another way again, we can 'erase the picture of the self common to Greek metaphysics, Christian theology and Enlightenment rationalism: the picture of an ahistorical natural centre, the locus of human dignity, surrounded by an adventitious and inessential periphery'.[23]

The suggestion one can accordingly now consider is that what Rorty actually repudiates is the idea of a human nature in the third of the meanings earlier signalled. On this meaning – (3) – a human nature would be a set of characteristics common to human beings that provided also a moral reference point: for shaping or constraining our thinking about human dignity, how to live well, or moral obligations, and so on.

The suggestion is supported by one other feature of his work, namely a distaste for the language of emancipation. That is, once again, a typically 'post-modern' stance. Rorty is opposed to the 'conviction that there is an interesting general theory about human beings or their oppression'; refers to 'the disappearance of the transcendental subject – of "man" as something having a nature which society can repress or understand'.[24] By the same token, utopia for him, a good society, is not what it is on account of being in harmony with some such putative nature. We would be wrong, Rorty says, to think of a 'common humanity' as the philosophical foundation for democratic politics. Followers of Dewey like himself 'would like to praise parliamentary democracy and the welfare state as very good things, but only on the basis of invidious comparisons with suggested concrete alternatives, not on the basis of claims that these institutions are truer to human nature …'.[25] The 'pragmatist utopia is … not one in which human nature has been unshackled', and pragmatists do not want 'narratives of emancipation'.[26] What they favour is cultural pluralism, as being apt to the spirit of tolerance in democratic politics – a spirit 'neutral on questions of what is central to human life, questions about the goal or point of human existence'.[27]

So, there is a lot in Rorty to support the suggestion that a major concern of his in disparaging the idea of a human nature is its normative usage. There may be readers who will find this suggestion problematic nevertheless, in view of some of what has already passed before us. Focusing, for example, on Rorty's denial of an ahistorical centre as the locus of human *dignity*, they might wonder then about the common human susceptibility to *humiliation*; or equally about the ability he says language gives us to attain purposes that are *higher*. Both humiliation and higher purposes can be related in familiar ways to notions of human dignity. There could, though, be a persuasive response to this sort of doubt. Rorty perhaps intended 'higher', in that usage of it, in some purely technical sense, and means 'humiliation', likewise, as a descriptive concept only (the kind of pain people feel in such and such circumstances etc.), and consequently is not involved by either term in the sort of moral evaluation which, on the other hand, he maybe does reckon 'human dignity' to carry. Thus there is nothing here to show that, rejecting the idea of a human nature as moral reference point, Rorty himself also relies on the idea of a human nature as moral reference point. All the same, he does rely on it as that.

(e) *The worst thing you can do to someone, beyond causing them acute pain, is to use that pain so that they will be unable to reconstitute themselves when it is over.* According to Rorty, 'cruelty is the worst thing we do'. This is a central, repeated point with him and he follows Judith Shklar in making it definitive of liberal belief.[28]

Cruelty *is* the worst thing we do. But cruelty is deliberately inflicting suffering; it is delight in, or indifference to, the pain of others. Rorty knows these obvious connections. One way for him of being 'very cruel' is to cause that special sort of pain which is humiliating people.[29]

The normative priority of this concern of his is something about which Rorty is himself emphatic. He discourages his readers 'from slipping into a political attitude which will lead you to think that there is some special goal more important than avoiding cruelty'.[30] And he warns, correspondingly, against the figure of the 'ascetic priest' – whose goal is 'the ineffable', and a bit of whom there is in every philosopher. Ascetic priests are impatient with 'mere happiness or mere decrease of suffering'; or with 'the mere pursuit of pleasure and avoidance of pain'.[31] Rorty proffers to them the rejoinder (as he says this is) of the novelist: 'It is comical to think that *anyone* could transcend the quest for happiness, to think that any theory could be more than a means to happiness, that there is something called Truth which transcends pleasure and pain.' As a liberal is someone who thinks cruelty the worst thing we do, so a democratic utopia would be one in which 'nobody would dream of thinking that there is something realer than pleasure or pain'.[32]

Ability to suffer pain, remember, is one of the intrinsic features human beings share with the brutes; and the special pain of humiliation is a common susceptibility we share with other human beings, however socialized, although not with the brutes. The worst thing we do, therefore, Rorty characterizes by reference to a human nature in both of meanings (1) and (2). But as it is precisely the *worst* thing we do, the idea of a human nature serves him as a moral reference point – that is, in meaning (3) as well, and his disclaimers with respect to this meaning in turn notwithstanding.

Rorty's reliance upon what he also simultaneously disclaims finds some concentrated forms of expression in his pages. Here is one example:

> A society which took its moral vocabulary from novels ... would not ask itself questions about human nature, the point of human existence, or the meaning of human life. Rather, it would ask itself what we can do so as to get along with each other, how we can arrange things so as to be comfortable with one another, how institutions can be changed so that everyone's right to be understood has a better chance of being gratified.[33]

There is, doubtless, good enough reason for withholding descriptions, 'the point of human existence' and 'the meaning of human life', from the purposes of getting along and being comfortable with one another. Where some have thought the glorification of God, the flourishing of high culture, self-actualization and what have you to be that point or meaning, Rorty says we should just do what we can to get along together without bothering to think of this in such terms.

Is there really no question here at all, though, 'about human nature'? His own favoured goal, it is true, is one that is more open, less specific, than are alternatives of this ilk. But it is not so obviously so in relation to every such alternative, as 'self-actualization' in the foregoing list may remind us. Perhaps the important difference is supposed to be that where these other purposes have been consciously grounded by their sponsors on an idea of human nature – grounded, as upon a foundation – Rorty for his part offers his benign goal as ungrounded; merely free-floating advice. Except that we already know what for him defines some of the parameters of getting along and being comfortable with one another. Everyone's 'right to be understood', for example, is clearly related to the goal of sparing people that specially human pain of being humiliated.

Here is a second example of that same kind of concentrated tension:

The view I am offering says that there is such a thing as moral progress, and that this progress is indeed in the direction of greater human solidarity. But that solidarity is not thought of as recognition of a core self, the human essence, in all human beings. Rather, it is thought of as the ability to see more and more traditional differences (of tribe, religion, race, customs, and the like) as unimportant when compared with similarities with respect to pain and humiliation.[34]

This seems to me again to reintroduce the character it has just ejected, presenting her merely in different shoes. Solidarity may well not merit being designated part of a core self or human essence. Still, there they are, those similarities with respect to pain and humiliation, compared with which so much diversity for Rorty is unimportant – unimportant from a moral point of view.

A third and last example takes us back to the issue of emancipation:

There is no human nature which was once, or still is, in chains. Rather, our species has – ever since it developed language – been making up a nature for itself … Lately our species has been making up a particularly good nature for itself – that produced by the institutions of the liberal West. When we praise this development, we pragmatists drop the revolutionary rhetoric of emancipation and unmasking in favour of a reformist rhetoric about increased tolerance and decreased suffering.[35]

From one angle, this is the familiar discourse of historicist denial of human nature: there is no such thing as human nature, it is said, because we form and transform ourselves, or are formed by our social relations; we make up our own nature. In fact, we do and we also don't, as is borne out by, amongst other things, the important similarities with respect to pain and humiliation.

My concern now, however, is not so much with the existence of these similarities as with their simultaneous renunciation and use by Rorty as a moral reference point. In this regard, dropping the rhetoric of emancipation changes nothing. 'Human nature unshackled' or 'in chains' does have a somewhat archaic ring, of which the talk of 'increased tolerance and decreased suffering' is free. But where the former has explicit recourse to an underlying human constitution as moral reference point, the latter has implicit recourse to it, that is all. It has implicit recourse to it via a notion of the ills human beings will generally want to avoid; whether in virtue of being, like other animals, susceptible to pain; or of being, unlike them, attached to beliefs, values, identities and so on, which are crucial to their well-being, so making them vulnerable to further awful, humanly specific kinds of hurt. It is this vulnerability that makes the value of tolerance appropriate in human affairs. The less, as much as the more, archaic rhetoric, therefore, aims at or hopes for a set of social and political arrangements that can be said, perfectly meaningfully, to be in greater conformity with some intrinsic and shared human characteristics. And since it comes to this, what then is actually wrong with the rhetoric of emancipation? But I leave that question and return to it later.

Let us pause here. Before going further, I want to review the path we have travelled so far. I shall do so by offering a short quotation from Rorty to represent each of the previous sub-sections (a) to (e).

(a) There is nothing to people except what has been socialized into them – their ability to use language, and thereby to exchange beliefs and desires with other people.

(b) ... all we share with all other humans is the same thing we share with all other animals – the ability to feel pain.

(c) ... human beings who have been socialized – socialized in any language, any culture – do share a capacity which other animals lack. They can all be given a special kind of pain: They can all be humiliated by the forcible tearing down of the particular structures of language and belief in which they were socialized (or which they pride themselves on having formed for themselves).

(d) ... there is nothing deep inside each of us,' no common human nature, no built-in human solidarity, to use as a moral reference point.

(e) ... the worst thing you can do to somebody is not to make her scream in agony but to use that agony in such a way that even when the agony is over, she cannot reconstitute herself.

Each of these passages raises a question about the content of one or more of its neighbours. Readers may now like to confirm for themselves that the headline summaries with which I began the five sub-sections (a) to (e) above were based, loosely, on these passages: (a) there on (a) here, and so forth for (b) through (e). They will be able to confirm for themselves also that these five passages all come from the same place. They all come from page 177 of *Contingency, Irony, and Solidarity*.

As displayed here, of course, the passages are not embedded in their native context. This is a recontextualization of them. But I do not believe that, using them so, I have misrepresented the several meanings and – as I have sought to bring out – logical tensions present in Rorty's thinking on this issue. On the contrary, the procedure I have followed has attempted to document the wide extent of their presence there. The only more particular interest of these five passages is the fact that they all come from the one page. Can further light be thrown on this strange (or so I perceive it, anyway) state of affairs? Perhaps some can, if we now look at one other kind of usage. It, too, can be exemplified from the same page.

(f) To be a person is to speak a *particular* language, one which enables us to discuss particular beliefs and desires with particular sorts of people.,

A recurrent suggestion in Rorty's work is that to believe in a common human nature you must be, not just aware of some human universals, but blinded by them. Thus, you must think of human nature as 'an inner structure which leads all members of the species to converge to the same point, to recognize the same theories, virtues, and works of art as worthy of honour'. You must dream 'of an ultimate community which will have transcended the distinction between the natural and the social'.[36] And you must refuse individual diversity. Rorty writes of Freud that he enabled us to understand 'both Nietzsche's superman and Kant's common moral consciousness' as alternative forms or strategies of life:

There is much to be said for both. Each has advantages and disadvantages. Decent people are often rather dull. Great wits are sure to madness near allied. Freud stands in awe before the poet, but describes him as infantile. He is bored by the merely moral man, but describes him as mature ... He does not see a need to erect a theory of human nature which will safeguard the interests of the one or the other. He sees ... neither as 'more truly human' than the other.[37]

What can one say? Indeed, there are conceptions of human nature so narrow as to obscure or repress real differences, societal and individual, to flatten out the enormous variety of human motivation and potentiality. To get off the starting block, a persuasive conception of human nature must clearly be able to accommodate particularity: the moral person and the poet, divergent patterns of belief and value, different languages. Still, a particular language, to take only this, is a language; it is dependent as such on 'an ability which distinguishes us from other intelligent animals';[38] and language is crucial, on Rorty's own account of things, to every human enterprise, moral, poetic or whatever.

Nor need referring particular languages to the general human capacity they depend on tie one to a hopeless notion of one day 'transcending' the distinction between the natural and the social. On the contrary, so referring them is just a reminder that there is that distinction, irreducibly – as there would not be if socialization really did go all the way down. In saying (when he does say it) that the sole intrinsic traits are ones we share with animals, like 'the ability to suffer and inflict pain', Rorty qualifies 'intrinsic' to mean 'untouched by historical change'.[39] But why should anyone understand it so: as indicating some pristine, altogether umodified nature? The most elementary bodily needs – to eat, to excrete, for rest – are in an important sense not untouched by historical change. Nor even is the ability to inflict pain, however it may be with the ability to suffer it. But such needs and abilities are also not *wholly* determined by the historical change that touches them. To deny that they are constitute an inherent nature is merely to dissolve one kind of reality in favour of another. There is no nature here, supposedly, because there is a history. One could with equal validity say – the very sort of thing Rorty is so concerned to have us abjure – that there is no history here because it is all down to a (human) nature. Or on the other hand: one can abjure both ways of speaking, in favour of maintaining an indispensable distinction.

Rorty's rhetorical strategy in this, the affirmation of particularity and historical change as telling against any common human nature, is standard in historicist argument on the topic. The strategy is to insist that the concept of human nature must carry more weight than it plausibly can carry and then to reject it because it cannot. With respect again to solidarity, for instance, Rorty proffers the contrasting standpoints of two characters he dubs, not entirely neutrally, the liberal ironist and the liberal metaphysician – the latter wanting to reference to a human nature, whilst the former eschews it. The metaphysician, we are told, wants our wish to be kind 'to be bolstered by an argument ... which will highlight a common human essence, an essence which is something more than our shared ability to suffer humiliation'. The ironist for her part just makes do with pain and humiliation.[40] Now, perhaps some people do want something more than this. But they need not want it. In the context of the present discussion, it is quite enough. To add, as Rorty does here, that the ironist's feeling of solidarity 'is based on a sense of a common danger, not on a common possession or a shared power' is only camouflage. Call it, at this point, a danger and not a power or possession; but it is in any case common to us as humans, part of a make-up or a constitution we share, which is just what many understand by a human nature; and the thing is also called by Rorty a susceptibility, an ability and a capacity, all of them, these, a little bit like a power.

They are not the sort of power, however, that Rorty has in mind upon the moment, and this is the real business now. For, the something more you must want of human beings for there to be a common human nature, is 'their relation to a larger shared power – rationality, God, truth, or history, for example'. I pass over rationality: one name, currently much maligned, for an important human capacity. But the presence of the Deity in this list, and of truth and history as hypostatized, free-standing – 'larger' – powers, yields the secret. Belief in a human nature is *ipso facto* belief in some telos or destiny. It is belief in a goal that is precisely metaphysical, one lodged perhaps at the end of an inexorable history. Here is Rorty insisting on the openness of the future:

> I take Orwell to be telling us that whether our future rulers are more like O'Brien or more like J. S. Mill does not depend ... on deep facts about human nature. For, as O'Brien and Humbert Humbert show, intellectual gifts – intelligence, judgement, curiosity, imagination, a taste for beauty – are all malleable as the sexual instinct. They are as capable of as many diverse employments as the human hand... What our future rulers will be like will not be determined by any large necessary truths about human nature and its relation to truth and justice, but by a lot of small contingent facts.[41]

Contingent ones, yes; though one may wonder why they may not be both large and small, comprising structural causes and trends as well as little accidents. But in any event if those rulers turn out to be more like O'Brien, things will go worse for human beings – on account of some facts and truths, whether deep or not, about their nature. And although a metaphysical teleology may sometimes be a conception of human nature, this is like Valéry being a petty-bourgeois intellectual. Not every conception of human nature is a metaphysical teleology.

II

I offer now a few concluding observations. The first of them anticipates this question: do we not have though, it might be asked, in the sort of matter just surveyed under (f), a resolution of any outstanding problem or puzzle concerning Rorty's anti-human nature discourse? The resolution would be that what he really means in dismissing the idea of a human nature is not what I mean in defending it. He means rather a conception in which – (4) – to affirm a human nature is to overlook or seriously understate cultural and individual diversity and/or to believe in some telos or destiny, a pre-given point of human existence. As it is not sensible thus variously to overlook, understate and believe, Rorty has sound reason for denying a human nature in his preferred sense, even while others like me continue to affirm one in our preferred sense. Everything is level then, surely.

No. For, while it is indeed the case that Rorty does mean something like (4), it is not all he means. Or at any rate it is not all he says. He also avails himself freely of rhetorical conveniences not pertinent to that meaning: telling us that there are no intrinsic or permanent features of human beings; that the self is simply what acculturation makes of it; that all we share as humans we also share with other species; that there is nothing universal or common to us to use as a basis of ethical judgement, nothing to repress or understand; and so on. What is all this for? One could after all just say, for example, 'there is no human nature in the sense of a metaphysical purpose or destiny implanted in each human being' – and leave it at that.

What we have with (4) is not Rorty's 'real' or only meaning but a meaning, so to say, of last resort. It is the inner, defensible core of a fighting position with a number of outlying rhetorical fortifications, all of which are visibly fragile and in one way or another soon abandoned by the people behind them. Thus it is always, with the radical, the comprehensive, denial of a human nature. The defensible core turns out to be less interesting than the outer wall. That there is nothing at all common to human beings or inherent in their make-up is at least startling when you think about it. But that there is no human nature *just* in the sense of there being no inner link of the human individual to an imma- nent theological or meta-historical purpose (or to a preordained order of lord- ship and servitude, capitalist forms of ownership, purely procreative sexuality, benevolent malign intent, etc.); *even though* some common characteristics are to be allowed when all is said and done – this can also be rendered by saying that there is only the sort of human nature there is, and not the sort that there isn't. it is a less than arresting proposition.

Second, I anticipate also, now, the objection that Rorty's core position can be taken separately from whatever he may say inconsistently with it. Isolating this position analytically from anything that so obscures it, we will do better to stay with it as a conception of human nature than to go with the sort of notion

I am here defending. This is because such common traits of human beings as there actually are do not add up to anything substantial enough to constitute a useful notion.

A short response to this is that definition is free. You can stay or go with what you want. You can define 'human nature' in so narrow a way that there will not be one. You may then want a word for what there nonetheless is in that domain. A longer response is that the judgement as to what does and does not count as substantial or useful can, however, also be put under scrutiny. By what criterion or in what context, bearing on the understanding of the ways of human beings, is a notion of their nature according to which they are susceptible to pain and humiliation, have the capacity for language and (in a large sense) poetry, have a sexual instinct, a sense of identity, integral beliefs – and then some other things too, like needs for nourishment and sleep, a capacity for laughter and for play, powers of reasoning and invention that are, by comparison with other terrestrial species, truly formidable, and more shared features yet – not substantial enough? Singly or together, these features all seem to be of some practical consequence. Consider only the sort of difference it might have made to their world if the beings called human were *not* susceptible to pain and humiliation. That would appear, so far as it is possible to think it through, to be a difference as substantial as any that are typically argued over when human nature is at issue: whether or not people are universally greedy and competitive, or are intrinsically moral, or are 'essentially' wedded to some larger hidden purpose or design.

We now know, in any case, how Rorty himself regards some of the human characteristics just collected – a collection shaped, indeed, according to his own especial emphases. And it is instructive to set those characteristics down side by side for a moment with the more radically historicist formulations he goes in for. One can do this by asking why people need ever actually be in pain, ever suffer or be oppressed. If they truly do just make up a nature for themselves, they could make up one that was proof against all that. It is hard to think why they have not done so, given how much suffering there has been all told. If we are machines, why do we not just 'invent the use for ourselves': reacting with joy or equanimity to (what formerly was) being tortured or being humiliated? Why not tinker with ourselves so that we will never, under any circumstances, be hungry? Or never feel weary under a burden of toil? Or cherish any belief or person so much as to be made vulnerable by doing that? Think how hard life would become for any would-be oppressor.[42] However, I do not genuinely mean any of this to be taken seriously. For it cannot.

There is, of course, *something* in it. People do find ways of making unavoidable suffering more bearable, forms of adaptation by which they seek to mitigate what they can of even the most brutal oppression, where it cannot be thrown off. Still, there are limits to human adaptability; and limits are part of what the discourse of human nature has been about. People can be pushed to, or close to, those limits and then they die or their lives become a torment. Or if they are a bit further back from the limits, their lives may be just harsh. Where human beings find themselves in these sorts of situation, there are at least a rhetoric of emancipation seems not entirely inappropriate. The idea is of a setting free from restraint or bondage: a setting free from restraint or bondage, here, of beings of a particular, not infinitely flexible, nature. How is this idea already useless, in a world where torture and hunger, political, religious, ethnic and other persecutions, are still rather prominent; where, as Richard Rorty for his part seems pretty well aware, large numbers of our species continue to live with, or under, social and political arrangements very far from comfortable?

The rhetoric of emancipation, it may be added, is not so distant from the rhetoric of 'utopia', which Rorty seems quite happy to employ. And even if the scope of the utopia projected by him may be less ambitious than the scope of many another – comfort simply and not the moon – there is an enormous, a world-transforming, amount to be said for that nonetheless, is there not?[43]

A final point. Rorty claims in one place to follow Sartre in this matter.[44] For Sartre, there is no human nature because 'Man is nothing else but that which he makes of himself' – he is 'a project ... instead of being kind of moss, or a fungus or a cauliflower'. So 'every one of us must choose himself', and that involves surpassing or widening, or else accommodating to, limitations of one kind and another.[45] Rorty's gloss on this is 'that man is always free to choose new descriptions (for, among other things, himself)'. The search for any putatively ultimate description or vocabulary, as he also contends, amounts to an attempt 'to escape from humanity'. That he should characterize it so is surely not surprising from a thinker who wants '[t]o say with Trilling that the mind is a poetry-making faculty'.[46]

I am reminded here, however, of other voices: most recently of Saul Bellow, writing about the genius of Mozart; and referring in this connection to our 'curious nature' and our 'inner freedom' with respect to the influence of external forces. And of Primo Levi, according to whom 'all of us are born poets' and 'the need to make poetry ... is of all countries and all times'. And then, more distantly, of the young Marx's 'free, conscious activity'; and of the mature Marx's 'free development of every individual'. And of John Stuart Mill, reflecting on just how much Bentham overlooked in his too simple conception of 'man': on 'the love of *beauty*, the passion of the artist', and 'the love of *action*, the thirst for movement and activity'.

Yet Bellow is content to put what he says under the rubric of our 'trans-historical powers' and 'our common human nature'. Levi locates poetry amongst the 'activities to which we are predisposed genetically'. Marx invokes 'the forces ... of humanity's own nature'. And Mill speaks likewise of 'these powerful

constituents of human nature'. It is not clear to me that there is a difference
of any substance between the idea they severally articulate – with whatever
variations – and the Rorty-Sartre one.[47]

Notes

1 *Objectivity, Relativism, and Truth* (ORT), Cambridge. 1991, p. 99.
2 See *Essays on Heidegger and Others* (EHO), Cambridge, 1991, p. 1; 'Thugs and Theorists', *Political Theory*, 15, 1987, pp. 564, 572, 578 n. 3; 'Feminism and Pragmatism',
   Radical Philosophy, 59, Autumn 1991, pp. 5, 12 n. 18.
3 *Consequences of Pragmatism* (CoP), Hemel Hempstead, 1982, p. 97. Cf. J.L. Austin,
   Sense and Sensibilia, Oxford, 1962, p. 2.
4 *Contingency, Irony, and Solidarity* (CIS), Cambridge, 1989, pp. 4, 21; cf. p. 6.
5 EHO, p. 132.
6 CoP, p. 203; CIS, pp. 59, 60.
7 CIS, pp. 64, 185.
8 EHO, p. 77; 'Feminism and Pragmatism', pp. 3–14.
9 CIS, p. xiii; ORT, p. 176.
10 'Feminism and Pragmatism', p. 4.
11 CIS, p. 94.
12 See the text to note 4 above.
13 CIS, pp. 91–92.
14 CIS, p. 178.
15 CIS, p. 89.
16 CIS, p. 36 and n. 12.
17 See the text to note 8 above.
18 EHO, p. 18.
19 *The Guardian*, 13 March 1992, p. 25.
20 'Thugs and Theorists', pp. 164–180.
21 ORT, p. 197; EHO, p. 132.
22 EHO, pp. 144, 152.
23 ORT, p. 176.
24 'Feminism and Pragmatism', p. 12; n. 22; CoP, p. 207.
25 CIS, p. 196; ORT, p. 211.
26 ORT, p. 213.
27 EHO, pp. 132–133.
28 CIS, pp. xv, 74, 146, 173, 190, 197.
29 CIS, p. 89.
30 CIS, p. 65.
31 EHO, pp. 71–72.
32 EHO, pp. 74–75.
33 EHO, p. 78.
34 CIS, p. 192.
35 ORT, p. 213.
36 ORT, pp. 31, 22.

37 CIS, p. 35.
38 See the text to note 19 above.
39 'Feminism and Pragmatism', p. 4; and see the text to note 10 above.
40 CIS, pp. 88–93.
41 CIS, pp. 187–188
42 See the text to notes 22 and 35 above.
43 Cf. my 'Marxism and Moral Advocacy', in Norman Geras, *Discourses of Extremity*, London, 1990, pp. 7–8.
44 ORT, p. 182 n. 17.
45 Jean-Paul Sartre, *Existentialism and Humanism*, London, 1984 (reprinted 1966), pp. 27–29, 46.
46 Richard Rorty, *Philosophy and the Mirror of Nature*, Oxford, 1980, pp. 361–362 n. 7, 377; CIS, p. 36.
47 'Saul Bellow on Mozart', *The Guardian*, 2 April 1992, p. 25; Primo Levi, *The Mirror Maker*, London, 1990, pp. 110–114; Karl Marx and Frederick Engels, *Collected Works*, London, 1975, vol.3, p. 276; Karl Marx, *Capital*, Vol.1, Harmondsworth, 1976, p. 739; Marx, *Grundisse*, Harmondsworth 1973, p. 488; J.S. Mill, 'Bentham', in Mary Warnock, ed., *Utilitarianism*, London, 1962, pp. 100–101.

3

Minimum utopia: ten theses

(Originally published in Leo Panitch and Colin Leys (eds), *Socialist Register 2000: Necessary and Unnecessary Utopias*, Merlin Press, London, 1999)

I offer here some reflections on utopia. I make no extravagant claim for them. They do not trace out a history of the concept, nor do they attempt to explore its thematic range and variety. They are simply one person's thoughts on the subject as we approach a new century and millennium. I have arranged them into ten summary theses.

1. Socialism is utopian

As a goal socialism is, and it always has been, utopian, including in its most influential version to date, namely Marxism. This is despite Marx and Engels's attempt, in the *Communist Manifesto* and elsewhere, to take their distance from utopia as mere abstraction or speculation, to ground their own thinking in present tendencies, in an analysis of real historical possibilities and of the social and political agencies for bringing them about. Everyone knows that in this sense the Marxist tradition sought from the beginning to be reso-lutely, *anti*-utopian. Re-read the relevant passages from the *Manifesto*. Of some of their predecessors – Saint-Simon, Fourier, Owen – Marx and Engels say that, faced with a proletarian class not yet sufficiently developed, faced likewise with material conditions still insufficient for the emancipation of the prole-tariat, these thinkers could but invent in place of what they lacked, so they, invented 'fantastic pictures of future society'.[1]

This was not to be the way of the founding thinkers of historical materi-alism. Indeed it was the source of one of classical Marxism's great strengths that, committed to the goal of a fundamentally different kind of social order, it sought to provide a political economy, a sociology and a politics of the present and the emergent future. This is, too, what its numberless detractors have most deeply begrudged it. For, whatever the changing fortunes of the movement for socialism, taken all in all there is still no more compelling theory of society than historical materialism, even once all the necessary qualifications to it have been made.

Notwithstanding any of this, however, it remains true that from the outset socialism was utopian. It was a distant land, another moral universe. It was radically other vis-a-vis the order of things it aspired to replace. And that is what it still is. A society beyond exploitation is in the realm of the ideal. Furthermore, so far from being any kind of inevitability, its achievement is an unsolved problem and – not to beat about the bush – the very possibility of it is in question. In this way socialism partakes also of one of the pejorative meanings of utopia. Until its realisation establishes otherwise, it partakes of the meaning of being an unattainable ideal. We may hope that it can be achieved, but we do not yet know that it can. Nor do we yet know how.

2. We should unashamedly embrace utopia

We should be, without hesitation or embarrassment, utopians. At the end of the twentieth century it is the only acceptable political option, morally speaking. I shall not dwell on this. I will merely say that, irrespective of what may have seemed apt hitherto either inside or outside the Marxist tradition, nothing but a utopian goal will now suffice. The realities of our time are morally intolerable. Within the constricted scope of the present piece, I suppose I might try to evoke a little at least of what I am referring to here, with some statistics or an imagery of poverty, destitution and other contemporary calamities- But I do not intend to do even this much. The facts of widespread human privation and those of political oppression and atrocity are available to all who want them. They are unavoidable unless you wilfully shut them out. To those who would suggest that things might be yet worse, one answer is that of course they might be. But another answer is that for too many people they are already quite bad enough; and the sponsors of this type of suggestion are for their part almost always pretty comfortable.

3. There have been two ingredients of socialist utopia

I distinguish from within the Marxist tradition two broad elements of the socialist vision, which, simplifying, I style maximum and minimum, ingredients. Informing discussions of the socialist future there has been, on the one hand, a dream or promise of ultimate liberation, one not generally filled out in very much detail but present nevertheless in certain pregnant words and phrases. It might be, from Marx's early works on, the dream of disalienation, of all-round individual self-development. Or it might be the promise in the slogan 'to each according to their needs', lavishly interpreted. It might be the implicit vision of a world of peacefully resolved conflicts without any need of policing or enforcement, or an anticipation of what used to be called 'fraternity'.

One should take care not to exaggerate. The influential thinkers of Marxism were serious people, not fools. They did not believe – as, in that caricature of the 'smiling Marxist' so dear to many critics, they are often represented as having believed[2] – in the possibility of a world free of all limitation and difficulty. They did not expect heaven on earth. Still, the image was there of a condition of uncoerced social peace and of free and ample individual self-realisation, with the sign against it of the radically, the incomparably different. Not as in all 'end of time' or a realm of concurring uniformity; this is merely part of the same caricature. But as in a fundamentally new beginning, the self-conscious history of humankind as opposed to a previously opaque prehistory.[3]

On the other hand, there was also – a mark, this, precisely of the materialism – the conception of a simple *sufficiency* of the means and conveniences of life. It was contained in the socialist demand for a release from extreme want and toil, a demand based on the elementary fact (which pro-capitalist liberals typically disguise from or soften for themselves) that the possibility, of individual flourishing is seriously undermined by poverty and grave need, as it is by the tedium of a lifetime of unwanted forms of labour. Within, or perhaps behind, any greater was this more modest objective: of providing everyone with the proper platform for a life of free self-development. Might each member of our species one day rise to the level of an Aristotle, a Goethe or a Marx? I don't know, although Leon Trotsky famously asserted so.[4] But the hypothesis was predicated on having to bring about an underlying sufficiency for all.

4. Maximum notions of utopia have their indispensable place

People will continue to long for what may be beyond their reach. Yearnings of this kind are merely the other face of finitude and limitation, of the regular troubles and the harsher oppressions of the world. As, in the normal way of things, fear of death, protracted pain or illness, close bereavement; and loneliness, disappointed love, personal betrayal or other inner hurts; more generally, excessive burdens and wretched long-term predicaments, are a cause of suffering, so do they also prompt ideas of a release from it. Here the reconstructive capacities of human thought – abstraction, projection, imagination – can always move through various levels of conceivable improvement right up to the furthermost negation. Hence, eternal life, ultimate redemption and the like, as well as some of the more common fictions of many a personal existence.

Hence, the most ambitious utopias.

At the same time, elements of the transcendent are lodged within mundane experience, thereby nourishing in a more positive way, too, visions of a radically different human realm. For if the extraordinary is already within the ordinary, why may it not be extended? And why may it not be extended again? Great art – or just good music, of all kinds – could be invoked at this point to exemplify

the way in which the aesthetic, the elevating or powerfully affective, inhabits
the quotidian world. But another less often used example demonstrates as
tellingly how even within the ordinary, at the most seemingly unremarkable
sites, there are moments of grace, joy and excitement capable of lifting those
present and transmuting the quality of their experience. I refer to the example
of modern sport, not much reflected on in meditations about Utopia. It is a
mistaken neglect, in my own view, since sport today gives as much genuine
and memorable pleasure to millions upon millions of people as can be claimed
for most other human pursuits. In the unexceptional context of what are no
more than idle games, and for all of the accompanying ugliness currently to
be found there – abusively exaggerated hatreds, boorishness, the corruptions
of a rampantly invasive commodification – there is a communal enjoyment of
competitive effort, and there are feats of impressive, sometimes breath-taking
skill, and uniquely specific moments of great beauty under pressure not repro-
ducible in any other setting. This is on top of the more common enjoyments
of time passed shooting the breeze with friends. C.L.R. James already said it
many years ago: 'the popular democracy of our day, sitting ... watching Miller
and Lindwall bowl to Hutton and Compton [or, for that matter, watching
Edwards, Bennett and J.P.R. Williams, or Cantona, Beckham and Giggs] in
its own way grasps at a more complete human existence'.[5] There could be
other examples still: of feelings of deep or intense love, outstanding acts of
friendship, compassion, courage. But from both kinds of cause, whether the
psychological and moral needs arising from suffering, or possibilities faintly
discerned within the lived experience of the real, we will continue to long for
what may be beyond our reach. We not only will continue to, we also should.
For, set against this wider human-natural background, maximum notions of
utopia can be seen to have their value. This value is the very dream of deliver-
ance. It is in the liberating fantasy that yields a different vantage point from the
one confining it and claiming the privilege, all too often, of being the sole *realistic* reality. We have to think about the seemingly impossible in order to be
able to discriminate what is generally possible. There are few things as bizarre
anyway, as Terry Eagleton observes elsewhere in this volume, as the futurist
vision trapped within assumptions of a putative realism. 'Those with their
heads truly in the sands or the clouds are the hard-nosed realists who behave
as though chocolate chip cookies and the International Monetary Fund will be
with us in another three thousand years time.'

5. Politically, we should be guided as socialists by the aim of minimum utopia

These above considerations notwithstanding, the political thought of socialism
should now be centred, not on notions of ultimate liberation or of other too
distant ambition, but on a world cured of its worst remediable deprivations and

horrors. The goal should be modest or minimum utopia. This is a thesis I have suggested in passing once before in the pages of *Socialist Register*, defining minimum utopia as a form of society which could generally provide for its members the material and social bases of a tolerably contented existence, or (put otherwise) from which the gravest social and political evils familiar to us have been removed.[6] Several reasons can be offered for thus limiting the horizon of left programmatic thinking for the time being.

The first and most important of these is simply that, could it but be achieved, minimum utopia would be a remarkable good in itself. To me the most compelling thing in Marxism – along with the broad truth of historical materialism – has always been, not its most far-reaching perspective, but its most basic one. Today more than ever it provides a good enough vision to be getting on with. The world as it is and as it has been presents us with a picture of cruelty, slaughter, gross forms of exploitation and oppression, dire need. If we could hope to achieve merely – *merely* – a condition in which people had enough to eat, adequate water, shelter, health care, and the fundamental rights of expression, belief and assembly; and in which they were free from arbitrary imprisonment, torture, 'disappearance', threat of genocide; now wouldn't that be something. Even to articulate the thought is to bring home how remote this objective is. But why should any human being have to settle for less? Remote therefore as it may be, it is indeed the minimum, even while being utopia in a more than powerful enough meaning of the concept. To have only this: it would be humankind's most magnificent accomplishment. Note that insisting on minimum utopia as a political guideline, a sufficient practical objective, does not in itself entail any renunciation of the more maximal ingredients of the socialist vision. These can either wait, or some of them may take care of themselves more or less. Others may turn out to have been misconceived. The question can just be left open. Relatively, it is of less importance.

A second reason is that we should not frame our projection of possible futures in terms that exclude the less benign, the more troublesome, features of the human make-up as it has revealed itself historically. Since I have argued this point before at length, I will be brief about it here. It is not a matter of denying the extent to which human beings can and do change – individually, histori-cally, culturally – nor the scope there might be, consequently, for a radically different human type, with different social and moral traits, in the dwellings and on the streets of a better future world. It is only a matter of cautioning against a too presumptive optimism in this regard: of drawing attention to how much there is in ordinary and extraordinary experience alike, from the most familiar situations of daily life to the torture chambers and the killing fields, to suggest some enduring human limitations such as could continue to blemish and unsettle even the best-placed social order.[7]

Third, there is a more general reason for scepticism towards any vision composed only of shades of light and nothing darker. For it comes to us from the two extremes of reflection about the social world, both from thinking about utopia itself and from thinking about the lowest depths humanity has sunk to, that we cannot fully comprehend an idea of perfect or complete happiness, let alone deliberately aim for it. This is why pure utopias can seem so flat and dull, whatever the intentions of those designing them. They lack the necessary contrasts that in any actual world make the goods of life what they are, to be valued and striven for against the basis. It is a point that was argued by George Orwell in a pseudonymous essay about notions of utopian thought recently traced to his authorship: happiness is scarcely conceivable except by way of its juxtaposition – in life as in thought – with more problematic and ambiguous states.[8] At the same time Primo Levi, pondering for his part on his experiences at Auschwitz, expressed a similar truth in terms of mundane finitude and complexity. Perfect happiness and perfect unhappiness are equally unattainable, he wrote, the obstacles to them deriving from the human condition itself 'which is opposed to everything infinite'.

> Our ever-insufficient knowledge of the future opposes it: and this is called, in the one instance, hope, and in the other, uncertainty of the following day. The certainty of death opposes it: for it places a limit on every joy, but also on every grief. The inevitable material cares oppose it: for as they poison every lasting happiness, they equally assiduously distract us from our misfortunes and make our consciousness of them intermittent and hence supportable.

The elusive nature of happiness, Levi also wrote, arises from an incomplete knowledge of 'the complex nature of the state of unhappiness':

> so that the single name of the major cause is given to all its causes, which are composite and set out in an order of urgency. And if the most immediate cause of stress comes to an end, you are grievously amazed to see that another one lies behind; and in reality a whole series of others.[9]

The point of adverting to these observations is emphatically not one of fatalistic pessimism: as would seek to encourage, on account of run-of-the-mill facts of daily life, a resigned countenancing of the vaster avoidable evils that have plagued humankind. The point is only to get more sharply into focus that it is eliminating those evils, or levelling them as far as we can, that should be the prime contemporary objective of socialist thought and politics, and this does not require any whitened vision of a future existence frankly unrecognisable to us, if it is indeed desirable. Enough, for now, the known and more easily imaginable forms of human fulfilment.

6. Minimum utopia is a revolutionary objective

The use of the language of 'minimum' and 'maximum' in the present context makes it necessary to forestall one possible misunderstanding that could arise from an older meaning of that distinction. Minimum utopia, as here envisaged, entails so fundamental a transformation of the existing structures of economic wealth and power and of the distributional norms relating to need, effort and reward that it is revolutionary in scope. This must be made explicit against an argument I anticipate roughly as follows: that formulated within, for example, a discourse of human rights, minimum utopia loses all socialist specificity; there is nothing in it that speaks against capitalism is such. For the achievements of capitalism, it will be said, and the reforms it has already accommodated, when set against the disasters witnessed in this century under the banner of socialism, make capitalism the better ground for minimum utopian aspirations.

Different lines of response are possible here, among which these.

First, the comparison reverses an admonition of J.S. Mill's by contrasting actual (so-called) socialism with an idealised capitalism[10] The latter's undoubted achievements are given to us as admirable and wholesome by the simple ruse of editing out of the picture the rolling catastrophe that capitalism has been for uncounted numbers of the world's population and continues to be to this day. It in no way minimises the moral and political calamities for which the left broadly, and despite its many currents and subdivision, is answerable, to say that capitalism and its apologists are answerable for as much and of their own. Second, the presentation of this socioeconomic form, virtually always by well-shod beneficiaries of it, in the guise of achievement and reformability is a piece of rank complacency that should be a cause for shame. Indeed it would be a cause for shame for most of them if its defenders ever had to stand naked, so to say, justifying their apologetic view to all audience of severely disadvantaged others, without benefit of the mediations and distances that usually protect them from this sort of encounter. So much, at least, is the force of contemporary 'discourse ethics', whatever its other problems. Third, with the complacency goes a manifestly one-sided form of patience: I mean patience towards a type of economic relation that has been with us for a few hundred years, unceasingly dealing out human misery together with its achievements, when the prospects of socialism, on the other hand, are discounted after one inauspiciously-placed and historically much briefer experiment gone wrong.

For the rest, the crucial issue here, concerning feasible economic models of minimum utopia, is one I cannot handle and so leave to others. The claim that there could not be, even with all the burgeoning facilities of today's information technology, anything better than capitalist economic organisation and capitalist markets, I am content to meet with a simple counter-assertion. I don't believe it.

7. Minimum utopia is to be conceived not only as socialist but also as liberal

The aim of a minimum utopia is, then, anti-capitalist, but in so far as there are tenets of liberalism not indissolubly bound up with capitalism it should not be anti-liberal. This is a thesis likely to discountenance some socialists. Either they will associate it with an outlook that essentially redefines socialism as a reformed capitalism, an outlook, as I have just made clear, I do not share. Or they will have in mind other associations more repugnant still, thinking of liberalisms – the dominant ones in fact – with a tolerance for vast poverty and inequality, and which find it no problem that a footballer, rock musician or director of companies should be able to earn in the fraction of a life what most working people cannot hope for in a lifetime.

It has to be said, nevertheless, that liberalism historically has also been about trying to set limits to the accumulation and abuse of political power, about protecting the physical and mental space of individuals from unwarranted invasion, and about evolving institutions and practices, political and juridical, that contribute to such ends. That even here a concern for capitalist property has been amongst the motivating objectives does not undermine the more general value of these institutions and practices, and they should not be lightly set aside, whatever other institutional discontinuities may turn out to be necessary in achieving a more democratic and egalitarian social order. They should not be set aside, in particular, on the basis only of a present confidence in some future spontaneous harmony. The great evils we hope to be able to remedy include precisely evils against which liberal institutions have given some protection.

8. Embracing utopia means embracing an alternative ethics

A different moral culture would be required to create and sustain a condition of minimum utopia. In some ways this point will seem so obvious as not to be worth stating. Inhabiting a world used by millennia of practice and acculturation to the 'normality' of some people being able to live by the efforts of others, used, and ever more used, to the most flagrant inequalities, the coexistence of widespread want and suffering with an overflowing luxury, we look towards the possibility of a different and better world, one that would have set its face against this kind of thing and whose watchwords would encompass at least a rough equality. How even to formulate the contrast without supposing a marked change in the moral culture?

The point is only less obvious to the extent of there having been a resilient left tradition, for which Marxism bears much of the responsibility, of diminishing the place of specifically ethical discourses and ethical advocacy within the wider struggle for socialism. It may simply be noted, therefore, that if attempts to reshape moral consciousness are likely to be by themselves insufficient – a thought that was at the heart of classical Marxism in giving the priority it did to analysis of the social tendencies and agencies which might bring socialism about – it does not follow from this that attempts to reshape moral consciousness are unnecessary. In fact the task of finding a path from where we presently are to a planet on which some moderately decent norms have at last come to prevail is unthinkable without a transformation of values. It is improbable, too, that that transformation could be wholly the effect, and not also a contributory cause, of other necessary changes, social, economic and political. This is too mechanical a supposition. The very business of trying to identify, persuade and mobilise the more likely social constituencies of wider change is bound to involve fostering new forms of social consciousness, given how much present forms of it are influenced by prevailing practices. How can it make sense to envisage the desired change of consciousness as not centrally including a change in moral thinking? No serious case for socialism can now bypass the most direct and careful effort of moral persuasion.

I go on, finally, to propose what I see as two components of a minimum utopian moral philosophy.

9. The moral universe we inhabit is (as if) governed by a contract of mutual indifference

The first component is negative. It consists of a critical characterisation of the existing state of affairs. Here I put forward the gloomy proposition that we live in a world not only replete with injustices large and small and the most appalling horrors, but, what is nearly as bad, also oversupplied with a toler-ance for such things on the part of most of those not suffering from them. I have tried to encapsulate this idea – the great tolerance people have for the sufferings of others, the living comfortably with them, the attitude of practical unconcern – in the hypothesis of a *contract of mutual indifference*. According to this, the relationship holding between most of the earth's inhabitants may be thought of as governed by the implicit agreement, 'in exchange for being released by you from any putative duty or expectation calling upon me to come to your aid in distress, I similarly release you.'[11] The core argument for imputing this agreement to people may be stated as follows. If you do not come to the aid of others who are under grave assault, in acute danger or crying need, you cannot reasonably expect others to come to your aid in similar emergency; you cannot consider them so obligated to you. Other people, equally, unmoved by the emergencies of others, cannot reasonably expect to be helped in deep trouble themselves, or consider others obligated to help them. Imagine, as a limit position, a world in which nobody ever came to the aid of anyone else under grave assault or cognate misfortune. Even though no formal agreement had been made between the individuals of this world to the effect that they owed one another, under threat or misfortune, nothing in the way of aid or care, the case for imputing such an agreement to them would be compelling. For, given their bystanding dispositions, no one could reasonably entertain a contrary expectation towards the generality of his fellows: along the lines, for example, 'even though I shall do nothing for others very unfortunately placed myself, nevertheless I think they would be obliged to help me and I shall look forward to their help should I ever need it'. No one could persuasively defend such an expectation to other people.[12]

Now, I do not say that the actual world is exactly like the one just described. There are obviously qualifications needed to that description. The most important of them is that people do also act altruistically; they act, at times, in sympathy or solidarity with others; they come to their aid or rescue. I have myself written about some brave examples of this.[13] I claim, even so, that the idea of a contract of mutual indifference captures rather too well the moral logic operating in the world in which we live. Most people, most of the time, do not do enough to oppose or remedy the moral enormities and ensuring forms of wretchedness which they know about.

This is not an uplifting thesis, and in proposing it at length I have made a point of emphasising that it is not.[14] Its unedifying character is evident from one type of response when it has elicited: namely, expressions of a plain scepticism and reluctance towards it. They are based – so far as any reasons have been articulated – on questioning the notion of an *imputed* agreement; and on questioning whether it is plausible to represent people as willing to accept a potentially self-damaging agreement like the one I hypothesise. Nobody venturing this response has yet troubled, however, to answer the argument set out above: to say how, doing nothing or very little to help others in grave difficulty when she could do something or a lot, a person might convincingly defend an expectation of help for herself when in grave difficulty.

The moral logic is discomfiting all right, but the mere discomfiture cannot show that it is not compelling in its way. Minimum utopia would have to rest upon an alternative moral logic.

10. Minimum utopia presupposes a pervasive culture of mutual aid

To achieve a minimum utopia we would need to find ways of overturning, reversing, the contract of mutual indifference so that a different ethic, an ideal of multivious care, could come to prevail. To be sure, some notion of this kind has always been implicit in socialist versions of utopia, whatever socialism's more unilaterally 'scientific' adherents might have reckoned to the contrary. The contrast between a society that would give proper weight to individual need and one regulated at every level by deep inequalities of wealth already tells us this to a degree. All the same, to the extent that the strategic focus of much socialist theorising has been on economic and political structures and institutions and on how to change them, not enough attention has been devoted to exploring the specific contours of a socialist ethic. My final thesis is that the latter would have to incorporate – integrally – duties of aid and rescue, though I do not have space here to address the question of the scope and limits of such duties.[15]

We should not simply assume that the institutional framework, or a 'spontaneity' of attitudes arising from it, would suffice to result in the requisite behaviour on the part of individuals in a future utopia, all doing what was necessary to keep each other safe and well. Any set of projected minimum utopian institutions is open to potential ruin if these are not actively supported and surrounded by a rich moral consciousness of the duty of care. This is in fact the principal burden of my hypothesis of the contract of mutual indifference: it brings out just how the structural and procedural provisions of a utopia, a projectedly good or well-ordered society, are rendered nugatory – actually ineffective, literally uncompelling – by the absence of a vigorous culture of reciprocal help to meet the threat and the incidence of violation. Such a vigorous culture will need a corresponding institutional framework in order to flourish – the framework of, among other things, a robust and self-active democracy, but the institutional framework will likewise depend upon the moral culture. Without it, it will either not come into being or not survive.

Intellectually, the road to minimum utopia goes by way of looking into the moral darkness.

Conclusion

In an essay composed now more than sixty years ago, Herbert Marcuse gave expression to a clear tension within left utopian thinking. Writing with Nazism triumphant in Germany, with Stalin's baleful regime consolidated in Russia as well as in the misguided loyalties of much of the international left, he posed a question that is unavoidable for anyone thinking inside the Marxist tradition, and so for 'critical theory', his chosen idiom there. 'What if the development outlined by the theory does not occur?' Marcuse asked. 'What if the forces that were to bring about the transformation are suppressed and appear to be defeated?' He answered this question by continuing to insist, on the one hand, that 'critical theory always derives its goals only from present tendencies of the social process'; but by affirming also, on the other hand, that critical theory has no fear of accusations of utopia. It has no fear of them, he said, because what cannot be realised within the established social order 'always appears to the latter as mere utopia'. However, this very transcendence speaks in its favour rather than against it. 'Critical theory preserves obstinacy as a genuine quality of philosophical thought.'[16]

One must be careful, naturally. Obstinacy can be blind. But an obstinate utopianism is much needed against the potent forces of privilege and indifference. The issue – that is, the outcome between utopia and the brute persisting power of injustice – is ever uncertain. Still, Marcuse's answer remains more attractive half a century on than is a style of thought which, beginning from supposedly neutral general assumptions, ends by landing you in the thinker's own back yard. To be for hope.[17]

Notes

1 Karl Marx and Frederick Engels, *Collected Works,* Vol. 6, pp. 514–515.
2 See my 'Seven Types of Obloquy: Travesties of Marxism', in Ralph Miliband and Leo Panitch (eds), *Socialist Register 1990: The Retreat of the Intellectuals,* London: The Merlin Press, 1990, pp. 1–34.
3 Karl Marx, 'Preface' to *A Contribution to the Critique of Political Economy.*
4 Leon Trotsky, *Literature and Revolution,* Anne Arbor, 1960, p. 256.
5 C.L.R. James, *Beyond a Boundary,* London: Hutchinson, 1963, p. 200.
6 See Norman Geras, 'Socialist Hope in the Shadow of Catastrophe', *The Contract of Mutual Indifference: Political Philosophy after the Holocaust* (hereafter CMI), Verso, 1998, pp. 83–120.
7 'Socialist Hope in the Shadow of Catastrophe'.
8 Orwell's essay was first published under the title 'Can Socialists Be Happy', in the Christmas 1943 issue of *Tribune.*
9 Primo Levi, *If This Is a Man* and *The Truce,* London, 1987, pp. 23, 79.
10 See John Stuart Mill, *Principles of Political Economy,* Longmans, 1909, Book II, chapter 1, section 3.
11 The present section draws on CMI, especially pp. 25–48. For the quoted formulation, see p. 43. See note 6.
12 CMI, pp. 28–29.
13 See 'Richard Rorty and the Righteous Among the Nations', in Ralph Miliband and Leo Panitch (eds), *Socialist Register 1994: Between Globalism and Nationalism,* London: The Merlin Press, 1994, pp. 32–59.
14 CMI, pp. 40–41.
15 See CMI, pp. 49–77, where I do address this question.
16 'Philosophy and Critical Theory', in Herbert Marcuse, *Negations: Essays in Critical Theory,* London, 1968, pp. 142–143.
17 The positions taken in this essay draw on long (mostly email) discussions and disagreements with my friend Eve Garrard, whom I accordingly thank.

4

The controversy about Marx and justice

(Originally published in 'A Marxian Approach to the Problem of Justice', *Philosophica* (Ghent), Vol. 33 (1), 1984, pp. 33–86)

In this essay I review a fast-growing sector of the current literature on Marx and the controversy that has fuelled its growth. During the last decade or so, the keen interest within moral and political philosophy in the concept of justice has left its mark on the philosophical discussion of his work. It has left it in the shape of the question: did Marx himself condemn capitalism as unjust? There are those who have argued energetically that he did not; and as many who are equally insistent that he did — a straightforward enough division, despite some differences of approach on either side of it. To prevent misunderstanding, it is worth underlining at the outset that the question being addressed is not that of whether Marx did indeed condemn capitalism, as opposed just to analysing, describing, explaining its nature and tendencies. All parties to this dispute agree that he did, agree in other words that there is some such normative dimension to his thought, and frankly, I do not think the denial of it worth taking seriously any longer. The question is the more specific one: does Marx condemn capitalism in the light of any principle of justice?

I shall survey the case for thinking he does not and the case for thinking that he does; the textual evidence adduced and supporting argument put forth on behalf of each. Given the extent of the literature being surveyed – some three dozen items (all but one of which have appeared since 1970; and incidentally, of largely, indeed overwhelmingly, North American provenance, twenty-one of the twenty-four authors cited here either writing or hailing from that continent) – each case as I present it is a kind of composite. No one of its proponents necessarily makes use of all the texts and arguments I shall enumerate and they sometimes emphasize or formulate differently those that they do use in common. Still, I give what I hope is an accurate overall map of this dispute, before going on to venture my own judgement on it. The main body of the essay falls, therefore, into three parts. First, I review the texts and arguments put forward by those who deny that Marx condemned capitalism as unjust.

Second, I review the texts and arguments put forward by those who claim he did so condemn it. I try in these two sections to present each case broadly as made, with a minimum of critical comment. Third, I then offer some conclusions, and argument in support of them.[1]

Before getting under way, however, there is one indispensable preliminary and that is to sketch briefly a part of the theoretical background to this debate, the general lines of Marx's account of capitalist exploitation. One may speak for this purpose of the 'two faces' of it distinguishable in the wage relation. The first and more benign of them is seen in the sphere of circulation, where there is according to Marx an exchange of equivalent values, wages on the one side for labour-power on the other. The workers sell their commodity – the capacity to work – and from the capitalist they receive in exchange, in the form of wages, the value of the commodity they sell, which is to say the value of what goes into producing it, of the things workers consume by way of their historically defined subsistence. What they receive from the capitalist, Marx goes out of his way to insist, is the full equivalent in value of what they sell and so involves no cheating. The second and uglier face of the relationship now shows itself, however, in the sphere of production. Here the workers, whose labour is itself the source of the value that commodities contain, will have to work longer than the time which is necessary to reproduce the value of their own labour-power, longer than is necessary to replace the value of the wage they have received. They will perform, that is to say, surplus labour, and the surplus-value they create thereby will be appropriated by the capitalist as profit. Labour-power in operation creates a value greater than the value labour-power itself embodies and is sold for. The two faces by turns reveal their contrasting features across the pages of *Capital,* complementary aspects of the wage relation: in the sphere of circulation, an equal exchange freely contracted; in the sphere of production, the compulsion to labour some hours without reward.

This, then, is the character of capitalist exploitation. Does Marx think it unjust?

1. Marx against justice

i. A first and, on the face of it, compelling piece of evidence against supposing so is that he actually says it is not. Once the purchase of labour-power has been effected, according to Marx, this commodity belongs to the capitalist as of right, and so therefore does its use and so do the products of its use.[2] Or, expressed from the worker's point of view, 'As soon as his labour actually begins, it has already ceased to belong to him'.[3] The capitalist, Marx says in the passage most often referred to in this connection, has paid for the value of labour-power, and the fact that the use of the latter now creates a greater value, this 'is a piece of good luck for the buyer, but by no means an injustice towards the seller'.[4] Similarly:

The fact that this particular commodity, labour-power, possesses the peculiar use-value of supplying labour, and therefore of creating value, cannot affect the general law of commodity production. If, therefore, the amount of value advanced in wages is not merely found again in the product, but augmented by a surplus-value, this is not because the seller has been defrauded, for he has really received the value of his commodity; it is due solely to the fact that this commodity has been used up by the buyer.[5]

ii. Consistently with this denial that the wage relation is unjust, Marx also rails against socialists who want for their part to appeal to considerations of justice. The best-known occasion is his polemic, in 'Critique of the Gotha Programme', against the notion of a fair distribution of the proceeds of labour. 'What is "a fair distribution"?' he asks pointedly. 'Do not the bourgeois assert that the present-day distribution is "fair"? And is it not, in fact, the only "fair" distribution on the basis of the present-day mode of production? Are economic relations regulated by legal conceptions or do not, on the contrary, legal relations arise from economic ones? Have not also the socialist sectarians the most varied notions about "fair" distribution?' Shortly afterwards, he refers to such notions as 'obsolete verbal rubbish' and 'ideological nonsense about right and other trash so common among the democrats and French Socialists' – the gist of all of which seems clear enough.[6] Again, in a letter of 1877, he writes contemptuously of 'a whole gang of half-mature students and super-wise diplomaed doctors who want to give socialism a "higher, idealistic" orientation, that is to say, to replace its materialistic basis (which demands serious objective study from anyone who tries to use it) by modern mythology with its goddesses of justice, Liberty, Equality, and Fraternity'.[7] On the one occasion when Marx himself makes use of some phrases about rights and justice – in his Inaugural Address to, and Preamble to the Rules of, the First International – he explains carefully in a letter to Engels: 'I was obliged to insert two phrases about "duty" and "right" into the Preamble to the Rules, ditto about "truth, morality and justice", but these are placed in such a way that they can do no harm.'[8]

iii. What motivates the above polemics, as well as Marx's denial of any injustice in the wage relation, is perhaps already evident. It is what is suggested to many, including those whose interpretation we are presently rehearsing, by another formulation from 'Critique of the Gotha Programme'; namely, that 'Right can never be higher than the economic structure of society and its cultural development conditioned thereby'.[9] Standards of justice, this may be taken to mean, are relative or internal to specific historical modes of production. It is not merely that they are generated by these – that juridical relations and the 'forms of social consciousness' corresponding to them 'originate in the material conditions of life[10] – but that, in addition, they are only applicable to and valid for them. The only principles of justice which are appropriate to judging a particular mode of production are those that in fact 'correspond' to it, that are functional to sustaining and legitimating it. In the words of another much-quoted passage:

> It is nonsense for Gilbart to speak of natural justice in this connection [interest payment on loans – N.G.]. The justice of transactions between agents of production consists in the fact that these transactions arise from the relations of production as their natural consequence. The legal forms in which these economic transactions appear as voluntary actions of the participants, as the expressions of their common will and as contracts that can be enforced on the parties concerned by the power of the state, are mere forms that cannot themselves determine this content. They simply express it. The content is just so long as it corresponds to the mode of production and is adequate to it. It is unjust as soon as it contradicts it. Slavery, on the basis of the capitalist mode of production, is unjust; so is cheating on the quality of commodities.[11]

Now, if by relativism in this regard we understand a conception in which what is just is simply a matter of subjective viewpoint, then Marx's conception may be said not to be a relativist one. It has, on the contrary, a firmly objective basis, since it construes the standards of justice appropriate to any society as being so by virtue of the real social function they perform.[12] It remains relativist, however, in the different sense of tying every principle of justice to a specific mode of production in the way described, and thus rendering each such principle unfit to provide a basis for trans-historical judgement. On this account of things, there cannot be an independent standard of justice, external to capitalism, yet appropriate to assessing it. There can be no principle transcending historical epochs and in the light of which Marx would have been able to condemn capitalism as unjust.

iv. We can put the same point in another way. Moral norms and notions come within the compass of Marx's theory of ideology. Not only, therefore, do ideas about justice, but so does morality more generally, belong to the superstructure of any social formation. As *The German Ideology* has it, 'Morality, religion, metaphysics, and all the rest of ideology as well as the forms of consciousness corresponding to these, thus no longer retain the semblance of independence'.[13] It is not consistent with his views on ideology that Marx should have found capitalist society to be unjust by reference to historically quite general norms of justice.[14]

Reformism
v. Justice being an essentially distributive value, it is argued furthermore, to attribute to Marx a concern with it is to inflect his critique of capitalism in a direction he explicitly repudiated and leads to a reformist conclusion he did not accept. For it focuses attention too narrowly on the distribution of income and the differentials within it: on the share of the social product received by the workers, the inadequate level of their remuneration. And it suggests that their

exploitation might be eliminated by alteration and regulation of this sphere, in other words, merely by reforms in the distribution of income. As we know, however, for Marx exploitation is in the very nature of capitalism, integral to its relations of production on which the distribution of income largely depends. His preoccupation is with this more fundamental issue of the production relations and the need for a thoroughgoing revolution in them. As important as they are, reforms in the matter of wage levels simply cannot lead to the abolition of exploitation.[15] So, Marx chides the authors of the Gotha Programme with having made a fuss about 'so-called *distribution*'. The distribution of 'the means of consumption' cannot be treated independently of the mode of production.[16] So too, in *Wages, Price and Profit,* he speaks of 'that false and superficial radicalism that accepts premises and tries to evade conclusions', and he goes on: 'To clamour for *equal or even equitable retribution* on the basis of the wages system is the same as to clamour for *freedom* on the basis of the slavery system. What you think just or equitable is out of the question. The question is: What is necessary and unavoidable with a given system of production?' Later in the same work Marx proclaims, 'Instead of the *conservative* motto, "A fair day's wage for a fair day's work!" they [the workers – N.G.] ought to inscribe on their banner the *revolutionary* watchword, "*Abolition of the wages system!*"'[17]

vi. The focus on distributive justice, some say, is also reformist in another way. It leads back from Marx's materialist enterprise of seeking the real revolutionary tendencies which will overturn the capitalist order to projects of moral enlightenment and legal reform. As one commentator puts this, it 'directs attention toward confused abstract ideals of justice and away from concrete revolutionary goals'.[18] The line of thought here is that for Marx it is a form of idealism to believe historical progress occurs through a change for the better in people's moral or juridical ideas. Such a change is secondary, derivative of the transformations in society's production relations. What counts, therefore, is to identify the actual historical tendencies that make for this sort of transformation and the social forces and movements at work that are capable of consummating it. Relative to this materialist task, a critique of capitalism in the name of justice represents a retreat — just equipping the would-be revolutionary, determined and passionate as may be, 'to deliver the keynote address at the next Democratic Convention'.[19]

vii. Principles of justice are, in any case, precisely *juridical* principles. As such, they have their place within that whole institutional apparatus of state, law, sanctions and so on, by which obligatory modes of conduct are imposed upon the members of a social order. According to Marx, however, a communist society will not have this sort of apparatus. The state here withers away. Communism as envisaged by him cannot then be seen as realizing a juridical principle like one of distributive justice, as conforming to and institutionalizing this where capitalism is to be criticized for violating it.[20]

Beyond scarcity

viii. A communist society as Marx envisages it, indeed, is a society beyond justice. That is the claim of the commentators whose case we are presenting and the main textual authority for it is the same section from 'Critique of the Gotha Programme' we have already cited, in which Marx speaks his mind about 'fair distribution' and about 'right'. For, in that context, he also anticipates two sorts of distributional criterion for the different phases of a post-capitalist society and discusses them in a way these commentators take to prove their point. For convenience, I refer hereafter to the two principles involved as, respectively, the *contribution principle* and the *needs principle*. The former will apply, Marx thinks, during an earlier period of emergent communism, 'still stamped with the birth marks of the old society'. After some necessary deductions from the total social product have been made – for infrastructural and similar social purposes and the provision of public goods – each individual will receive from it, by way of means of personal consumption, an amount in proportion to his or her labour contribution. Each will be rewarded, therefore, according to an equal standard, constitutive of a situation of 'equal right'. But this is an equal right, Marx says, 'still constantly stigmatized by a bourgeois limitation'. Though it no longer permits class differences or privileges, nevertheless by measuring people solely according to their labour contribution, it allows those relatively well endowed, whether with physical or with intellectual ability, to benefit from the greater contribution they can thereby make, and it entails, conversely, for those with relatively large needs or responsibilities, greater burdens and disadvantages than others will have to bear:

> *It is, therefore, a right of inequality, in its content, like every right.* Right by its very nature can consist only in the application of an equal standard; but unequal individuals (and they would not be different individuals if they were not unequal) are measurable only by an equal standard in so far as they are brought under an equal point of view, are taken from one *definite* side only, for instance, in the present case, are regarded *only as workers* and nothing more is seen in them, everything else being ignored.

Such a one-sided approach, so to speak levelling the complex individuality of persons, is unavoidable, Marx holds, in the initial stage of communism. Only in a later period will it be possible to implement the needs principle, better able, this, to match each person's individuality:

> In a higher phase of communist society, after the enslaving subordination of the individual to the division of labour, and therewith also the antithesis between mental and physical labour, has vanished; after labour has become not only a means of life but life's prime want; after the productive forces have also increased with the all-round development of the individual, and all the springs of co-operative wealth flow more abundantly – only then can the narrow horizon of

bourgeois right be crossed in its entirety and society inscribe on its banners: From each according to his ability, to each according to his needs![21]

Now, it is argued in the light of these passages that the needs principle – which I shall render henceforth: 'From each according to their ability, to each according to their needs!' – is not a principle of distributive justice; and that in the higher phase of communism Marx speaks of, the very circumstances, of scarcity and conflict, that make such principles necessary will no longer exist. The formula is not intended by him as a principle of justice, so the argument goes, since it is clear here that he regards principles of justice, and concepts of rights associated with them, as inadequate by their nature, unable in their generality and formalism, indeed unable owing to their egalitarianism, to take account of the specific individuality of each person. The needs principle is not such a general or formal rule, because it does not subsume people under any equal standard or point of view but takes them in their specificity and variety. It is not, some even suggest, a prescriptive principle at all but simply a description of how things will eventually be. When Marx talks, therefore, of the narrow horizon of bourgeois right' being crossed, we must take him to mean that it is considerations of rights and justice as such that are transcended and left behind: 'to mean, not merely that there will be no more *bourgeois* right, but that there will be no more *Recht,* no more legal and moral rules'.[22] This possibility is based upon the hypothesis of a progressive disappearance of those conditions which create the need for codes of rights and norms of distributive justice. It is predicated, that is, on the elimination of scarcity and of other sources of human conflict, or at least on their diminution to a point of insignificance. With increasing material productivity yielding an abundance of resources; with less selfish, more sympathetic and generous interpersonal attitudes and qualities; with more harmonious and co-operative relationships all round – what from Hume to Rawls have been perceived as 'the circumstances of justice' will be present no more. If Marx sees this communist society as being 'higher' than all preceding social forms, then obviously, given what has gone before, this cannot mean he regards it as *more just.* No, it is higher according to some other standard of value.[23]

ix. For – finally, in our review of this side of the argument – Marx is committed to certain other values. As was made clear at the very beginning, no one here is denying that he condemned capitalism, and he did so in the light precisely of values other than justice: the most commonly mentioned in this connection being freedom; but also self-realization, well-being and commu-nity.[24] Unlike norms of justice, it is held, such values are not wholly relative or internal to historically specific modes of production and so are able to serve as universal criteria of judgement. There is a subordinate dispute, 'on this side of the line' as it were, as to whether they are themselves also moral values or are, rather, values of a different, non-moral sort, but I shall ignore that issue as of secondary significance, in view of the position I take in the last section of this essay on the principal issue of disagreement.

2. Marx for justice

i. If Marx sees no injustice or fraud in the wage paid by the capitalist to the labourer, then that is because these two, as he insists, exchange fully equivalent values. However, it is only in the narrow and preliminary perspective of the circulation process (so says our second group of interpreters in reply) that he does treat the wage relation as an exchange of equivalents. Only within the sphere of exchange itself, where commodities are bought and sold, and only in accordance with the criteria internal to it, with the law of value which governs the purchase and sale of commodities, does Marx depict the relation in that way. Once he moves forward, the wage contract behind him, to deal with the surplus labour that must be rendered by the worker to the capitalist within the production process, and once he sets this individual relationship in its broader class context, with the capitalist class facing the workers and exploiting them repeatedly and continuously, he goes on to represent the wage relation as not in fact an exchange of equivalents, not a genuine exchange at all. That the capitalist advances anything in exchange for labour-power, let alone something of an equivalent value, this, Marx now says, is 'only illusory' and a 'mere semblance' or 'form'[25] It is an 'appearance', a 'mere pretence'.[26] There is no true equivalence in the exchange, for the worker must perform .more labour than that which is necessary to replace the value of the wage; and thus Marx speaks of the surplus labour involved as done 'gratis' for the capitalist and as 'uncompensated', or often calls it simply 'unpaid labour'.[27] And the exchange is only an apparent one anyway since the capitalist just contributes to it what has been appropriated – *gratis!* – from the product of the labour of other workers. As Marx puts it in *Capital*:

> The exchange of equivalents, the original operation with which we started, is now turned round in such a way that there is only an apparent exchange, since, firstly, the capital which is exchanged for labour-power is itself merely a portion of the product of the labour of others which has been appropriated without an equivalent; and, secondly, this capital must not only be replaced by its producer, the worker, but replaced together with an added surplus. The relation of exchange between capitalist and worker becomes a mere semblance belonging only to the process of circulation, it becomes a mere form, which is alien to the content of the transaction itself, and merely mystifies it. The constant sale and purchase of labour-power is the form; the content is the constant appropriation by the capitalist, without equivalent, of a portion of the labour of others which has already been objectified, and his repeated exchange of this labour for a greater quantity of the living labour of others.[28]

There is a parallel to be noted here between Marx's treatment of the apparent equivalence in the wage contract and his treatment of the freedom the worker enjoys in choosing to enter that contract. For the worker may appear to do this quite voluntarily and the sphere of circulation to be, therefore, 'a very Eden of the innate rights of man ... the exclusive realm of Freedom, Equality, Property and Bentham'.[29] But the reality is different and, again, not so benign: 'the "free" worker', Marx writes, 'makes a voluntary agreement, i.e. is compelled by social conditions to sell the whole of his active life, his very capacity for labour'; and 'the period of time for which he is free to sell his labour-power is the period of time for which he is forced to sell it'.[30] As, in the one case, unilateral appropriation of the labour of others is the reality behind an appearance of equal exchange, so in the other, compulsion is the real content of the appearance of voluntary contract: 'capital ... pumps out a certain specific quantum of surplus labour from the direct producers or workers, surplus labour that it receives without an equivalent and which by its very nature always remains forced labour, however much it might appear as the result of free contractual agreement'.[31] The supposed justice of the wage relation is comparable, then, to the worker's freedom in it. It is an appearance whose real content or essence is a radically different one. It is asserted by Marx provisionally and in the context only of the circulation process where capitalist and worker treat with one another exclusively as individuals, but is then revealed in due course as mere appearance, within the overall perspective of the relations of, and in, production, a perspective this, by contrast, of the relationship of class to class.[32]

Exploitation as theft

ii. But if Marx, so to speak, takes back his assertion of an equivalence in this matter, does he also clearly take back his denial that there is any injustice involved? Does he say, in fact, and in defiance of his own strictures of other socialists, that the real and exploitative content of the wage relation is *unjust* or is in violation of anyone's *rights*? In so many words he does not, but in effect – this case continues – he does. For he often talks of the capitalist's appropriation of surplus-value in terms of 'robbery', 'theft' and the like, which is tantamount to saying that the capitalist has no right to appropriate it and that his doing so is, therefore, indeed wrongful or unjust. Thus, referring in one place to the surplus product as 'the tribute annually exacted from the working class by the capitalist class', Marx goes on: 'Even if the latter uses a portion of that tribute to purchase the additional labour-power at its full price, so that equivalent is exchanged for equivalent, the whole thing still remains the age-old activity of the conqueror, who buys commodities from the conquered with the money he has stolen from them.'[33] That is not a maverick usage on Marx's part. On the contrary. He also speaks of the annual surplus product 'embezzled from the English workers without any equivalent being given in return', and he says that 'all progress in capitalist agriculture is a progress in the art, not only of robbing the worker, but of robbing the Soil.'[34] He refers to 'the booty pumped out of the workers' and 'the total surplus-value extorted ... the common booty' and 'the loot of other people's labour.'[35] The prospective abolition of capitalist property he describes as 'the expropriation of a few usurpers.'[36] And the wealth produced under capitalism, he says, is based on the 'theft of alien labour time.'[37] Now it is perfectly possible, of course, to use the language of robbery without intending, for one's own part, any charge of injustice and wrong. One may mean by it simply to invoke, and not to endorse, some prevailing or conventional standard of rightful ownership. Thus, Robin Hood stole from the rich to help the poor, and so forth. But the whole point here is that according to Marx, as should be clear enough by now, exploitation is not robbery by prevailing and conventional standards, wrong by the norms of capitalist society. This point has been well put by Jerry Cohen: 'since ... Marx did not think that by capitalist criteria the capitalist steals, and since he did think he steals, he must have meant that he steals in some appropriately non-relativist sense. And since to steal is, in general, wrongly to take what rightly belongs to another, to steal is to commit an injustice, and a system which is "based on theft" is based on injustice.'[38]

Some see it as significant, moreover, that in his discussion of primitive capitalist accumulation in the concluding part of the first volume of *Capital*, Marx should have emphasized, amongst other violent and bloody methods, the robbery that marked this process too – robbery of 'all their own means of production' from the direct producers, theft of the common lands from the people.[39] Not right and labour, as in the idyll of political economy, but 'in actual history ... conquest, enslavement, robbery, murder, in short force, play the greatest part'.[40] This actual history may not be decisive from a purely theoretical point of view, since one could envisage a capitalism with clean origins or at least with cleaner origins than these, and it is capitalism in general, and by its very nature, that falls foul of Marx's charge of wrong, irrespective of how salubrious or otherwise its origins. Nevertheless, if he highlighted the robbery that actually occurred, he did so in order to draw attention to capitalism's unjust historical foundation. And since the context of this condemnation is precisely a transition period between modes of production, it shows surely, against what is argued on the other side, that not every standard of justice was, for him, internal to a particular mode of production.[41]

iii. From what Marx says about capitalist robbery, therefore, we can infer a commitment to independent and transcendent standards of justice, and further evidence of the same thing is provided by his way of characterizing the two principles of distribution that he anticipates for post-capitalist society. I shall come presently – at 2.viii – to the interpretation of the second of them, the needs principle, that responds to what we have seen the other group of commentators aver about it. Of import here is that, and how, Marx ranks these principles relative both to what precedes them historically and to one another. The contribution principle, by which distribution of consumption goods is based exclusively on the labour one has done, he explicitly calls an 'advance'. This principle – where 'no one can give anything except his labour, and ... nothing can pass to the ownership of individuals except individual means of consumption' – is a superior one, then, to the norms of capitalist distribution. But on the other hand, because as was earlier explained, it takes no account either of differential individual endowment or of differential needs, Marx says also that it possesses 'defects' relative to the needs principle which will eventually replace it, so that we must take the needs principle as being a yet superior one. He proposes, in other words, a hierarchy of distributive principles; and as they are not ranked by him according to any extrinsic standard of value, it is a reasonable supposition that he simply sees some principles as fairer or more just than others intrinsically, on a trans-historical standard of justice.[42]

Moral realism
iv. Marx's seemingly relativist statements in this area are not, in fact, what many have taken them to be. They are statements not of moral relativism but rather, as we may call this, of moral realism. That standards of right are, for him, sociologically grounded or determined means that the norms people believe in and live by will be powerfully influenced by the nature of their society, their class position in it, and so on.

It means, more particularly, that what standards of right can actually be implemented effectively and secured – this is constrained by the economic structure and resources of the given society. It does not mean that the standards to be used in evaluating or assessing a society must necessarily also be constrained by the same economic configuration; that the only valid criteria of assessment are those actually prevalent, those harmonious with the mode of production.[43] Marx's assertion that right cannot be 'higher than the economic structure' is a case in point. Its context makes clear – that it is a realist, not a relativist, one. He first speaks of the contribution principle as an advance over capitalism, then explains why it is defective none the less, and says that the defects are inevitable, however, during the first phase of communism. Then he makes the statement in question and says, immediately afterwards, that the different conditions of a higher phase of communism will permit the implementation of the needs principle. Implanted in this context, Marx's statement is plausibly one concerning the real prerequisites of achieving progressively higher or more advanced standards of right. It is obviously not a statement that there can be no higher or lower in this matter on account of each such standard being relative to its appropriate economic structure.[44]

v. There is nothing at all either reformist or contrary to the cast of Marx's thought, it is argued in addition, about a preoccupation with distribution as such. He does object to any over-restricted focus upon the social *division of income*, but that is because he sees the latter as more or less a consequence of the relations of production, and it is both politically misguided and theoretically senseless to condemn the necessary effects of a cause which is itself left uncriticized. On any broader view of distribution, however, Marx is clearly concerned with it: with the distribution of free time, of opportunities for fulfilling activity, of unpleasant or rebarbative work; with the distribution of welfare more generally, of social and economic benefits and burdens. And he is concerned, in particular and above all, with the distribution of productive resources, on which according to him this wider distribution depends. That is clear even in the passage of 'Critique of the Gotha Programme' from which his putative anti-distributive orientation is usually derived. For, insisting that the distribution of the means of consumption cannot be viewed as independent of the mode of production, Marx speaks of the mode of production as itself a kind of – more basic – distribution: 'the distribution of the conditions of production.'[45] His belittling of the 'fuss' about distribution, therefore, is aimed at distribution too narrowly construed and not in general. His own attention to the production relations is precisely a preoccupation with distribution, with for him the most fundamental one of all, namely that of the means of production; and as such this preoccupation is revolutionary *par excellence.*[46]

vi. Equally, there is nothing inherently reformist or idealist, from Marx's point of view, in criticism of capitalism by appeal to ethical norms or ideals, like justice. True, if such is the sole and self-sufficient, or even the principal, burden of a critical discussion of capitalism, then he does find it so wanting, but while clearly inadequate for him as an impulse to, or instrumentality of, revolutionary change, moral criticism and argument are in no way incompatible with the sort of materialist analysis – of the real historical tendencies towards revolution – that he sees as indispensable. In conjunction with that analysis, and with the actual movement and the struggles of the workers against capitalism, and with the social and economic transformations which these struggles and other developments bring about, a normative critique is perfectly in place and the denial of this just a form of what is called economism. Moral censure and justification are certainly the accompaniment of, and arguably they are a relatively independent contribution to, processes constituting the human agency of revolutionary change, the formation of a desire and a consciousness for socialism.[47]

vii. So, whatever else may be the force of categorizing principles of justice and right as juridical ones, the categorization is unacceptably narrow if it is meant to bind them indissolubly to the existence of law, in a strict and positivist sense. They are, of course, as Marx knew well, standardly embodied in legal codes, backed up by the apparatus of enforcement that is a part of the state. However, such principles can be too, in the first instance, simply ethical ones concerning what is and what is not a morally defensible distribution of goods and bads; and it is possible to conceive their realization without the paraphernalia of state coercion. If these points do not make a juridical conception, then Marx had, or he *also* had, a non-juridical conception of justice.[48]

The needs principle
viii. That is what the principle, 'From each according to their ability, to each according to their needs!', amounts to. It is in substance a principle of distributive justice even if its attainment is envisaged together with the death of the state. There are some differences worth noting in the way this is argued, amongst the writers whose interpretation is being outlined, but the common ground is that, whether knowingly or not, Marx retains a notion of rights even for the higher phase of communism. Severe as his 'Critique of the Gotha Programme' may be about a certain sort of formalism exemplified by the contribution principle, the strictures there do not finish by disposing of all types of right, or of general rules as such. They simply reveal, in effect, what rights and rules Marx finds morally inadequate. As one commentator has written, 'it is only the horizon of bourgeois right, not that of rights *Überhaupt*, that is superseded in the transition to the higher stage'.[49] The general rule, indeed, marked down for this higher stage is the fulfilment of individual needs, and the right that it generalizes a right, amongst other things, to the means of personal development or self-realization. Its complement (expressed in the first half of the famous slogan) is that each person makes an effort commensurate with her or his abilities, in taking on a share of the common tasks. If they succeed, these standards, in making good the defects of the principle they supplant – which, sensitive only to the magnitude of labour contribution, gives out larger rewards to greater capabilities and talents – this is not because they are free of either the generality or the prescriptive force characteristic of rights. It is only because Marx obviously regards need and effort as morally more appropriate, in a word fairer, criteria of distribution than individual endowment. Why else should he say of the contribution principle that 'it tacitly recognizes unequal individual endowment and thus productive capacity as natural privileges',[50] whilst looking forward to the implementation of the needs principle, quite happy therefore to countenance its recognition of unequal need, forgoing with respect to this any such talk of privilege? The element of plain good fortune in the possession of great or exceptional abilities he clearly does not see as meriting any larger reward than is inherent in the very exercise and enjoyment of them. That Marx himself thinks of the needs principle as less formalistic, or more concrete, than the one it supplants, more exactly attuned, morally speaking, to the specific individuality of each person, does not for all that undo its generality as a normative principle.

Now, it is just because of the idea of its greater responsiveness to the specificity of every individual that some of the writers who view the needs principle, along the above lines, as a standard of right and justice, agree nevertheless, with those who reject that view, that it is not a principle of equality: under it, different individuals are accepted as being, by definition, unequal individuals.[51] Others – a majority – of these writers, however, do not agree. Marx must be understood, they think, as proposing, in place of a false equality, a truer or a better one. For, the sole charge laid by him, by way of its aforesaid 'defects', against the contribution principle, is in essence that it yields unjustifiable inequalities, unequal rewards based on differences in individual ability that are for him of no moral relevance. What Marx foresees in its stead is equality not in the sense of a right to equivalent rewards for equivalent amounts of labour, nor yet in the sense of the right of each person to exactly the same things or to an identical share of social wealth; it is, rather, an equality of self-realization – everyone's right, equally, to the means of his or her own.[52] As for the prospect of an eventual abundance of resources, this is either not discussed at all here or else, acknowledged as the precondition of giving effect to the needs principle, obviously not thought incompatible with construing the latter as a principle of distributive justice. Only one writer explicitly — though another perhaps implicitly – treats the assumption of unconditional abundance as a problematic one.[53]

ix. The claim, finally, that Marx's condemnation of capitalism rests on values such as freedom and self-actualization, though not on any conception of justice, involves an inconsistent usage of his texts. Whether these other values are said themselves to constitute an ethic ('of freedom') or morality ('of emancipation'), or are regarded, on the contrary, as being non-moral goods,[54] it makes no difference in this matter; the claim sets up a distinction in his thought between two sorts of values: on the one hand, those – to do with rights and justice – necessarily dependent on and relative to historically particular social formations and hence unsuitable for the revolutionary criticism of them; on the other hand, those – like freedom and self-realization – not so dependent or relative and apt consequently for critical use. The distinction is unfounded. To the extent that Marx does postulate an ideological limitation or relativity of values, his theory of ideology is perfectly general in its reach, encompassing every sort of normative concept and not only ideas about justice. Sociology of normative belief in attempting to explain the historical bases of different values, it is consistent, however, with his also making evaluative judgements of universal range on his own behalf. Marx does, of course, condemn capitalism for its unfreedom, oppression, coercion, but so does he in substance condemn it for its injustice. And just as, conversely, he does indeed identify principles of justice that are internal to and functional for the capitalist mode of production, so also does he identify conceptions of freedom and of self-development historically relative in exactly the same way.[55] To take account only of texts in which he does the first is in the circumstances exegetically arbitrary.[56]

3. Marx against Marx

In the face of two so opposed construals of a single author's meaning, each apparently supported by a plethora of both direct citation of, and inferential reasoning from, his works, it is probably as well to begin by posing, point-blank, the question of whether a definitive resolution of this issue is possible by reference only to the letter of Marx's texts. I think there are reasons for doubting that it is. I shall mention two such, at any rate, one a consideration of a general kind, the other a more specific doctrinal point.

The first is that Marx was not a moral philosopher and there is more than likely to be some incoherence in what he gives out on these matters. To say he was no moral philosopher actually understates the relevant point. For, it is not just that he was primarily something else, scientific historian, critic of polit-ical economy, theoretician of proletarian revolution, or what have you; but in any case mere non-practitioner of moral philosophy and neutrally disposed towards it. It is that Marx, as is well known, was quite impatient and dismissive of overt theoretical reflection about normative questions, condescending only rarely to engage in it himself. He was hostile, not neutral, towards the explicit elaboration of socialist ethical theory, disdained in this area the kind of rigorous examination of problems and concepts he so insisted upon elsewhere. At the same time, and despite this, like just about everyone else he was given to the use of moral judgement. Normative viewpoints lie upon, or just beneath the surface of, his writings, and they lie there abundantly, albeit in an unsystematic form. This being so, some, perhaps even major, inconsistency here on his part is not to be excluded. The details of our two antithetical interpretations do at least suggest the possibility of it.

The second reason needs more extended exposition. It concerns what I should like to call the 'dialectical play' indulged in by Marx as to whether or not the wage relation constitutes an exchange of equivalents. Does it? The answer is: yes and no. Viewed as an exchange of commodities in the market, it does. The capitalist pays for the value of labour-power; the worker gives this commodity and receives, in exchange, a wage of equal value. But, viewed as a relation in production, the wage relation is not an exchange of equivalents. For, here the worker has still to give something: not in the sense of selling it, since the sale has already been concluded, but in the sense of personal effort; and this personal effort is the substance of a value that is larger than the value of the wage. The same thing can be expressed in other terms. Does the accumulation of value and capital which takes place result from labour that is the capitalist's? Yes and no. The labour which is its source belongs to the capitalist, for it has been bought and paid for; but it is not the labour of his (more rarely, her) own body, not the sweat of his (or her) brow. It is, if you like, labour that the capitalist owns but not the capitalist's own labour. Now, there is nothing myste-rious about all this (leave alone whether the theory of value that it depends on is defensible) – it is spelled out plainly by Marx himself and careful readers of *Capital* have no trouble grasping it. Considered from one point of view, the wage relation is an exchange of equivalents and the accumulation of capital due only to the use of what is the capitalists. Considered from another point of view, the wage relation is not an exchange of equivalents and the accumulation of capital is due to the labour of the worker. The two points of view are simply that, two different angles of vision on a single phenomenon. They depend on two different senses of what counts as an exchange of equivalents. They are in no way contradictory, but mutually consistent parts of the doctrine that labour is the source and substance of all value: that labour-power, sold for what it is worth as a commodity, in operation creates something that is worth more.

An equivocal dialectic

Which of them, however, is the appropriate point of view in the present context, the controversy about Marx and justice? Those according to whom he sees no injustice in the wage relation privilege the first, that there is an exchange of equivalents. Many (not all) of those according to whom he does regard the wage relation as unjust privilege the second, that there is not. Each side says, in effect, '*This* point of view is the only one relevant to the question of whether or not capitalism is for him unjust'.[57] But what of Marx himself? Well, Marx has it both ways, and that is at least one root of the difficulty. Note, here, that the problem is not that he affirms both points of view. As has just been said, they are mutually consistent parts of one doctrine. The problem is that he equivocates as to which of them is the one relevant to the moral question, so that it is legitimate in a way for each side to claim, about the two different perspectives: Marx *really* means us to adopt this one. For, he does say that, so far as justice is at issue, all that matters is that equal values are exchanged, in accordance with the laws of commodity production, and he thereby legitimates the view of one side in this dispute. But then, by a piece of dialectical wizardry in Chapter 24 of the first volume of *Capital*, he has these same laws turning into their very opposite. In his own words, 'the laws of appropriation or of private property, laws based on the production and circulation of commodities, become changed into their direct opposite through their own internal and inexorable dialectic'. He speaks here, similarly, of the occurrence of a 'dialectical inversion'. The exchange of equivalents has now become, accordingly, only apparent, not an exchange of equivalents – in fact theft. A passage from the *Grundrisse* tells us, in the same vein, that 'the right of property undergoes a dialectical inversion, so that on the side of capital it becomes the right to an alien product'.[58] If the laws of commodity production and exchange have actually turned into their opposite, then that legitimates the view of the other side in this dispute as well, that, when all is said and done, there is no genuine equivalence or reciprocity here.

But this turning into opposites is just a logical trick, or more generously perhaps – though that point stands – the enjoyment of intellectual paradox and surprise. It is a game with the two different senses of equivalence. Nothing, in fact, changes into its opposite in this matter. Everything persists. In so far as the laws of commodity production require that equal values be exchanged in the market, they are, and this remains so when labour-power is sold as a commodity. And in so far as these laws allow that labour-power may indeed be sold as a commodity, being itself alienable, they allow *ab initio* a relation other than, but consistent with, equal exchange in the market, a relation in which the capitalist uses the worker to reap a profit over the wage, while the worker for her or his part simply works, just giving the portion of value that the other just takes. The right of property involved is always a right of persons to use what they own, thus what they have paid the value of in exchange; and it is, consistently with that, always a right to profit from the labour of others. Both the equivalence or reciprocity and the lack of it are there from beginning to end. Marx knows all this — it is, after all, his own theory — and he says as much even in expounding the 'dialectical inversion'. But, as is so often the way with it, the dialectic here only muddies the water. A thing cannot be its opposite. If the wage relation is an exchange of equivalents and just, then that, finally, is what it is, and this can be maintained, even to the point of extreme stubbornness,[59] in the face of Marx clearly speaking otherwise. But if it does indeed turn into its direct opposite, then it is not, finally, an exchange of equivalents or just, and therefore Marx cannot really mean what he says when he says that it is. The confusion amongst his commentators is a fruit, then, of his own: of his prevarication over which perspective, equivalence or non-equivalence, really counts for this purpose; of the consequent willingness and ability to assert, to all appearances in his own voice, both that the wage relation is not unjust and that it is theft. There are other and perhaps more important causes of Marx's confusion, causes I shall come to shortly. But the path is certainly smoothed for it by his use in this context of the language of the dialectic.

In view of these considerations, any attempt to resolve the central issue in dispute must bring with it some measure of reconstruction beyond mere exegesis, and I will contend for my own part that the most cogent such reconstruction broadly vindicates those who say Marx did think capitalism unjust. It gives them the better of this argument. The enterprise requires that one be as faithful as possible to the spirit of all the pertinent texts, both those already adduced on each side and others to be cited in what follows. One should not deny the elements of confusion and inconsistency in them, a common though not a universal temptation in this debate. Rather, acknowledging their presence there, one should seek to make the best sense that can be made of them. A reconstruction along these lines, however, broadly vindicates the view that Marx thought capitalism unjust, because it is better able to explain the apparent evidence to the contrary than are those who gainsay that he did able to explain what speaks against them. The issue turns, in my opinion, on two questions. Each of them is sorely embarrassing to the case I shall henceforth here oppose, and neither has elicited a satisfactory response from its proponents. On the principle that a good test of any intellectual position is the answers it has to the strongest questions that can be put against it, the view that Marx did not condemn capitalism as unjust must be judged to be uncompelling, for all the passages from his work seemingly in its favour. I shall, in any case, now take the two crucial questions in turn, interposing between them, though, what I think needs to be conceded on account of those passages. First, I endorse the claim, against inadequate attempts to explain such talk of his away, that in characterizing exploitation as robbery, Marx was impugning the justice of it. Second, I qualify this claim in the light of his own disavowal of a critique of capitalism in the name of justice. Third, I argue that the counter-claim, that his real critique was, instead, one on behalf of freedom and self-actualization, bears within it a fatal logical flaw: probed, this reveals, at the heart of his very critique on behalf of these other values, a concern for distributive justice.

'Explanations'
Why then, firstly, does Marx use 'robbery' and cognate terms in describing the realities of capitalism, unless it is because he thinks them unjust? The force of this question is not lost on those who deny that he thinks so and, in general, they do not flinch from responding to it.[60] Nor are they short of suggested answers. On the contrary, they offer, between them, a surprisingly large number. I shall set down their suggestions here. (1) In some of the usages in question, Marx has in mind the theft, not of surplus-value, but of the worker's health or time. (2) As regards the robbery involved in particular in the primitive accumulation of capital, this has the 'straightforward' sense that some people took what did not belong to them: wrong, therefore, according to prevailing standards of rightful ownership, it does not necessarily entail a charge of injustice on Marx's own part. (3) Similarly, but with regard now to capitalist exploitation in general, this is robbery only on bourgeois society's own conceptions of justice, and not by any standard that he himself entertains. At any rate, 'it appears that' the passages under discussion can be accounted for in this way. (4) Marx's model here might be a relationship of more or less regular plunder, as of a conquering from a conquered people, and in that case 'it is not so clear that' the robbery is unjust, since, being regular, such plunder must be based on existing material possibilities, hence correspond to the given mode of production, and if it corresponds to the mode of production, then it is, we know, just, on Marx's conception of justice. (5) His talk of theft and the like is aimed in fact at the disguised coercion, or merely at the coercion, whether disguised or open, rather than at the injustice of capitalist exploita-

tion. (6) Or it is 'rhetoric pure and simple', 'Marx … speaking figuratively', or 'speaking falsely', misrepresenting his own view of things. (7) In any event, it simply cannot be taken as levelling a charge of injustice on the basis of a principle that transcends capitalism, for Marx's views on ideology prohibit him from doing that.[61]

The secret of these attempted explanations is discovered in the last of them. It might be thought that the plurality of their number testifies to the soundness and security of the interpretation of Marx they are deployed to defend, able to throw so much against a potentially damaging criticism. But it only testifies, in fact, to the feebleness of each one. If the texts themselves pointed to some strong and obvious explanation, then the authors of the above suggestions might have been expected to converge on it. In the absence of this, they do the best they can, each in his own particular way. The first three suggestions merit some detailed individual comment. Briefer and more generalized treatment then disposes of the rest of them.

As to (1), Marx does sometimes say that capital robs the workers of their time and health, or that it 'usurps' these things.[62] But, with respect to the passages in dispute in this debate, that accounts only partially for one or two of them, as open-minded readers may satisfy themselves. The main point of these passages is the theft of surplus labour and surplus value. More importantly, even where it is time and health that is the point, does not this, as one commentator has observed, 'show *at least* that on Marx's view capitalist production essentially involves the theft of the worker's time and health, and is for *that* reason unjust?'[63] As for (2), the argument has some logical force but is for all that wanting. That is, it is possible that, in speaking of the robbery that marked the dawn of capitalist society, Marx meant only to register the violation of pre-existing property rights and not himself to condemn it; to record a wrong by the then prevailing standards rather than injustice by his own. Abstractly considered, therefore, the circumstance that he was dealing with a transition between modes of production does not in itself conclusively prove that he subscribed to some trans-historical principle of justice. He might simply have been speaking relative to positive property rights.[64] But what tells us that this abstract possibility is a fact – that Marx in reality did mean what he possibly might have meant? Nothing does, absolutely nothing in the relevant texts. On the contrary, the passion of his treatment of primitive accumulation indicates the opposite, that his description of this process is also a denunciation of the brutal methods it involved. We are offered no reason here for thinking that his talk of robbery was not intended in his own name – unless inconsistency with the view that he did not consider capitalism to be unjust can itself be counted as such a reason. The argument, in other words, is merely an explanation of convenience. It responds to a need that must be met if that view is to be sustained, and has no independent textual foundation.

The same goes for the argument – (3) – that, in calling capitalist exploitation 'robbery', Marx implicitly invokes standards of justice internal to capitalism and records an injustice relative only to these. Since he never says explicitly that exploitation is unjust, whether by standards internal to capitalism or by standards external to it, how do we know that such is the burden of the robbery passages? We do not. It just 'appears that' they can be accounted for in that way. What appears, however, to others is Marx himself simply saying that the capitalist robs the worker, and as the passages themselves give not so much as a hint of any appeal to someone else's norms of justice, saying it in his own right. It is again, not the texts, but the needs of the interpretation that are the real foundation of the argument. I shall digress briefly to point out that the latter is part of a subordinate difference amongst those who concur that Marx does not himself view capitalism as unjust. Some of them claim that he does, at least, see it as unjust by its own criteria.[65] It is true that he seeks to expose an ideology of bourgeois society according to which the worker receives full recompense for all the value his or her labour-power creates. The worker, Marx holds, receives the equivalent only of some of that value, of a part of it equal to the value of labour-power itself. However, this is all that the capitalist is required to pay according to the laws of commodity production and exchange, and it is these which Marx plainly takes as the real standard of bourgeois right in this matter. If, therefore, the ideology is a deception or hypocrisy, the relation between capitalist and worker still satisfies what are for him the sole effective juridical norms of capitalist exchange.[66] So the claim is unconvincing. But, convincing or not, it makes no difference it cannot establish that when he terms exploitation, repeatedly – without qualification – 'robbery', 'theft', 'embezzlement', and surplus value 'loot' or 'booty', and capitalists 'usurpers', this does not imply that, right or wrong by bourgeois society's standards, exploitation is an injustice by Marx's own lights. It cannot establish it save via the pure presumption that exploitation cannot be that, on account of other things he says, which is the presumption generating speculation as to what else these usages might mean.

Double-counting

And this is the crux of it all. What we have here are precisely *ad hoc* and speculative attempts to explain away material that embarrasses the interpretation of Marx these writers favour. They are speculative attempts because there is nothing in the robbery passages themselves, or in their context, to confirm that they in fact have the character attributed to them in the explanations suggested. Detailed consideration of the remainder of these would involve unwarranted repetition. (7) *just asserts* that the talk of robbery cannot carry a charge of injustice, on the basis of this presumption of consistency. Doubtless on the same basis (6) equally, and very conveniently, just discounts such talk as rhetoric and self-misrepresentation. (5) is a quite arbitrary displacement; 'robbery' has a meaning distinct from 'coercion' and we are given no reason to believe either that Marx was ignorant of the distinction or that he chose to overlook it. And the tautological inadequacy of (4) is manifest. It tells us in essence, albeit with a tentativeness surely due to its own inadequacy, that 'it is not so clear that' Marx regards this particular form of robbery as unjust, because we know that it is for him not unjust if it corresponds, as regular plunder necessarily would, to the prevailing mode of production. But the question remains, why then does he characterize it as robbery? This attempt at a response, like all the others, is just based on a kind of exegetical double-counting: there must be some such explanation as these, for we already know that Marx says capitalist exploitation is not unjust and so he cannot *really* mean robbery. One can just as well reason, as others in effect do: we *know* he thinks exploitation is robbery, so he cannot *really* mean it is not unjust. Either way the reasoning begets a forced and conjectural reading of some passages from Marx's work, a reading strained against the evidence internal to them.

The assumption of some consistency is, of course, a rational principle of textual interpretation. Where an author's work reveals the clear commitment to a certain intellectual position and we nevertheless find there also some few formulations which seem to contradict that, interpretative charity demands that we should enquire whether the inconsistency is not merely an apparent one or seek some other way of explaining the formulations in question. Elsewhere, for example, I have myself argued that Marx obviously did have a concept of 'human nature' and that the one lonely – and ambiguous – passage which has encouraged many to believe otherwise is susceptible to such treatment and must be given it. The same applies to a single phrase, concerning 'uninterrupted revolution', in Lenin's writings before 1917, a phrase often used to denature the sense of his conception of the Russian revolution up to that year.[67] However, the assumption of consistency has its limits. It cannot be absolute. Otherwise, one will simply presume complete theoretical coherence where it may be lacking. When not just one or a few formulations, but a whole body of formulations, arguments, concepts, stands in the way of one of a thinker's putative intellectual commitments, then an assumption of full consistency is no longer either rational or justified. The whole of section 2 of this essay, and the literature there summarized, is testimony to the fact that this is the case with respect to Marx's disavowal of any critique of capitalist injustice. In such circumstances, the argument that he cannot have held one viewpoint because to have done so would have been inconsistent with another he affirmed, is not a good one.

In the absence, therefore, of any convincing answer to the question, why Marx should have called exploitation 'robbery' if not because he considered it unjust, one must accept the most natural reading of the passages where he so characterizes it, which is that he did consider it unjust. To treat exploitation as theft is to treat the appropriation of surplus-value and, with it, capitalist property rights as wrongs. That such was Marx's view of things, however, is a claim that has to be qualified – and this brings me to the second part of my argument. For one can no more wish away the material that is troubling to this claim than one can Marx's talk of robbery. He does explicitly deny that there is injustice in the relationship between capitalist and worker, eschews and derides any appeal on behalf of socialism to the language of rights or justice, and appears more generally to underwrite a conception wherein standards of justice are merely relative to each mode of production. Some commentators have been tempted to propose that it is in fact this sort of material which is not to be taken at face value: that his denial of any injustice in the wage relation is made 'tongue-in-cheek' or with satirical, 'ironic' intent; that he means by it to say simply – this is what is called or what is taken to be just, or this is what is just by capitalist criteria, or this is a mere appearance of justice inasmuch as the exchange to which it relates is itself a mere appearance; and that, correspondingly, the object of his impatience with socialist appeals to notions of what is just or fair is only the rhetoric of justice and not its substance.[68] In other words Marx, on these proposals, is either not speaking literally and seriously here or not speaking in his own voice. As I have already intimated, I think the temptation to have recourse to this kind of explanation is mistaken. It gives us a mirror-image of the procedure of those who would explain away Marx's assertions of robbery, just switching from one side of the intellectual profile to the other the values of what he means literally and what he does not; conveniently discounting, exactly as do writers of the opposite viewpoint, what cannot readily be accommodated within the interpretation proffered: in the present case, not the charge of theft but rather the relativizing discourse about justice.

An unacknowledged thought

But the procedure is equally unconvincing with respect to this. On internal textual evidence Marx speaks in these matters both seriously and for himself. It is true, to be sure, that it is on criteria internal to capitalism that his judgement of the equity of the wage relation is based. But then, according to the only direct and explicit statements Marx makes concerning justice, it is precisely and solely such internal and, thus, relative criteria that are relevant to deciding what is just and what is not. If the relation is just by capitalist standards, it is also just on the only explicit conception of justice that Marx himself puts forward. There is at any rate no conscious irony involved – if one does not, in the manner I have criticized, simply presume that there *must* be, given other things we know. So far as his own intentions are concerned, Marx has to be taken as meaning both that the wage contract is not unjust according to the appropriate, internal, bourgeois standards and – therefore! – that it is not unjust according to him, that is, according to the relativist definition of justice to which he expressly commits himself. From this it should be clear that in my view one cannot plausibly dispose of all of what I have termed his relativizing discourse by representing it as only apparently that and really something else. It may be true of some of his statements standardly read as relativist ones that they are not. The argument, in particular, that the proposition, 'Right can never be higher than the economic structure of society', signifies rather a sober moral realism, seems to me from the details of the proposition's context to be a cogent one, in any case no less plausible than the common relativist interpretation of these words. More generally, such a sense of or care for moral realism is unquestionably an important dimension of Marx's thought, thereby also of the problem under discussion, and it is one to which I shall later advert. All the same, I think it idle to hope to liquidate, by appeal either to this or to other considerations, what is at the very least a strong tendency on his part, one that pervades his mature writings, whatever else he may *also* do or say inconsistently with it; a tendency to relativize the status of norms and values, and whose most incontrovertible manifestation is the treatment of these as ideological, hence superstructural and merely derivative, without independent validity or trans-historical reach.

Is there, then, no way of resolving the conflict between Marx's explicit statements that are the product and reflection of this tendency and his implicit charge that capitalism is unjust, borne by, amongst other things, his usage of the terminology of robbery? I believe there is, although what I propose has itself an air of paradox about it. Not only is it perfectly coherent, however; it is the virtually mandatory conclusion in the light of all the relevant textual evidence. The proposal is: Marx did think capitalism was unjust but he did not think he thought so.[69] This is because in so far as he indeed thought directly about and formulated any opinion concerning justice, which he did only intermittently, he expressed himself as subscribing to an extremely narrow conception of it. The conception was narrow in two respects: associating justice, firstly, in more or less legal positivist fashion, with prevailing or conventional juridical norms, the standards internal to each social order; and associating it, secondly, with the distribution of consumption goods or, as this relates to capitalism, the distribution of income, and hence with a too partial focus upon the process of exchange in the market. This double association is manifest in the material cited at section 1, paras. iv above and it is obvious why on the basis of it Marx should have treated the wage contract as not unjust and justice as not a revolutionary notion. But it is these two conceptual associations that are, along with the 'dialectical inversion' discussed earlier, the source of his confusion.[70]

For neither of them is obligatory in estimating the justice of a society, which is to say that there are alternative and broader conceptions of distributive justice than they define. One may consider what is proper in virtue of a supposed set of *moral*, rather than legal or conventional, rights or entitlements – the rational content of notions of natural right – and one may also take account, in doing so, of the distribution of advantages and disadvantages quite generally, including here consequently the distribution of control over productive resources. And that is exactly what Marx does and does frequently, even if the concept, 'justice', is not expressly present to his mind and under his pen when he does it. Not compelled by the aforementioned conceptual associations, we can legitimately say, therefore, that inasmuch as he obviously finds the distribution of benefits and burdens under capitalism morally objectionable, impugning the capitalist's right to the best of it, he does think capitalism is unjust. Implicit in his work is a broader conception of justice than the one he actually formulates, notwithstanding the fact that he never himself identifies it as being such. This is not a question of simply imputing to Marx something alien to his own ways of thought. On the contrary, it is *he* who clearly, albeit *malgré lui* (despite himself), challenges the moral propriety of the distributive patterns typical of capitalism – distribution in this context, mark you, taken in its widest sense – and that he does not realize what he is doing in challenging it, precisely criticizing capitalism as unjust, is merely a confusion on his part about the potential scope of the concept of justice and thus neither here nor there so far as the substance of the issue is concerned. The challenge, by its nature, cannot be anything else than a critique of injustice. We have seen this with respect to the matter of robbery: to say that this is what capitalists are engaged in just *is*, so long as one has no well-founded alternative explanation of its meaning, to question their right to what they appropriate and so the justice of that appropriation. We may now go on to adduce further confirmation of the resolution of this controversy I have here proposed, by examining how things stand with the third matter for discussion previously signalled: Marx's commitment to the values of freedom and self-development.

The distribution of freedom

It is this commitment, remember, that is urged upon us, by those who deny his attachment to considerations of justice, as being the real basis of his condemnation of capitalism. But such a delineation of putative alternatives is a false one, as immediately becomes clear if we proceed to put the second of the two questions I have said are embarrassing to the case these writers make. Whose freedom and self-development or self-realization are at issue? The answer to this question, Marx's answer, is – tendentially everybody's. Tendentially, because of course for Marx universal freedom can only come through class struggle, the dictatorship of the proletariat, a transitional economic formation and so on, in the course of which there should be, certainly, a progressive enlargement of freedom and of opportunities for individual self-realization, but only over time and in the face of social and also material obstacles. Everybody's, however, because it is after all a universal freedom and self-development that he both envisages and looks forward to at the end of the line. And this is to say that it is the distribution and not just the extent of these, not just the aggregate quantity so to speak, that matters to him. Communist society is a better society in Marx's eyes and capitalism condemned by him at least partly because of the way in which the former makes such 'goods' available to all where the latter allots them unevenly and grossly so. His concern with distribution in the broad sense, in other words, takes in the very values said to distance him from any preoccupation with justice, so that these do not in truth supply the foundation of a separate and alternative critique of capitalism. His critique in the light of freedom and self-actualization, on the contrary, is *itself* in part a critique in the light of a conception of distributive justice, and though it is so in part only, since there is also an aggregative aspect involved, Marx clearly believing that communism will provide greater freedoms overall than has any preceding social form,[71] the identity is none the less real or important for all that.

Considering, indeed, this point's logical centrality to the whole controversy, it is surprising how little discussion there has been of it in the literature here being reviewed. For it vitiates a claim quite fundamental to the 'anti-justice' interpretation. That Marx does care about distribution broadly construed has, as I have made clear, been effectively argued by opponents of this. But the theoretical hole, the incoherence, in the interpretation that is revealed once the goods themselves of freedom and self-development are seen to fall within the scope of this distributive concern of his is something noted by few commentators and then only fleetingly, in passing.[72] In any event, the distributive dimension of Marx's treatment of these values may now be documented. I cite material relevant both to the distribution of advantages and disadvantages in general and to the distribution of freedom and self-development in particular.

In *The German Ideology,* Marx refers to the proletariat as 'a class ... which has to bear all the burdens of society without enjoying its advantages'. One sort of advantage he has in mind is evident from the following, in the same work:

> All emancipation carried through hitherto has been based ... on restricted productive forces. The production which these productive forces could provide was insufficient for the whole of society and made development possible only if some persons satisfied their needs at the expense of others, and therefore some – the minority – obtained the monopoly of development, while others – the majority – owing to the constant struggle to satisfy their most essential needs, were for the time being (i.e., until the creation of new revolutionary productive forces) excluded from any development.[73]

This disparity is also registered in the later, economic writings. Marx speaks on one occasion, for example, of 'the contradiction between those who have to work too much and those who are idlers' and of its projected disappearance with the end of capitalism.[74] Amplifying the point in *Capital* itself, he writes:

The intensity and productivity of labour being given, the part of the social working day necessarily taken up with material production is shorter and, as a consequence, the time at society's disposal for the free intellectual and social activity of the individual is greater, in proportion as work is more and more evenly divided among all the able-bodied members of society, and a particular social stratum is more and more deprived of the ability to shift the burden of labour (which is a necessity imposed by nature) from its own shoulders to those of another social stratum. The absolute minimum limit to the shortening of the working day is, from this point of view, the universality of labour. In capitalist society, free time is produced for one class by the conversion of the whole lifetime of the masses into labour-time.[75]

Some readers will think they detect, in Marx's way of putting things here, the signs of a definite evaluative attitude to the distributive imbalance he describes, and they will be right to think so. Lest it be said, however, that this thought is just prompted by their, and my, own intellectual predilections, not by anything Marx himself says, we can point to other passages of the same general type, in which a charge of moral wrong is not merely signalled obliquely but is there black on white. Thus, speaking, in a famous summary paragraph, of the cumulative processes of capitalist development, Marx says *inter alia:* 'Along with the constant decrease in the number of capitalist magnates, who usurp and monopolize all the advantages of this process of transformation, the mass of misery, oppression, slavery, degradation and exploitation grows.'[76] Note: the capitalists not only monopolize all advantages, they also *usurp* them, which is just to say that they have no right to what they monopolize. And included under this rubric of the usurpation of advantages is, once again, self-development; in the *Grundrisse* Marx writes: 'Since all *free time* is time for free development, the capitalist usurps *the free time* created by the workers for society.'[77] So, the distribution of advantages, amongst them free time and free development, and also, conversely, of burdens, is morally illegitimate, and this entails a commitment to some more acceptable, some fairer, distribution of both the first and the second.

That such indeed is what Marx is committed to, another and a better standard of distributive justice than prevails under capitalism, is also brought out clearly in a passage from the third volume of *Capital,* concerning capitalism's 'civilizing' mission. He states first: 'It is one of the civilizing aspects of capital that it extorts this surplus labour in a manner and in conditions that are more advantageous to social relations and to the creation of elements for a new and higher formation than was the case under the earlier forms of slavery, serfdom, etc.' Then, proceeding to elaborate on this statement, Marx says immediately after it: 'Thus on the one hand it leads towards a stage at which compulsion and the monopolization. of social development (with its material and intellectual advantages) by one section of society at the expense of another disappears.'[78] It could not be more direct. The social formation in prospect is 'higher', and it is higher in part because compulsion disappears, but *also* because so does the monopolization of social development by some at the expense of others. The positive distributive principle that is implicit in this judgement is spelled out by Marx elsewhere. He refers, in the first volume of *Capital,* to: 'those material conditions of production which alone can form the real basis of a higher form of society, a society in which the full and free development of every individual forms the ruling principle.'[79] Or, in the celebrated formula of the *Communist Manifesto*: 'In place of the old bourgeois society, with its classes and class antagonisms, we shall have an association, in which the free development of each is the condition for the free development of all.'[80]

Justice and class interests

So soon, therefore, as the ambit of 'distribution' is extended to cover the generality of social advantages, especially the relative availability of free time, time, that is, for autonomous individual development, itself a crucial component in Marx's conception of human freedom, it becomes evident that his critique of capitalism is motivated by distributive considerations, at least amongst others. Do those who claim that he did not think capitalism unjust have any persuasive answer to this apparent evidence against their claim? None that I have been able to discover. In fact, for the most part they do not even attempt one, either ignoring or being unaware of the problem for them here. Taking those who do have something to say about this, however, we may quickly pass over, as not worthy of serious attention in view of the texts just cited, the bare assertion of one author that 'Marxist freedom' should not be thought of as a social good to be distributed. Those texts, I submit, suffice to show the opposite. We can be nearly as quick with the argument of the same author that, since the capitalist like the worker is in a significant sense unfree so long as capitalism persists, it is not the point of Marx's critique that the former enjoys freedoms which the latter lacks.[81] It is unquestionably true, on the doctrine of alienation, that everybody is to some degree unfree under capitalism. But the passages I have quoted demonstrate, equally, that it is also part of Marx's criticism of this society that it privileges some with advantages, opportunities for free development included, which others are denied, by contrast with what he envisages as the principle of a communist society.

More space needs to be given to the only substantial attempt at a counter-argument in this matter. It is to be found in a recent paper by Allen Wood, whose earlier articles played so prominent a part in stimulating the whole debate. Wood concedes that Marx 'clearly objects to the prevailing distribution of such entities as effective control over the means of production, leisure time, and the opportunity to acquire education and skills'; but such objection, he claims, cannot be counted a criticism of capitalism as unjust, since to be that it would have to be urged on the basis of 'disinterested or impartial considerations' and it is not consistent with what Wood calls the 'class interests thesis' that Marx should have urged it on this kind of basis. The class interests thesis, part and parcel of historical materialism, is stated thus: 'Marx believes that our actions are historically effective only in so far as they involve the pursuit of class interests, and that the historical meaning of our actions consists in their functional role in the struggle between such interests.' For a rational or self-conscious historical agent, Wood argues, practical recognition of this thesis is incompatible with taking justice, in the sense of impartially grounded distributive principles, as a primary concern.[82]

Two things may be said in response to Wood's argument. The first is that the incompatibility it alleges is open to question. It is Marx's belief, certainly, that where there are classes and class struggle, disinterested or impartial consideration of the interests of everyone is merely an ideological illusion, and he aligns himself unambiguously with one set of interests, the proletariat's, against those of its exploiters. The goal of communism, furthermore, he treats as being in the interests of the proletariat and absolutely not in the interests of the capitalist, as a capitalist, and it is a goal for him that cannot be effectively secured except on the basis of proletarian interests and of the social and political movement that pursues them. However, to limit the 'historical meaning' of action along this path to its functional role within a struggle so characterized, just one sectional interest against another, is radically to diminish, to impoverish, the sense which Marx himself – everywhere – gives it. For, as partial and as 'interested' as he unashamedly proclaims it to be, such action also has a universal aspect, in virtue of the character of its historical objective, of what the proletariat's struggle is a struggle for. This universality, I have already said, is tendential; it cannot be immediate. Some genuine social interests, of really existing people, first of all the interest of the beneficiaries of exploitation in its continuance, are not allowed by Marx morally to count for anything. That is the truth in Wood's argument. But if the proletariat's struggle for its own interests can still be viewed as being of ultimately universal significance, it is just and indeed because, considered from an impartial and disinterested standpoint, the goal of this struggle, 'the free development of all', is for Marx a moral advance on the sectional monopoly of social advantages that capitalism entails. Is it, after all, a feature special to his intellectual outlook that in the pursuit of just arrangements, the interests some will have in the preservation of injustices from which they benefit must be set aside? Scarcely. In returning to someone what rightfully belongs to her, you may legitimately disregard, so far as it is only justice that is at issue, any interest that, say, I may have in holding on to it. Nor, for the rest, is there anything in itself remarkable about the fact that the historical objective or ideal which Marx adumbrates he also sees as not being immediately or straightforwardly realizable, but rather as mediated by obstacles, opposed by vested interests, as something therefore that must be

fought for through a long and difficult process on which 'causes' other than
the ideal in view will inevitably leave their mark. This is in the nature of many
political ends and it is a problem for everyone, although some give themselves
the luxury of pretending that it is not.[83]

The second thing to say is that even if one does not – as I do – contest
the incompatibility Wood argues there to be between the so-called class interests thesis and any too central preoccupation with disinterested principles of
justice, but grants him it for the sake of exhausting exegetical possibilities, it will
not suffice for his defensive purpose. For it only shows that if Marx expressed
a commitment to disinterested distributive principles, he did so inconsistently with other beliefs he held. It cannot show that he did not express such a
commitment, because he in fact did, as is manifest from the textual evidence
assembled above. Wood himself in some sort acknowledges the existence of
this evidence. In his own words,

> Marx often describes the results of the communist revolution in terms which
> suggest that if one accepts the description, then one has reasons for considering
> these results as impartially or disinterestedly good. For example, Marx claims that
> the revolution will put an end to alienation, that it will enable *every member of
> society* to develop his or her capacities, that it will promote community and soli-
> darity between people, and that it will facilitate the expansion of human produc-
> tive powers and the *universal* satisfaction of human needs.[84]

But then the passages in which these claims are made are promptly
discounted as 'the liturgy which self-styled "Marxist humanism" never tires of
chanting'. Sharp stuff, but what is, its justification? What, in other words, saves
Wood from giving their due weight to the passages which he himself so aptly
characterizes? Well, just the class interests thesis and other passages said to be
its consequence, and which he takes – wrongly, but we have decided here to let
this pass – as evincing a contempt on Marx's part for humanitarianism. Exegetically, however, it is no more legitimate to set aside the first sort of passage for
not squaring with the second than it would be to set aside the second sort,
therefore the class interests thesis itself, for not squaring with the first. If the
object is to understand Marx's own thought, as for Wood it emphatically is,
then the only proper procedure would be to register a large inconsistency
there. Simply to decide that the apparent evidence of a disinterested concern
with the distribution of human goods – and, *Wood says it,* such is what the texts
in question suggest – cannot really be what it gives every appearance of being,
is to indulge in that double-counting we have already, in the matter of robbery,
uncovered and dismissed.

On this issue as on that, proponents of the 'anti-justice' interpretation default.
They are unable satisfactorily to answer the questions they must, unable to
explain the data they must if they are to render plausible the interpretation
they propose. Their account of Marx, one must conclude, is mistaken. The

negative part of my critique of it is here completed, and it remains only to spell out positively what the substance of the conception of justice is that is implicit in his writings. The strands of it already run through the foregoing discussion and it is just a matter now of trying to draw them out more clearly.

The conditions of production

Fundamental to that conception is that there is no moral right to the private ownership and control of productive resources.[85] Treating exploitation as theft, Marx challenges the legitimacy of some people being in a position to appropriate the surplus product of social labour, and he thereby challenges the legitimacy of the system of property rights whose consequence such appropriation is. The positive titles to property embodied in capitalist law, therefore, are condemned as unjust by reference to a generalized moral entitlement – to control over the means of production – which for him has precedence over them. Some will doubtless find it mildly shocking that I attribute to Marx what is in effect a notion of natural right, and this is understandable in view of his overt hostility to the natural rights tradition. Consider, however, how he regards the private ownership of land:

> From the standpoint of a higher socioeconomic formation, the private property of particular individuals in the earth will appear just as absurd as the private property of one man in other men. Even an entire society, a nation, or all simultaneously existing societies taken together, are not the owners of the earth. They are simply its possessors, its beneficiaries, and have to bequeath it in an improved state to succeeding generations, as *boni patres familias* [good fathers of families].[86]

What *can* he be saying? That no one owns or that no one can own land? But Marx knows all too well that individuals both can and do privately own it. Their positive legal titles to such ownership are no mystery to him. That no one, then, legal titles notwithstanding, *truly* owns it – truly *owns* it – in the sense of having a right to it which *legitimately* excludes others? Exactly. He is saying no more nor less than that people are not morally entitled to exclusive use of the productive resources of the earth; saying that private ownership of these constitutes a wrong. What else could his meaning be? There is even, according to the above passage ('they ... have to bequeath it in an improved state' etc.), a moral obligation in this matter to later generations. The same judgements are betrayed by the tenor of other, similar texts. Thus, in connection with rent, Marx writes that 'the tremendous power [of] landed property when it is combined together with industrial capital in the same hands enables capital practically to exclude workers engaged in a struggle over wages from the very earth itself as their habitat. One section of society here demands a tribute from the other for the very right to live on the earth.' And of capitalist agriculture he says: 'Instead of a conscious and rational treatment of the land as permanent communal property, as the *inalienable* condition for the existence and reproduction of the chain of human generations, we have the exploitation and the squandering of the powers of the earth.'[87]

Taken together with the language of usurpation and robbery, passages like these put beyond doubt Marx's conviction that the 'distribution of the conditions of production' in capitalist society is unjust.[88] Now, I have said that this conviction is fundamental to his conception of justice, but it does not exhaust it. The normative principle it entails, that of collective democratic control over productive resources, is complemented by another, the needs principle, covering the distribution, broadly speaking, of individual welfare, with this second principle seen by Marx as the eventual consequence of realizing the first. And I do not agree with a suggestion which has been made on both sides of the debate that it is not the particular content of the needs principle, or of any other distributive principle which might govern access to individual welfare in a classless society, that is of moment, but just the fact that any such principle will be the result of collective democratic decision.[89] I do not agree with this because one can easily imagine distributive norms or practices which, endorsed by the most democratic procedures of a social collective, will be morally objectionable none the less.

Not to put too fine a point on it: a stable majority, whatever the basis of its self-definition, arbitrarily, regularly and over an extended period votes advantages and benefits for its members and relative disadvantages for the members of some minority, whatever, in turn, the basis of its identification.[90] Of course, Marx himself plainly did *not* envisage the possibility that a classless society might so combine collective control over the conditions of production with sheer moral arbitrariness in the distribution of welfare. Whether that was simply a sign of utopian optimism on his part, as non-socialists and perhaps even some socialists may be likely to think, or rather evidence of a bold, far-sighted realism, is an issue that may be left aside, for the point here is a different one. It is that if Marx himself upholds the principle of collective control over resources with the clear expectation that its implementation will have a certain kind of further distributive consequence and will not have a certain other kind of distributive consequence for the enjoyment of basic human goods, then it is a strange caprice to make abstraction from this expectation concerning distributive consequences and impute to him an ethical conception in which it is just collective control that matters, more or less irrespective of the nature of its ulterior distributive results. Such results must surely participate in defining the value he attaches to a future communist society. It is, in any case, a fact that he expressly formulates a principle to cover them.

So I take the principle he formulates, 'From each according to their ability, to each according to their needs!', as also integral to his notion of a just society and I want now to say something additional to the arguments reported at 2.viii, in defence of construing it thus as a standard of distributive justice. There are essentially two reasons advanced against regarding it as such, and I shall consider these in turn. They are (A) that the needs principle is not a standard of equality but meant on the contrary to respond to the unique individuality of' each person, to the variety of personal character and need, and is therefore a formula for' treating people differentially; and (B) that by anticipating a time when 'all the springs of co-operative wealth flow more abundantly', Marx envisages an end to scarcity and so to the very circumstances requiring principles of justice.[91]

Needs and equality

As to (A), attention should be drawn to another text that is of interest in this connection, yet neglected in the argument over Marx's meaning in 'Critique of the Gotha Programme'. For there is also a passage in *The German Ideology* which, from the standpoint of a sort of needs principle, takes issue with a version of the contribution principle, criticizing the view 'that the "possession" and "enjoyment" of each should correspond to his "labour"'.

> But one of the most vital principles of communism, a principle which distinguishes it from all reactionary socialism, is ... that differences of *brain* and of intellectual ability do not imply any differences whatsoever in the nature of the *stomach* and of physical *needs;* therefore the false tenet, based upon existing circumstances, 'to each according to his abilities', must be changed, in so far as it relates to enjoyment in its narrower sense, into the tenet, 'to *each according to his need*'; in other words, a *different form* of activity, of labour, does not justify *inequality,* confers no *privileges* in respect of possession and enjoyment.[92]

What this passage rejects, it rejects precisely as justifying inequality, and therefore the needs principle which it commends by contrast cannot reasonably be regarded as anything but a standard of equality. The passage, however, was probably written by Moses Hess and not by Marx and Engels, who are thought only to have edited the chapter of *The German Ideology* from which it comes.[93] Needs are here construed, moreover, in an explicitly narrow sense, as basic physical needs, and as I shall argue shortly, one cannot take that as having been Marx's intention in 'Critique of the Gotha Programme'. We must be circumspect, then, as to what may legitimately be made of this passage in the present context. It would plainly be wrong to jump, without more ado, to the conclusion that, because of the manifestly egalitarian import of lines penned some thirty years earlier by another hand, the kindred formulations of Marx in the later text just have to be of identical import. But if such quick certainty would be unwarranted on our part, we may fairly ask how, in the light of these lines, the diametrically opposite certainty can be warranted on the part of those insisting that the principle he puts forward is not one of equality. The need for circumspection here cuts both ways. And these commentators, it should be noted, simply ignore this passage from *The German Ideology*.

Exercising all due care and caution, we are entitled none the less to make the following observations about it. First, there is no other passage in the Marx-Engels Works that has so obvious a bearing on the famous slogan from 'Critique of the Gotha Programme' as this one does, notwithstanding the assumption concerning its probable authorship. Second, it provides a salutary reminder that the tenet, 'to each according to their needs', was already part of the tradition of socialist discourse before Marx himself employed it. Third, the passage shows that this tenet was understood by others as a principle of equality and that one of these others, an erstwhile collaborator, openly proposed it as such within a work that was intended to bear Marx's name. These three points must surely suffice to open anyone's mind to there being at least a reasonable possibility – let us say no more yet than that – that Marx in turn espoused the principle in question out of a similar, egalitarian concern. In any case, fourthly and decisively, between the earlier passage from *The German Ideology* and the text of 'Critique of the Gotha Programme' there is an undeniable internal likeness which confirms that this possibility is a fact. For just as the burden of the former is that 'differences of ... intellectual ability' and thus of 'labour' cannot justify '*inequality*' or '*privileges*', so part of the burden of the latter is to find fault with the contribution principle because 'it tacitly recognizes unequal individual endowment and thus productive capacity as natural privileges' and so amounts to '*a right of inequality*'.[94]

Consideration of the earlier passage, therefore, just serves to highlight the fact that when Marx speaks of the 'defects' of the contribution principle, he clearly refers to inequalities entailed by it which are morally unacceptable in his eyes. That he does this, and in accordance, we can now see, with a pre-existing tradition of argument, supports the claim that the needs principle as he presents it is a principle of equality. It is obviously true, on the other hand, that in envisaging equal treatment from one point of view, that principle necessarily countenances unequal treatment from other points of view. All people, equally, will be able to satisfy their needs. But the means of consumption will not be divided into exactly equivalent individual shares; even equal labour contributions will not, or will not invariably, be matched by such shares being of the same size; some but not all, only those who need them, will have access to expensive drugs or medical treatment; and so forth. There is nothing unusual in this, however. The same applies to absolutely every substantive conception of social justice or principle of equality. If distribution is to be according to some standard of need, then people who make the same labour contribution, or people for that matter of the same height or born under the same astrological sign, may well not receive equivalent resources. But likewise, if distribution is according to some standard of achievement or merit, then those with identical needs or who have made similar efforts may just as well find that their needs are not equally provided for or their efforts not equally rewarded, as the case may be. It is indeed a truism of the philosophical analysis of both justice and equality that the *formal* principle involved here – 'Treat like cases alike and different cases commensurately with their differences' – is practically useless until one has specified *substantive* criteria regarding what sort of likenesses and what sort of differences are morally relevant; what kind of equality it is, in other words, that matters. Marx for his part comes down in favour of need, and against 'individual endowment', as the decisive criterion. There is no question that, in doing so, he himself emphasizes how adoption of this criterion – responding to the specific needs of each individual – must, *in some senses*, mean unequal individual treatment. It is a mistake, however, to get carried away by this emphasis of his, as are so many of the contributors to this debate. For they cannot, simply by verbal fiat, stipulate that there is not then *any* sense in which equal consideration and treatment are involved. There is, and Marx shows himself aware of it in the way he criticizes the contribution principle. The needs of all, irrespective of individual endowment, irrespective also of such other and many differentiating characteristics as will be judged to be morally irrelevant – the needs of all equally, therefore, are to be met.

Communist abundance

We may turn now to (B), the argument that since the prospective abundance of communist society will 'permit everyone's needs to be fully satisfied',[95] principles of distributive justice will have become. redundant there. There will no longer be any necessity for authoritative norms or rules that lay down what sort of distribution is fair, and thus the needs principle as proposed by Marx cannot be taken for one. The argument does not withstand close scrutiny. Some critical reflection on the concept of 'abundance', which means also on the concept of human 'needs', will show what is wrong with it. To this end, the following passage supplies a useful background to Marx's thinking on the subject. 'Man is distinguished from all other animals by the limitless and flexible nature of his needs. But it is equally true that no animal is able to restrict his needs to the same unbelievable degree and to reduce the conditions of his life to the absolute minimum.'[96] Now, when Marx anticipates the springs of wealth flowing 'more abundantly', what is his idea of abundance? He does not say directly. Indeed, there is no evidence that he gave the question any very rigorous consideration. We are obliged, in trying to answer it, to see what can be extrapolated from any texts that may be relevant — as accords with my earlier remarks about the need to find the best reconstruction we can. But there are, in any event, only three pertinently different 'possibilities' here, the terms of the above passage providing us with a convenient framework for distinguishing what they are. (a) There is abundance relative to an 'absolute minimum', a bare physical subsistence, definition of needs. (b) There is, at the other end of the scale, abundance relative to a 'limitless and flexible' notion of needs; in the sense, that is, of

everyone being able to have or do whatever they might conceivably feel themselves as needing to. (c) And there is abundance relative to some standard of
'reasonableness' — there could of course, be more than one such standard —
intermediate between (a) and (b).

We can discount (a) on the grounds that there is a lot of textual evidence
that it is not Marx's notion for a communist society. He thinks in terms not of
a minimum standard but of the expansion of individual needs.[97] And he has
in mind particularly needs of individual self-realization. This is clear from,
amongst much else that could be cited, his reference in 'Critique of the Gotha
Programme' itself to 'the all-round development of the individual' and from
the contrast he draws in *Capital* when he refers to 'a mode of production in
which the worker exists to satisfy the need of the existing values for valori-
zation, as opposed to the inverse situation, in which objective wealth is there
to satisfy the worker's own need for development.'[98] The needs principle as
Marx construes it is not distinct from the other principle we have seen that he
enunciates — namely, the 'free development' of each and of all[99] — but rather
encompasses it and is not therefore to be understood in any minimalist sense.
We can discount (b), on the other hand, on the grounds that it is absurd; it is
not really a possibility at all. For 'flexible' needs are one thing, but 'limitless'
needs quite another. If by way of means of self-development you need a violin
and I need a racing bicycle, this, one may assume, will be all right. But if I need
an enormously large area, say Australia, to wander around in or generally use
as I see fit undisturbed by the presence of other people, then this obviously will
not be all right. No conceivable abundance could satisfy needs of self-development of this magnitude, given only a modest incidence of them across some
population, and it is not difficult to think of needs that are much less excessive
of which the same will be true. While it will not do simply to take it as a matter
of course that Marx cannot have entertained an absurdity, it is also not legitimate to impute this sort of thing to him without some textual basis for doing
so, and there is no such basis. His reflections in the third volume of *Capital* on
the persistence of the realm of necessity' betoken an altogether more sober
vision of communist abundance.[100]

We are bound, consequently, to conclude in favour of (c), that this is
abundance relative to some standard of 'reasonable' needs which, large and
generous as it may be possible for it to be, still falls short of any fantasy of abundance without limits. It might be said against the reasoning by which I have
reached this conclusion that the very fact that the principle under discussion
is. a needs principle rules out the kind of fantastic and extravagant individual
requirements hypothesized in the last paragraph. Marx means precisely needs,
not any old wants or fancies. But this point changes nothing at all. It is only
another route to the same conclusion. So long as the relevant notion of needs
covers more than 'the absolute minimum', as we have seen for Marx it does, the

distinction between what may properly be counted the needs of communist women and men and what are merely wants, whims or fancies will require a standard of differentiation. It makes no difference whether this is said to distinguish reasonable from unreasonable needs, or needs *tout court* from wants and the rest. The substance is the same. There is still a determinate standard this side of unqualified abundance.

If we now ask how a standard of 'reasonableness' vis-à-vis the satisfaction of needs might be maintained without overt conflict, there are again two suggestions that we can safely reject. (i) It could be coercively imposed by a state-type body or other institution of social control. We know that this is not what Marx envisaged. (ii) The standard, if such it can be called in these circumstances, might simply be a spontaneous, unreflected one. That is to say, it might just 'so happen' that the needs of different individuals are, everywhere and always, of such a kind and such a level as to be all satisfiable in a harmonious way. I think there are good reasons for doubting that this was Marx's view of the matter. For one thing, it does not sit well with the idea of an economy subject to conscious regulation, of a *planned* use and distribution of resources. For another, the very idea of spontaneity here is open to question. These individuals will after all be 'social individuals', so that their overall needs cannot just, 'primitively', be thus and so. The prospect, in any case, of there never being any potentially conflicting needs of individual self-development is scarcely imaginable. So much the worse for a conception of communism that does depend on it. There is, finally (iii) the supposition that though there can be no primitively-given co-ordination or harmony of individual needs and though these might well sometimes potentially conflict, there will be authoritative social norms, including distributive ones, which people more or less voluntarily accept. Still plenty utopian enough for many tastes, this is a more realistic supposition and it renders Marx's principle from 'Critique of the Gotha Programme' in effect one of distributive justice. It is supported by at least these aspects of his thought: that although the state, in the Marxist sense of that term, withers away, public institutions in which the community collectively deliberates and decides on its common affairs will still exist; and that though labour will have become 'life's prime want'[101] ... there will continue to be a 'realm of necessity', in other words some work also that is not free creation or self-realization but 'determined by necessity and external expediency', a burden Marx explicitly envisages being shared by everyone, with the obvious exception of the very young, the very old, the infirm and so on[102] — even if shared only according to relative ability.

The claim, for the rest, that 'From each according to their ability, to each according to their needs!' is not meant as any kind of norm, but is merely a *description* of the future,[103] is not very plausible in the light of the fact that Marx speaks of a communist society inscribing it on its banners, no less, and with an exclamation point at that.

Conclusion

The viewpoint I have criticized in this essay may be regarded as a bogus solution to a genuine problem in Marx's thought. The problem is an inconsistency — or paradox[104] — in his attitude to normative questions. Disowning, when he is not actively ridiculing, any attachment to ideals or values, he is nevertheless quite free in making critical normative judgements, author of a discourse that is replete with the signs of an intense moral commitment. The 'anti-justice' interpretation attempts to smooth away this contradiction by representing its two sides as just applicable to different things: what Marx disowns and derides is justice, rights; the ideals of freedom, self-realization, community — these he invokes and affirms. It is a spurious resolution. The obstacle cannot be so easily levelled. Early and late, Marx's denials in this matter (efforts of repression, so to speak, of the normative dimension of his own ideas) are quite general in scope. Thus, in *The German Ideology*: 'Communism is for us not a *state of affairs* which is to be established, an *ideal* to which reality [will] have to adjust itself. We call communism the real movement which abolishes the present state of things.'[105] Similarly, twenty-five years on in *The Civil War in France*, the workers 'have no ideals to realize, but to set free the elements of the new society with which old collapsing bourgeois society itself is pregnant.'[106]

Not, then, be it noted, the ideal of freedom or of self-actualization *as opposed to* the ideal of justice: no ideals to realize, just the immanent movement and that is that. The generality of this negation leaves its mark, in fact, at the most strategic conceptual point, mocking the very disjunction of which some commentators here make so much. In the *Communist Manifesto*, a hypothetical opponent is imagined as charging that communism 'abolishes eternal truths, it abolishes all religion and all morality'. The response to the charge is not a rebuttal of it, but the acknowledgment that the communist revolution 'is the most radical rupture with traditional property relations; no wonder that its development involves the most radical rupture with traditional ideas'. But what are the eternal truths actually mentioned as being, with all morality, candidates for abolition? I quote: 'Freedom, Justice, etc.'.[107]

Marx's impatience with the language of norms and values is global in range. And yet he himself, despite it, does plainly condemn capitalism — for its oppressions and unfreedoms and also, as the argument of this essay has been, for its injustices. Denied publicly, repressed, his own ethical commitments keep returning: the values of freedom, self-development, human well-being and happiness; the ideal of a just society in which these things are decently distributed. One can perhaps go some way towards explaining this pervasive contradiction. But that does not mean either explaining it away or justifying it. It should be recognized, on the contrary, as a real and deep-seated inconsistency on Marx's part and one with not very happy effects. Some of these may have been innocent enough: the many socialists who have simply followed him in the same obfuscation, confusing both themselves and others, in one breath denying the normative standpoint clear as noonday in what they say in the next. Not so innocent, within the complex of historical causes of the crimes and tragedies which have disgraced socialism, is the moral cynicism that has sometimes dressed itself in the authority of traditional 'anti-ethical' pronouncements. Marxists should not any longer continue to propagate the aboriginal self-contradiction and confusion in this area, but must openly take responsibility for their own ethical positions, spell them out, defend and refine them. A properly elaborated Marxist conception of justice — to take only the example that is most relevant to this debate — would not be at all premature.

A certain salutary impulse, even so, can be detected in, and partially accounts for, Marx's disavowal of all commitment to ethical principle. It is what I have referred to earlier as a sense of moral realism. Expressed negatively in a distaste for easy moral rhetoric, mere moralizing, unconstrained by objective knowledge of historical realities, its positive core is the conviction that ideals alone are an insufficient tool of human liberation and the consequent dedication to trying to grasp the material preconditions of this (historically unavoidable alienations, unfreedoms and injustices included)[108] and the social agencies capable of bringing it about. Such a historical sense, all that is entailed by it in the work of Marx, is no small thing: it is Marx's strength, his greatness. The strength, I had better repeat, does not make good or excuse the deficiency. Normative analysis and judgement can be put in their proper place, a necessary if circumscribed one, without exaggerated denial or dismissive scorn. But it is relevant to remark upon the strength together with the deficiency, all the same. For there has been, and there is, no shortage of moral philosophy which, innocent of course of Marx's particular failure in this matter and generally delighted to be able to point it out, is guilty of a greater irresponsibility of its own: minute analysis of the right, the good, the just and what have you, conceptually *nice and far* from the messy throng, the scarred history of toil and comfort, power and protest, fear, hope, struggle. The contemporary discussion of precisely justice provides ample illustrative material, in the several conceptions of just social arrangements proffered in conjunction with more or less nothing, sometimes actually nothing, on how these might conceivably be achieved. The last and the largest paradox here — that Marx, despite everything, displayed a greater commitment to the creation of a just society than many more overtly interested in analysis of what justice is.[109]

Notes

1 For convenience of reference, bibliographical details of the literature under review are assembled here. In subsequent citation I then give just the author's name (followed, where there is more than one publication by the same author, by an identifying numeral in parenthesis as designated below in this note) and page

number(s). Several of the articles are cited from the following collections: M. Cohen, T. Nagel and T. Scanlon (eds), *Marx, Justice, and History,* Princeton 1980; K. Nielsen and S.C. Patten (eds), *Marx and Morality (Canadian Journal of Philosophy,* Supplementary Volume VII, 1981); J.R. Pennock and J.W. Chapman (eds), *Marxism (Nomos XXVI),* New York and London, 1983. Contributors to the debate may be grouped as follows:

[I] Those according to whom Marx did not criticize capitalism as unjust: D.P.H. Allen (1) 'Is Marxism a Philosophy?', *Journal of Philosophy,* 71, 1974, pp. 601–602 (2) 'Marx and Engels on the Distributive Justice of Capitalism', in Nielsen and Patten, pp. 221–250; G.G. Brenkert (1) 'Freedom and Private Property in Marx', in M. Cohen et al., pp. 80–105 (reprinted from *Philosophy and Public Affairs,* 8, No. 2, Winter 1979, pp. 122–147) (2) *Marx's Ethics of Freedom,* London, 1983, ch. 5; A. Buchanan (1) 'Exploitation, Alienation and Injustice', *Canadian Journal of Philosophy,* IX, No. 1, March 1979, pp. 121–139 (2) *Marx and Justice,* London, 1982, ch. 4 (a revised version of 'The Marxian Critique of Justice and Rights', in Nielsen and Patten, pp. 269–306; L. Crocker, 'Marx's Concept of Exploitation', *Social Theory and Practice,* Fall 1972, pp. 201–215; S. Lukes (1) 'Marxism, Morality and Justice', in G.H.R. Parkinson (ed.), *Marx and Marxisms,* Cambridge, 1982, pp. 177–205 (2) 'Morals', in T. Bottomore (ed.), *A Dictionary of Marxist Thought,* Oxford, 1983, pp. 341–342 (3) *Marxism and Morality,* Oxford, 1984 forthcoming, chs 3–5; R.W. Miller (1) 'Marx and Aristotle: A Kind of Consequentialism', in Nielsen and Patten, pp. 323–352 (2) *Analyzing Marx,* Princeton, 1984 forthcoming, chs 1 and 2; R.C. Tucker, *The Marxian Revolutionary Idea,* London, 1970, ch. 2 (which is reprinted from C.J. Friedrich and J.W. Chapman (eds), *Justice* (Nomos VI), New York, 1963, pp. 306–325); A.W. Wood (1) 'The Marxian Critique of Justice', in M. Cohen et al., pp. 3–41 (reprinted from *Philosophy and Public Affairs,* 1, No. 3, Spring 1972, pp. 244–282) (2) 'Marx on Right and Justice: A Reply to Husami', in M. Cohen et al., pp. 106–134 (reprinted from *Philosophy and Public Affairs,* 8, No. 3, Spring 1979, pp. 267–295) (3) *Karl Marx,* London, 1981, Part 3 (4) 'Marx and Equality', in J. Mepham and D.H. Ruben (eds), *Issues in Marxist Philosophy,* Volume 4, Brighton, 1981, pp. 195–221 (5) 'Justice and Class Interests', forthcoming in *Philosophica* (Ghent) 1984.

[II] Those according to whom Marx did criticize capitalism as unjust; R.J. Arneson, 'What's Wrong With Exploitation?', *Ethics,* 91, January 1981, pp. 202–227; G.A. Cohen (1) 'Freedom, Justice and Capitalism', *New Left Review,* 126, March/April 1981, pp. 3–16 (2) Review of *Karl Marx* by Allen W. Wood, *Mind,* XCII, No. 367, July 1983, pp. 440–445; J. Elster (1) 'Exploitation, Freedom, and Justice', in Pennock and Chapman, pp. 277–304 (2) *Karl Marx: A Critical Examination,* Cambridge, 1985 forthcoming, ch. 4; M. Green, 'Marx, Utility, and Right', *Political Theory,* 11; No. 3, August 1983, pp. 433–446; R. Hancock, 'Marx's Theory of Justice', *Social Theory and Practice,* 1, 1971, pp. 65–71; Z.I. Husami, 'Marx on Distributive Justice', in M. Cohen et al., pp. 42–79 (reprinted from *Philosophy and Public Affairs,* 8, No. 1, Fall 1978, pp. 27–64); P. Riley, 'Marx and Morality: A Reply to Richard Miller', in Pennock and Chapman, pp. 33–53; C.C. Ryan, 'Socialist Justice and the Right to the Labour Product', *Political Theory,* 8, No. 4, November 1980, pp. 503–524; H. van der Linden, 'Marx and Morality: An Impossible Synthesis?', *Theory and Society,* 13, No. 1, January 1984, pp. 119–135; D. van de Veer, 'Marx's View of Justice', *Philosophy and*

Phenomenological Research, 33, 1973, pp. 366–386; G. Young (1) 'Justice and Capitalist Production: Marx and Bourgeois Ideology', *Canadian Journal of Philosophy*, VIII, No. 3, September 1978, pp. 421–455 (2) 'Doing Marx Justice', in Nielsen and Patten, pp. 251–268.

[II*] *A* group not altogether distinct from [II] but rather more tentative, expressing reservations of one sort or another about the interpretation of [I] without directly challenging it: N. Holmstrom, 'Exploitation', *Canadian Journal of Philosophy*, VII, No. 2, June 1977, pp. 353–369; W.L. McBride, 'The Concept of Justice in Marx, Engels, and Others', *Ethics*, 85, 1975, pp. 204–218; J.H. Reiman, 'The Possibility of a Marxian Theory of Justice', in Nielsen and Patten, pp. 307–322; W.H. Shaw, 'Marxism and Moral Objectivity', in Nielsen and Patten, pp. 19–44; R.J. van der Veen, 'Property, Exploitation, Justice', *Acta Politica* (Amsterdam), 13, 1978, pp. 433–465.

2 Karl Marx, *Capital*, Volume I (Penguin edition), Harmondsworth, 1976, pp. 292, 303, and *Theories of Surplus Value*, Moscow, 1968–72, Volume I, p. 315.

3 *Capital* I, p. 677.

4 *Capital* I, p. 301.

5 *Capital* I, p. 731.

6 Karl Marx and Frederick Engels, *Selected Works*, Moscow, 1969–70, Volume 3, pp. 16, 19.

7 Karl Marx and Frederick Engels, *Selected Correspondence*, Moscow, n.d., pp. 375–376; see also *Capital* I, pp. 178–179 n. 2.

8 *Selected Correspondence*, p. 182; and see *Selected Works* 2, pp. 18–20, for the phrases in question.

9 *Selected Works* 3, p. 19.

10 Karl Marx, *A Contribution to the Critique of Political Economy*, London, 1971, p. 20.

11 *Capital*, Volume III (Penguin edition), Harmondsworth, 1981, pp. 460–461; see also *Capital* I, p. 178.

12 Wood (1), pp. 18–19 (3), pp. 131–132.

13 Karl Marx and Frederick Engels, *Collected Works*, London, 1975ff., Volume 5, pp. 36–37.

14 Brenkert (1), p. 90 (2), pp. 150, 154–155.

15 See Tucker, pp. 50–51; Wood (1), p. 27; Buchanan (1), p. 134, (2), pp. 56–57.

16 *Selected Works* 3, pp. 19–20.

17 *Selected Works* 2, pp. 56–57, 75.

18 Buchanan (1), p. 134.

19 Wood (1), p. 30 and see also (2), p. 133 (3), p. 143.

20 Wood (1), pp. 26–27, 30; Lukes (1), p. 198.

21 *Selected Works* 3, pp. 16–19.

22 Lukes (1), p. 200.

23 For this paragraph, see Tucker, p. 48; Brenkert (1), p. 91 (2), pp. 153, 162; Buchanan (1), p. 139 (2), pp. 57–59; Lukes (1), pp. 198–203 (3), chs 3 and 4; Wood (2), p. 131 (3), pp. 138–139, (4), pp. 203–211; Miller (1), pp. 338–339; Allen (1), p. 609.

24 See Tucker, p. 50; Wood (1), pp. 34–41 (2), pp. 119–128 (3), pp. 125–130, 138; Brenkert (1), pp. 81–86, 93–105 (2), ch. 4 and pp. 155–157; Allen (1), pp. 609–611; Lukes (1), p. 201 (2), p. 342, (3), chs 3 and 5; Miller (2), chs 1 and 2.

25 Karl Marx, *Grundrisse*, Harmondsworth, 1973, pp. 458, 509, 551, 674.

26 *Theories of Surplus Value* III, pp. 92–93, and I, p. 316.

27 *Capital* I, pp. 346, 680; and pp. 672, 689, 691, 693, 714, 715, 728, 729, 732, 733, 757, 769, 771; *Capital* III, p. 509; *Theories of Surplus Value* II, p. 29; *Grundrisse*, pp. 570–571.

28 *Capital* I, pp. 729–730.

29 *Capital* I, p. 280.

30 *Capital* I, pp. 382, 415.

31 *Capital* III, pp. 957–958; see also *Grundrisse*, pp. 247–249, 464.

32 This is the argument of Holmstrom, pp. 366–368; Husami, pp. 66–67; Young (1), pp 441–450 Ryan, pp. 512–513, Arneson, pp. 218–219 and of my own 'Essence and Appearance: Aspects of Fetishism in Marx's Capital', *New Left Review*, 65, January/ February 1971, at pp. 80–81, 84.

33 *Capital* I, p. 728.

34 *Capital* I, pp. 761, 638.

35 *Capital* I, p. 743; *Capital* III, pp. 312–313; *Theories of Surplus Value* II, p. 29.

36 *Capital* I, p. 930.

37 *Grundrisse*, p. 705.

38 Cohen (2), p. 443; and see Husami, pp. 45, 63, Young (1), pp. 431–433; Ryan, p. 513; Elster (1), pp. 291–293 (2), ch. 4; van der Linden, pp. 128–129.

39 *Capital* I, pp. 875, 885, 889, 895.

40 *Capital* I, p. 874.

41 See Arneson, p. 204 Cohen (1), p. 15; and especially on this last point Young (2), pp. 262–263.

42 See *Selected Works* 3, pp. 18–19; and Hancock, p. 66; van de Veer, p. 373, Husami, p. 58; Arneson, pp. 214–215; Riley, pp. 39–42; Elster (1), pp. 290–291, 296 (2), ch. 4.

43 van de Veer, pp. 371–373, Holmstrom, p. 368; Husami, pp. 49–51, Arneson, p. 216; Shaw, p. 28; Hancock, pp. 66–67.

44 *Selected Works* 3, pp. 18–19.

45 Ibid.

46 van de Veer, p. 376; Husami, p. 75; Cohen (1), pp. 13–14, Arneson, pp. 222–225; van der Veen, p. 455.

47 Holmstrom, p. 368; Husami, pp. 53–54, Ryan, p. 516 Elster (2), ch. 4.

48 Husami, pp. 78–79; Shaw, pp. 41–32 Riley, pp. 49–50 n. 40.

49 Arneson, p. 216; see also van de Veer, p. 372, and compare the text to n. 22 above.

50 *Selected Works* 3, p. 18.

51 Riley, pp. 39–43; Husami, p. 61.

52 Hancock, pp. 69–70; Arneson, pp. 214–216; Reiman, pp. 316–317, 321–322; Elster (1), p. 296 (2), ch. 4; Green, pp. 438–442.

53 Respectively Elster and – with the appearance of some inconsistency – Reiman.

54 Respectively, here, Brenkert, Lukes and Wood.

55 See *Collected Works* 6, pp. 464, 499–500, and *Grundrisse*, pp. 487–488, 651–652.

56 Young (2), pp. 266–268; Arneson, pp. 219–220 Husami, pp. 52–53.

57 See, for example, Allen (2), pp. 234–237, and Young (2), pp. 263–266.

58 *Capital* I, pp. 725–734 (the quoted material appears at pp. 729, 730 n. 6, 734); *Grundrisse*, p. 458.

59 See, for instance, Wood (3), p. 256 n. 21, and the apt comment on it by Cohen (2), p. 443.

60 But see Tucker, p. 46, having perhaps overlooked the relevant material, he says that Marx and Engels 'do not admit that profit derived from wage labour under the capitalist system is "theft"'.

61 See, for (1): Allen (2), p. 248; for (2): Brenkert (2), p. 148; for (3): Buchanan (2), pp. 187–188 n. 31; for (4): Wood (2), pp. 117–118 (3), pp. 137–138; for (5): Wood (2), p. 119 (3), p. 138, and Brenkert (2), pp. 147–148; for (6): Allen (2), pp. 246–249; for (7): Brenkert (2), pp. 149–150

62 *Capital* I, pp. 375–376, 553, 591, 599.

63 See the references at notes 33–37 above, and Young (2), pp. 256–258.

64 See text to n. 41 above.

65 See Allen (1), pp. 603–607; (2), pp. 240–241; Buchanan (1), p. 138, (2), pp. 54–55.

66 Ryan, p. 510; Brenkert (2), pp. 139–140

67 See *Marx and Human Nature: Refutation of a Legend*, London, 1983, and in particular the remarks at pp. 57–58; and *The Legacy of Rosa Luxemburg*, London 1976, pp. 70–100.

68 Holmstrom, p. 368; Husami, pp. 45, 67; Arneson, pp. 217–218; Young (1), pp. 441, 446 (2), p. 252; van de Veer, pp. 369–370.

69 Two other writers make this point: see Cohen (2), pp. 443–444 – also (1), p. 12 – and Elster (1), pp. 289–290, 303 n. 44 (2), ch. 4. Oddly, so does a third, Steven Lukes, from the other side of the debate: his essay on the subject, however, minimizes the force of the point, consigning to a footnote Marx's belief that capitalism was unjust and simply declaring it an 'unofficial' view; and while his forthcoming book appears to concede a larger place in Marx's thinking to this unofficial view, the appearance is basically deceptive since Lukes does not in fact concede what really matters here, that the belief in question shows Marx's attachment to some non-relativist standards of justice. See Lukes (1), p. 197 n. 83 (3), ch. 4.

70 See also, in connection with this paragraph and the next, Hancock, p. 66; Shaw, pp. 41–42; Ryan, pp. 516–517; van der Veen, pp. 434, 448, 455.

71 Here I disagree with Arneson, pp. 220–221.

72 See Arneson, pp. 220–221; Riley, p. 50 n. 40 and cf. Hancock pp. 68–69.

73 *Collected Works* 5, pp. 52, 431–432.

74 *Theories of Surplus Value* III, p. 256.

75 *Capital* I, p. 667.

76 *Capital* I, p. 929.

77 *Grundrisse*, p. 634.

78 *Capital* III, p. 958.

79 *Capital* I, p. 739.

80 *Collected Works* 6, p. 506.

81 See Brenkert (2), p. 158, for both arguments.

82 Wood (5).

83 See my 'Bourgeois Power and Socialist Democracy. On the Relation of Ends and Means', *The Legacy of Rosa Luxemburg*, ch. IV.

84 Wood (5), my emphasis.

85 See Cohen (1), p. 13; Ryan, p. 521.

86 *Capital* III, p. 911.
87 *Capital* III, pp. 908, 948–949 – my emphasis.
88 The bland assertion according to which (once again) 'it appears that' Marx's crit-
    icisms of capitalism are not based on any conception of 'productive-distributive'
    justice – and by this the assertion's author has in mind just what I have argued for
    in the text – is itself based, it appears, on his forbearing to give us some account
    of these passages. See Buchanan (2), pp. 59–60. And it is, candidly, no more than
    a desperate intellectual ruse to say – see Brenkert (2), p. 162 – that, collective
    property being 'a qualitatively different institution' from private property, it has
    to be regarded simply as something radically new, not as a different, more just
    arrangement, a redistribution, of the means of production. This is the discourse
    of the pure, unconstrained 'leap' and quite foreign to Marx's own sense of the
    continuities of history which, despite all novelty and change, and the growth in
    human productive powers, make the comparative analysis of social institutions a
    rational enterprise. The 'distribution of the conditions of production' (see text to
    n. 45 above) is, unproblematically, a trans-historical category for him.
89 See Crocker, p. 207, and Ryan, pp. 521–522.
90 A less 'extreme' example is given by Arneson, p. 226.
91 See I (viii) above.
92 *Collected Works* 5, pp. 537–538.
93 See Ibid., pp. 586 n. 7, 606 n. 143.
94 *Selected Works* 3, p. 18.
95 Wood (4), p. 211; and see also Lukes (1), p. 201.
96 'Results of the Immediate Process of Production', Appendix to *Capital* I, p. 1068.
97 *Capital* III, pp. 959, 986–987, 1015–1016; *Capital* I, p. 667.
98 See text to n. 21 above, and *Capital* I, p. 772.
99 See text to notes 79 and 80 above.
100 *Capital* III, p. 959.
101 See text to n. 21 above.
102 *Capital* III, pp. 959, 986 7, 1015–1016; *Theories of Surplus Value* III, p. 256; and see
    also the text to n. 75 above.
103 See I (viii).
104 See Lukes (3), for a clear statement of the paradox as well as this solution to it.
105 *Collected Works* 5, p. 49; and cf. p. 247.
106 *Selected Works* 2, p. 224.
107 *Collected Works* 6, p. 504. Allen Wood overlooks this conjunction in his use –
    consequently misuse – of this passage. See Wood (2), p. 128 (3), p. 129, and the
    comment of Arneson, p. 221.
108 See Hancock, pp. 66–67; Cohen (1), p. 16.
109 I should like to thank Michael Evans for comments of his on Marx's slogan from
    Critique of the Gotha Programme: and Jon Elster, Steven Lukes and Richard
    Miller for permitting me to see work not yet published.

5

What does it mean to be a Marxist?

(Originally published in Matthew Johnson (ed.), *The Legacy of Marxism: Contemporary Challenges, Conflicts, and Developments*, London and New York: Continuum, 2012, pp. 13–23)

I should like to begin by thanking the organizers of this conference for inviting me to take part. I am particularly glad of the opportunity to speak on this topic since it is one I have thought much about in recent times, feeling as I do that there are ways in which I continue to be a Marxist, but also that there is one way in which I don't. I'll get to that later. Let me also say at the outset, having brought up the subject of my own relationship to Marxism, that I shall be making further reference to it here. The issues I want to discuss are of quite general import; but I haven't found it possible to discuss them in a general way without at the same time touching on this individual, biographical dimension.

I shall distinguish three meanings of 'being a Marxist'. I don't say that these exhaust the field of possible meanings. They are merely three meanings of interest to me and around which I find it convenient to organize my thoughts. To signal the general shape of what I will go on to say, these three meanings may be labelled, for short, *personal*, *intellectual* and *socio-political* ways of being a Marxist. I deal with them in turn.

1. Personal

This first meaning is conceptually quite straightforward but it is not uninteresting for all that. For someone to be a Marxist, in the first – personal – sense I want to distinguish, he or she must (a) subscribe to a significant selection of recognized Marxist beliefs, and (b) describe him or herself as a Marxist. Let me elaborate on each of those two points.

(a) I put it the way I do – speaking of *a significant selection* of recognized Marxist beliefs – because I don't think there is any single essential, or obligatory, tenet of Marxist doctrine or theory without which a person must fail in their self-identification as a Marxist. In my experience this is not always agreed amongst Marxists themselves. I have come across people who regarded acceptance of the labour theory of value – or, more bizarrely, of the falling rate of profit – as a *sine qua non* of authentic Marxist identity. More famously perhaps, Lenin wrote in chapter 3 of *The State and Revolution* that 'Only he is a Marxist who extends the recognition of the class struggle to the recognition of the dictatorship of the proletariat'. But given the breadth as well as the historical age of Marxism, and the consequent intellectual diversification of it, such attempts to pin down a single compulsory requirement of Marxist belief strike me as absurd. As Stefan Collini wrote in *The Guardian* a week ago, 'A quite extraordinarily rich and sophisticated body of ideas developed, and continues to develop, under this label ...' – he is referring to Marxism – and as Marxism has not been a church (despite certain religion-like features displayed in some of its branches; despite the view of certain of its critics that it is a secular variant of religion), it is not up to anyone to decree that adherence to any single thesis is indispensable to being a Marxist.

Naturally, it would not be sensible to call someone a Marxist on the basis of her signing up to some isolated and inconsequential proposition(s) lifted from, say, *Capital* or the *Communist Manifesto*; and that is why I refer, in the first condition above, to adherence to some significant plurality of Marxist beliefs. I shall give an illustration of the point. When asked a few years ago [Geras's reference here is to an interview he gave to the magazine *Imprints*, Vol. 6, No. 3, 2002–3] whether I still thought of myself as a Marxist, I answered that I did, and gave three reasons why I did. They were: that (i) historical materialism is broadly true – or perhaps it would be more accurate to say here, where I'm not spelling out the whole answer with its qualifications, true enough; (ii) that Marxism involves an 'enduring commitment to the goal of an egalitarian, non-exploitative society'; and (iii) that I valued 'Marxism's focus upon what is sometimes called the problem of agency: the problem of finding a route, the active social forces, between existing historical tendencies and the achievement of a substantially egalitarian society'. I would still, today, give these reasons for my being a Marxist; and I offer them also as an example of how being a Marxist depends, in the first of the two conditions I have proposed, on affirming some significant conjunction of Marxist beliefs.

What about the second condition? This is (b) that the person who affirms the relevant beliefs *describes* him or herself as a Marxist. I add it as a second requirement not only because, Marxism not being a church, nobody is in a position to insist for anyone else on their membership of it: Marxism is a broad intellectual tradition, and one is free to adhere to it or not, as one chooses. But there is an additional reason for this possibility of choice, one that has long been clear to me as a matter of simple experience and that I shall now try to exemplify in quasi-formal terms.

Imagine someone who sees himself as a Marxist, but not in the sense of slavishly adhering to every important element of what he takes to be Marxist thinking; in the sense, rather, of using his critical faculties to distinguish what is right from what is wrong in that tradition and upholding only those elements he sees as viable. Thus, he says that he is a Marxist *because* of p, q and r, these all being aspects of Marxist thought which he takes to be true and/or valuable, and *despite* x, y and z, also aspects of Marxist thought but which he thinks are wrong and to be rejected. Now, here is a second person and she, it just so happens, reverses the weighting put on the very same pair of sets of components of Marxist thought. She says that she is not a Marxist, this because of x, y and z, which she, like the other guy, thinks are wrong, and *despite* p, q and r, which she too finds true and/or valuable, but not true or valuable enough to outweigh the wrongness and disvalue of x, y and z. These are two people, in other words, who agree that Marxism is good in the very same ways, and no good in the very same ways; and yet the two of them divide over whether to call themselves Marxists.

Thus, it is perfectly easy to imagine someone saying in response to my declaration of intellectual allegiance of eight years ago that, while agreeing with me that there's a lot of truth in historical materialism, *and* that the goal of an egalitarian, non-exploitative society is a good one, *and* that Marxism's focus on the problem of agency showed a commendable sense of social and political realism – nonetheless they do not subscribe to Marxism, preferring to identify with a radical left liberalism. Why they do not subscribe to Marxism is, let us say, that the insufficient attention of the tradition to ethical issues, and the lack of an adequate theory within it of political democracy, and the common dismissal by Marxists of the merits of liberalism, have all been seriously disabling features of the tradition, time and again leading its adherents astray. It is not by accident that I cite as weaknesses of Marxism features that I really do take to be such. I call myself a Marxist despite them. I can well understand why others might decline to call themselves Marxists because of them.

There is a sort of existential choice one makes. The choice is based on reasons, as I have tried to show; but the reasons are guiding rather than forcing ones, and other factors come into play, though I leave aside what those other factors are.

2. Intellectual

I turn to my second meaning of being a Marxist, the one that I have called the 'intellectual' meaning. What I have in mind here is that, as well as having some relevant combination of Marxist beliefs, a person can work – as writer, political publicist, academic, thinker, researcher – within the intellectual tradition begun by Marx and Engels and developed by later figures. They can work as Marxists, write as Marxists, by engaging with major themes or thinkers of the tradition, by wrestling with problems they perceive it to have left unresolved, by applying Marxist concepts in fresh domains, by doing new research to expand previously undeveloped aspects of Marxist thought, and so on. Here, too, I would want to emphasize the breadth and variety there has been in this way of being a Marxist.

For Marxist intellectual work embraces the work of historians who have seen themselves as applying the methods and insights of the materialist conception of history to the study of particular countries, social formations, historical periods; of political economists writing on the phases of capitalist development, today on globalization; political philosophers studying the ideas of Marxist thinkers, whether to clarify their meaning, take them further or remedy deficiencies they find there; literary and cultural theorists, interpreting literary texts and other cultural products in the light of Marxist concepts; sociologists of development; students of labour movements; those attempting to theorize the nature of fascism; etc. Whatever its weaknesses and its failures, one of the strengths of Marxism has surely been that it could animate the work of so many people across so many disciplines.

In this connection also, however, I want to propose that one shouldn't think of Marxist intellectual work in too fixed and narrow a way – so that writing history or doing political economy can be seen as a straightforwardly Marxist type of activity; whereas, say, doing moral philosophy is not, because moral philosophy isn't something Marx himself engaged in and it has not been a notable feature of Marxist discussion since Marx. For suppose, as is in fact the case, that Marxism has been deficient in certain areas, saying nothing, or nothing useful, or not much, or the wrong things; and one wants to try and make good the deficiency, help to fill the gap. I shall suggest two examples: one from my own work, the other more speculative.

What does each of us owe to other people in the way of aid or rescue when their situation is dire – life-threateningly dire? What is the *extent* of our duty to others under such circumstances, assuming there is one? Now, one can ask of these questions: are they Marxist questions? They're obviously not *specifically* Marxist since anyone could ask them; they are of quite general philosophical and indeed human concern. But they *should* be questions of interest to Marxists, since the notion of solidarity, including international solidarity, has been important to Marxists. They are, in any event, questions that I asked in my book *The Contract of Mutual Indifference*. They illustrate the fact that there are questions that have not been central in the Marxist canon but that it is proper for Marxists to pursue – proper because they are questions that arise directly from what are more specifically Marxist concerns. That someone could raise and try to answer the very same questions without relating them to any Marxist context is true, but it isn't relevant to the point I'm making: which is that the development of Marxist thought must sometimes involve working in intellectual regions, such as moral philosophy, where its presence has hitherto been weak to non-existent.

My second example I will merely gesture towards, sweepingly, as being a general requirement if political Marxism is to thrive again in future – a prospect I no longer take for granted. Marxism has been characterized by a huge deficit with respect to democracy. The deficit has been both theoretical and practical. Theoretical because, envisaging the transformation of the world, no less, Marxism never adequately projected the theory of political democracy that would be adequate to coping with so far-reaching a task. And practical because, partly in consequence, Marxist movements have time and again fallen into anti-democratic and murderous ways. I will do no more than allude to the Stalinist experience, because it is definitive for many as a warning of what Marxism could become. Unless, today and tomorrow, Marxists show themselves willing to engage fully with the intellectual resources of liberalism – yes, liberalism, this so often maligned figure on the Marxist left – and to absorb everything that liberalism knows and Marxists have either derided or belittled or ignored; unless a Marxist political theory comes to terms with the truths of liberal political theory, acknowledging the normative force of human rights, the idea of judicial independence and separation of powers, exploring different forms of representation, insisting on free elections and an untrammeled freedom of speech and opinion, understanding the virtues of political pluralism; unless all of that, Marxism as a political movement might as well shut up shop.

Note that I do not say Marxism should be *uncritical* of liberalism. Liberalism in many variants is too accommodating of unjust inequalities. Yet, if it is not willing to learn from liberalism, Marxism is unlikely to be of any benefit to anyone politically. It will deserve to have had its day. A frankly, unashamedly *liberal* Marxism – this too might look unfamiliar to many in the way of Marxist intellectual work. But it is not merely a possible, it is a vital, area for future Marxist work if Marxism itself is to have a worthwhile future. That leads, so to say organically, into the last part of this paper.

3. Socio-political

The third meaning of 'being a Marxist' that I want to discuss – the socio-political meaning – concerns not just the would-be Marxist's beliefs or the content of his or her intellectual work. It's about being part of something larger. On this meaning, a person is a Marxist if they belong to the Marxist left. Here I could refer to the old theme of the unity of theory and practice, or to the idea that Marxism as well as being a theory was a mass movement. There is a well-known pedigree for these claims, starting with the eleventh of Marx's *Theses on Feuerbach* – 'The point is to change it' – and taking in the idea of Marxism as the self-consciousness of the working class, a theory for the workers' movement. Whatever truth there may once have been in this notion of a theory providing guidance to a movement, however, it doesn't apply today. Politically, Marxism has become a very marginal presence.

Still, there is a Marxist left – both in an organized and in a looser sense. There are political organizations that profess Marxism; and beyond these there is a wider current of opinion formed by people who would call themselves Marxist or admit to being significantly influenced by Marxism; one might even count as on the periphery of the Marxist left people who would not acknowledge any direct Marxist influence on their thinking but who share with more avowed Marxists or semi-Marxists some important tenets of belief. Given what Marxism has now come to, it would surely be too strong to refer to this Marxist social presence as a *movement*. Despite that, I think we can continue to talk of a Marxist left of sorts. And one can be a Marxist in the sense of being part of this Marxist left.

At the risk of startling you, or some of you, but not just for that effect – rather in order to register my own conviction that here is a way of being a Marxist that no longer recommends itself – I am sorry to say that to be a member of the Marxist left today is to be part of something, a body of opinion, a political current, that is accursed. Steady on, you may think, that's a bit strong, isn't it? Accursed? Why that? And why now? In view of the history of the Soviet Union, or of the international communist movement that supported and excused it, or of China under Mao (to mention only those sorry examples of Marxism gone wrong), how has the Marxist left become accursed only today and not long before that?

I will not shirk the question, which is fair. This is my answer to it. It is partly personal, but also partly general. Like everybody else, I was – I am – of my generation. I was inducted into Marxism already knowing about Stalinism and all its horrors; but knowing also that that experience didn't exhaust the totality of Marxist thought or, as I thought and hoped, of Marxist possibility. Stalinism had been one grossly distorted realization of Marxism's anti-capitalist project, embarked upon under maximally unpropitious historical conditions, but other better realizations were still possible, and under the watchword this time of socialist *democracy*. Furthermore, what I knew in this regard, or at any rate hoped, I knew and hoped in the company of large numbers of others on the Western left, people not at all indulgent towards the crimes of Stalin. We were a part – for those who remember the 1960s and 1970s – of a *new* left, a left that had learned the lessons of the historic tragedy that the Stalinist experience had been. So, although there was even then a section of the Marxist left that one could aptly regard as compromised by an ugly past or indeed present, apologists for the crimes of Stalin and/or Mao, this was not the Marxist left as a whole, as we knew it.

Today, in the light of what has happened in the first decade of 21st century, it is not so easy, if you believe in human rights and the importance of the fundamental civic and political freedoms that we owe to historical liberalism, to find a Marxist left that is worth belonging to or being broadly identified with. In both its organized and its looser, more amorphous forms the Marxist left is a place of the most disgraceful apologetics and ambiguous or worse than ambiguous alignments. What makes this a matter for especial regret and criticism today, by those of us who still think of ourselves as Marxists in either or both of my first two senses but feel no identification with, and eschew membership of, the Marxist left as such, is that this is a Marxist left that can make no further appeal to historical 'innocence'. It already knows the consequences of undemocratic organization, the absence of liberal safeguards, the elevation of the great leader; and of turning a blind eye to all this so as, supposedly, not to give comfort to enemies on the political right. It *should* know better, but it doesn't.

What am I talking about? I'm talking about a Marxist left from within which after 9/11 there came voices ready to make excuses for an act of mass murder that the whole left should have forthrightly condemned. And which, more generally, is always free with forms of 'understanding' of terrorism – by another name, murder of the innocent – in a shallow root-causes sociology of grievance, alienation, poverty or what have you. And from within which there have been people willing to march side by side with radical Islamists – that is, anti-democratic and reactionary theocrats – and to shout 'We are all Hezbollah' (also not an organization renowned for its commitment to Enlightenment or, for that matter, Marxian universalist values, to say nothing of liberal and democratic ones). And within which there are still those who will sing the praises of Cuba as a post-capitalist society, its harsh way with political dissent notwithstanding. And those who will turn out in Camden to give a warm welcome to Hugo Chavez, just the latest in a line of adored leaders whose merit seems to be that they are from somewhere else. And who will speak up even for the likes of Mahmoud Ahmadinejad or the Chinese leadership where there is a matter of some criticism directed at them by Western politicians who enjoy the moral advantage of being leaders of countries with free electorates and free elections.

And who have been so convinced that there was only one possible, one legitimate, viewpoint on the left about the war in Iraq that they have reacted to others on the left who didn't share that viewpoint as if they could no longer *be* of the left. These are often the same people, incidentally – these unswervingly convinced-of-one-viewpoint ones – as opposed the US-led response to 9/11 that overthrew Taliban rule in Afghanistan, and as opposed Nato's intervention in Kosovo in 1999, and as opposed the eviction of Saddam Hussein's armies from Kuwait in 1991, and as opposed the eviction of Argentina from the Falklands in 1982. They are, in any case, unable to accommodate the idea that someone on the left might favour the overthrow of a genocidal and fascistic tyrant.

They are also, some of them, people who have worked tirelessly to put in place in British universities a policy of boycotting the academics of one country

– one country only – Israel; and irrespective of what the Israeli academics to be boycotted (in fact blacklisted) by them may individually think about the policies of their government; and irrespective of the historical pedigree of the idea of boycotts directed exclusively against Jews. And who, again some of them, treat the right of nations to self-determination as unproblematically to be recognized for many peoples but not, apparently, in the case of the Jews. [As too often, responses at the conference to these points of mine reached immediately for the easy convenience that I shouldn't confuse criticism of Israeli policy with anti-Jewish animus. As anyone can see for themselves, I took no exception in what I said to criticism of Israeli policy, an entirely legitimate activity. I took issue with (a) punitive actions directed against Israeli academics (which is not merely 'criticism'); and (b) the denial of the right to national self-determination of the Jews and the Jews alone, a denial implicit in the view that Israel is an illegitimate state (which, too, is not mere criticism, but a threat to the organized national existence of the Jewish people).]

This is a Marxist left that, in order to make its opposition to the Western military presence in Afghanistan more psychologically comfortable for itself, prefers not to talk about what the return of Taliban rule to that country would mean for its people, and its women and girls more especially, or when it does talk about it is not above mocking and belittling the genuine concern of others on that score. It is a Marxist left today which, in its Anglophone embodiment, is governed by one overriding impulse, 'anti-imperialism'; and, within this, opposition especially to any policy supported by the US or British governments, with all other considerations subordinate to that, if given any think-room at all.

I anticipate, as one possible response to all this, that these ideas and activities may be features of a small fragment, the 'far left', but that it is too quickly generalizing on my part to treat them as any more widespread than that, or as typifying the Marxist left in general. I am familiar with this response and I don't accept it. To put it briefly and bluntly, I read. I read what goes on in the opinion pages of the national press, and so far from these tropes being confined to the far left, the SWP and its like, they extend even beyond what I have referred to as the more amorphous Marxist left, into broadly 'progressive' circles that would not willingly own to the name Marxist. This is, if you want, an ironic and distorted coming to fruition of the notion of Gramscian hegemony. Even with Marxism as a body of thought in overt political decline, some of the most lamentable apologetic tropes and moral compromises of Marxism's least glorious realization have taken hold more widely amongst the left-liberal intelligentsia.

I do not say, just to be clear about this, that there are no distinctions within the body of opinion that I have here evoked, no gradations. Distinctions and gradations there certainly are. There are the 'hard' crowd: the out-and-out 'we-are-all-Hezbollah'-niks; unashamed apologists for terrorism, dressed up this in the obscuring language of 'the right to resistance' and of 'revolutionary violence', as if either formula could justify murdering the innocent; the apologists for Cuba, or China, or Iran. But there is a softer version too, offered by the practitioners of the mumble and evasion where authoritarian movements or regimes are up for assessment and possible condemnation; democrats to a man and a woman, and as insistent as anyone on the importance of basic rights when some misdemeanor of a Western government is under scrutiny, but much more 'nuanced' when patently undemocratic polities or organizations are the object of critical attention.

How to explain it, the continuing weakness, the persistent moral failure, of this sector of the left, with the Marxist left a substantial core of it? A full answer to the question would doubtless need to go much wider than I can on this occasion, but one part of the answer, I would suggest, is this. The failure has its source in a group of temptations regularly displayed by a section of the Western left when confronted by (a) the undemocratic practices of supposedly socialist or anti-imperialist or (in some assumed sense) 'progressive' states, and (b) the claims made for the democracies of the wealthier capitalist countries. There is, first, a temptation to look for considerations mitigating the lack of democracy in the kind of states I have just referred to: considerations such as blockade, encirclement (of the young Soviet state), underdevelopment, the legacy of colonialism, and so on. There is, second, an attempt to point to features compensating for that lack of democracy: principally social and economic achievements of one kind and another (rapid industrialization, Cuba's health care). Third, there are arguments to the effect that the democracies of advanced capitalist societies are themselves either flawed and limited as democracies or not really democracies at all but disguised forms of dictatorship.

Now, it is not that there is nothing at all to be said in support of these themes. In turn: (i) a country mired in poverty has fewer democratic resources than a wealthy one; (ii) where there are achievements to note, there is nothing wrong with noting them; (iii) the democracies of the capitalist world are indeed flawed in certain ways – differently, and some more than others, but invariably failing to offer all their citizens an equality of influence and rights. Nonetheless, there is a central piece of bad faith in the way that, for a section of the left, these three themes typically combine to enable their partisans to evade a single inescapable fact: namely that, flawed as they may be, the capitalist democracies are democracies, whereas none of the would-be anti-capitalist countries, anywhere, has managed to sustain comparably good or better democratic institutions over any length of time. I do not say that this means it could never happen. I do not believe that. What I do think, though, is that the democratic institutions we are familiar with have yet to be improved on in any of those places that some leftists are given to casting an indulgent eye upon even while they seek to distance themselves critically from the political institutions of their own countries, institutions from which they benefit and which are superior. Unwilling to profess a clear allegiance towards what is democratically better, a certain type of leftist is always ready to make allowances for what is democratically worse.

This is a standpoint more attached to its own anti-capitalism than it is to the struggle against political tyranny or, if it comes to it, to the opposition (obligatory for any principled socialism) to terrorist murder. Some may be upset by such a characterization of the evaluative priorities of the left I'm talking about here, for it is not a ranking openly avowed as a rule. Yet, *practically*, in terms of the dominant polemical rhetoric coming from the relevant quarter, this is how it too often goes: the democracies of the West flawed, at fault, hypocritical, aggressors, and so forth, while quite appallingly anti-democratic movements and regimes are made apology for, and bathed in the mitigation of that shallow root-causes sociology to which I earlier referred – root causes for which some proximate 'we' is always said to bear the ultimate responsibility. Tyranny, terrorism, even genocide, almost cease to be horrors in their own right, evils to be opposed alongside economic exploitation, inequality, poverty and other byproducts of global capitalism. They are, as it were, 'levelled' by always being traced back in their turn to capitalism and imperialism, so that they become lesser evils and their direct agents and perpetrators lesser enemies.

In conclusion, then, I have considered three meanings of 'being a Marxist'. They can go together or they can come apart. Marxists in the first and second meanings may also be Marxists in the third meaning; or they may not. However, unless a Marxism of personal belief and a Marxism of creative intellectual work both thoroughly renewed and wrested once and for all from the grip of anti-democratic and illiberal themes and concepts – unless *such* a Marxism can come to animate the Marxist political left, Marxism as a political force might just as well be dead and buried. A movement so slow to learn would have earned this fate.

6

The Euston Manifesto
For a renewal of progressive politics

(This text, outlining the principles for a democratic, anti-authoritarian left-wing politics, was first published online in 2006, garnering support from liberal, socialist and progressive thinkers in Europe and the United States. Geras was the principal author, with input from Damian Counsell, Alan Johnson and Shalom Lappin. See http://eustonmanifesto.org/the-eustonmanifesto/ and http://normblog.typepad.com/normblog/2006/04/the_euston_mani.html.)

A. Preamble

We are democrats and progressives.

We propose here a fresh political alignment. Many of us belong to the Left, but the principles that we set out are not exclusive. We reach out, rather, beyond the socialist Left towards egalitarian liberals and others of unambiguous democratic commitment. Indeed, the reconfiguration of progressive opinion that we aim for involves drawing a line between the forces of the Left that remain true to its authentic values, and currents that have lately shown themselves rather too flexible about these values. It involves making common cause with genuine democrats, whether socialist or not.

The present initiative has its roots in and has found a constituency through the Internet, especially the 'blogosphere'. It is our perception, however, that this constituency is under-represented elsewhere – in much of the media and the other forums of contemporary political life.

The broad statement of principles that follows is a declaration of intent. It inaugurates a new website, which will serve as a resource for the current of opinion it hopes to represent and the several foundation blogs and other sites that are behind this call for a progressive realignment.

B. Statement of principles

1 For democracy
We are committed to democratic norms, procedures and structures – freedom of opinion and assembly, free elections, the separation of legislative, executive and judicial powers, and the separation of state and religion. We value the traditions and institutions, the legacy of good governance, of those countries in which liberal, pluralist democracies have taken hold.

2 No apology for tyranny
We decline to make excuses for, to indulgently 'understand', reactionary regimes and movements for which democracy is a hated enemy – regimes that oppress their own peoples and movements that aspire to do so. We draw a firm line between ourselves and those left-liberal voices today quick to offer an apologetic explanation for such political forces.

3 Human rights for all
We hold the fundamental human rights codified in the Universal Declaration to be precisely universal, and binding on all states and political movements, indeed on everyone. Violations of these rights are equally to be condemned whoever is responsible for them and regardless of cultural context. We reject the double standards with which much self-proclaimed progressive opinion now operates, finding lesser (though all too real) violations of human rights which are closer to home, or are the responsibility of certain disfavoured governments, more deplorable than other violations that are flagrantly worse. We reject, also, the cultural relativist view according to which these basic human rights are not appropriate for certain nations or peoples.

4 Equality
We espouse a generally egalitarian politics. We look towards progress in relations between the sexes (until full gender equality is achieved), between different ethnic communities, between those of various religious affiliations and those of none, and between people of diverse sexual orientations – as well as towards broader social and economic equality all round. We leave open, as something on which there are differences of viewpoint amongst us, the question of the best economic forms of this broader equality, but we support the interests of working people everywhere and their right to organize in defence of those interests. Democratic trade unions are the bedrock organizations for the defence of workers' interests and are one of the most important forces for human rights, democracy-promotion and egalitarian internationalism. Labour rights are human rights. The universal adoption of the International Labour Organization Conventions – now routinely ignored by governments across the globe – is a priority for us. We are committed to the defence of the

rights of children, and to protecting people from sexual slavery and all forms of institutionalized abuse.

5 Development for freedom
We stand for global economic development-as-freedom and against structural economic oppression and environmental degradation. The current expansion of global markets and free trade must not be allowed to serve the narrow interests of a small corporate elite in the developed world and their associates in developing countries. The benefits of large-scale development through the expansion of global trade ought to be distributed as widely as possible in order to serve the social and economic interests of workers, farmers and consumers in all countries. Globalization must mean global social integration and a commitment to social justice. We support radical reform of the major institutions of global economic governance (World Trade Organization, International Monetary Fund, World Bank) to achieve these goals, and we support fair trade, more aid, debt cancellation and the campaign to Make Poverty History. Development can bring growth in life-expectancy and in the enjoyment of life, easing burdensome labour and shortening the working day. It can bring freedom to youth, possibilities of exploration to those of middle years, and security to old age. It enlarges horizons and the opportunities for travel, and helps make strangers into friends. Global development must be pursued in a manner consistent with environmentally sustainable growth.

6 Opposing anti-Americanism
We reject without qualification the anti-Americanism now infecting so much left-liberal (and some conservative) thinking. This is not a case of seeing the US as a model society. We are aware of its problems and failings. But these are shared in some degree with all of the developed world. The United States of America is a great country and nation. It is the home of a strong democracy with a noble tradition behind it and lasting constitutional and social achievements to its name. Its peoples have produced a vibrant culture that is the pleasure, the source-book and the envy of millions. That US foreign policy has often opposed progressive movements and governments and supported regressive and authoritarian ones does not justify generalized prejudice against either the country or its people.

7 For a two-state solution
We recognize the right of both the Israeli and the Palestinian peoples to self-determination within the framework of a two-state solution. There can be no reasonable resolution of the Israeli–Palestinian conflict that subordinates or eliminates the legitimate rights and interests of one of the sides to the dispute.

8 Against racism

For liberals and the Left, anti-racism is axiomatic. We oppose every form of racist prejudice and behaviour: the anti-immigrant racism of the far Right; tribal and inter-ethnic racism; racism against people from Muslim countries and those descended from them, particularly under cover of the War on Terror. The recent resurgence of another, very old form of racism, antisemitism, is not yet properly acknowledged in left and liberal circles. Some exploit the legitimate grievances of the Palestinian people under occupation by Israel, and conceal prejudice against the Jewish people behind the formula of 'anti-Zionism'. We oppose this type of racism too, as should go without saying.

9 United against terror

We are opposed to all forms of terrorism. The deliberate targeting of civilians is a crime under international law and all recognized codes of warfare, and it cannot be justified by the argument that it is done in a cause that is just. Terrorism inspired by Islamist ideology is widespread today. It threatens democratic values and the lives and freedoms of people in many countries. This does not justify prejudice against Muslims, who are its main victims, and amongst whom are to be found some of its most courageous opponents. But, like all terrorism, it is a menace that has to be fought, and not excused.

10 A new internationalism

We stand for an internationalist politics and the reform of international law – in the interests of global democratization and global development. Humanitarian intervention, when necessary, is not a matter of disregarding sovereignty, but of lodging this properly within the 'common life' of all peoples. If in some minimal sense a state protects the common life of its people (if it does not torture, murder and slaughter its own civilians, and meets their most basic needs of life), then its sovereignty is to be respected. But if the state itself violates this common life in appalling ways, its claim to sovereignty is forfeited and there is a duty upon the international community of intervention and rescue. Once a threshold of inhumanity has been crossed, there is a 'responsibility to protect'.

11 A critical openness.

Drawing the lesson of the disastrous history of left apologetics over the crimes of Stalinism and Maoism, as well as more recent exercises in the same vein (some of the reaction to the crimes of 9/11, the excuse-making for suicide-terrorism, the disgraceful alliances lately set up inside the 'anti-war' movement with illiberal theocrats), we reject the notion that there are no opponents on the Left. We reject, similarly, the idea that there can be no opening to ideas and individuals to our right. Leftists who make common cause with, or excuses for, anti-democratic forces should be criticized in clear and forthright terms. Conversely, we pay attention to liberal and conservative voices and ideas if they contribute to strengthening democratic norms and practices and to the battle for human progress.

12 Historical truth
In connecting to the original humanistic impulses of the movement for human progress, we emphasize the duty which genuine democrats must have to respect for the historical truth. Not only fascists, Holocaust-deniers and the like have tried to obscure the historical record. One of the tragedies of the Left is that its own reputation was massively compromised in this regard by the international Communist movement, and some have still not learned that lesson. Political honesty and straightforwardness are a primary obligation for us.

13 Freedom of ideas
We uphold the traditional liberal freedom of ideas. It is more than ever necessary today to affirm that, within the usual constraints against defamation, libel and incitement to violence, people must be at liberty to criticize ideas – even whole bodies of ideas – to which others are committed. This includes the freedom to criticize religion: particular religions and religion in general. Respect for others does not entail remaining silent about their beliefs where these are judged to be wanting.

14 Open source
As part of the free exchange of ideas and in the interests of encouraging joint intellectual endeavour, we support the open development of software and other creative works and oppose the patenting of genes, algorithms and facts of nature. We oppose the retrospective extension of intellectual property laws in the financial interests of corporate copyright holders.

The open source model is collective and competitive, collaborative and meritocratic. It is not a theoretical ideal, but a tested reality that has created common goods whose power and robustness have been proved over decades. Indeed, the best collegiate ideals of the scientific research community that gave rise to open source collaboration have served human progress for centuries.

15 A precious heritage
We reject fear of modernity, fear of freedom, irrationalism, the subordination of women; and we reaffirm the ideas that inspired the great rallying calls of the democratic revolutions of the eighteenth century: liberty, equality and solidarity; human rights; the pursuit of happiness. These inspirational ideas were made the inheritance of us all by the social-democratic, egalitarian, feminist and anti-colonial transformations of the nineteenth and twentieth

centuries – by the pursuit of social justice, the provision of welfare, the brotherhood and sisterhood of all men and women. None should be left out, none left behind. We are partisans of these values. But we are not zealots. For we embrace also the values of free enquiry, open dialogue and creative doubt, of care in judgement and a sense of the intractabilities of the world. We stand against all claims to a total – unquestionable or unquestioning – truth.

C. Elaborations

We defend liberal and pluralist democracies against all who make light of the differences between them and totalitarian and other tyrannical regimes. But these democracies have their own deficits and shortcomings. The battle for the development of more democratic institutions and procedures, for further empowering those without influence, without a voice or with few political resources, is a permanent part of the agenda of the Left.

The social and economic foundations on which the liberal democracies have developed are marked by deep inequalities of wealth and income and the survival of unmerited privilege. In turn, global inequalities are a scandal to the moral conscience of humankind. Millions live in terrible poverty. Week in, week out, tens of thousands of people – children in particular – die from preventable illnesses. Inequalities of wealth, both as between individuals and between countries, distribute life chances in an arbitrary way.

These things are a standing indictment against the international community. We on the Left, in keeping with our own traditions, fight for justice and a decent life for everyone. In keeping with those same traditions, we have also to fight against powerful forces of totalitarian-style tyranny that are on the march again. Both battles have to be fought simultaneously. One should not be sacrificed for the other.

We repudiate the way of thinking according to which the events of September 11, 2001 were America's deserved comeuppance, or 'understandable' in the light of legitimate grievances resulting from US foreign policy. What was done on that day was an act of mass murder, motivated by odious fundamentalist beliefs and redeemed by nothing whatsoever. No evasive formula can hide that.

The founding supporters of this statement took different views on the military intervention in Iraq, both for and against. We recognize that it was possible reasonably to disagree about the justification for the intervention, the manner in which it was carried through, the planning (or lack of it) for the aftermath, and the prospects for the successful implementation of democratic change. We are, however, united in our view about the reactionary, semi-fascist and murderous character of the Ba'athist regime in Iraq, and we recognize its overthrow as a liberation of the Iraqi people. We are also united in the view that, since the day on which this occurred, the proper concern of genuine liberals and members of the Left should have been the battle to put in place in Iraq a democratic political order and to rebuild the country's infrastructure, to create after decades of the most brutal oppression a life for Iraqis which those living in democratic countries take for granted – rather than picking through the rubble of the arguments over intervention.

This opposes us not only to those on the Left who have actively spoken in support of the gangs of jihadist and Ba'athist thugs of the Iraqi so-called resistance, but also to others who manage to find a way of situating themselves between such forces and those trying to bring a new democratic life to the country. We have no truck, either, with the tendency to pay lip service to these ends, while devoting most of one's energy to criticism of political opponents at home (supposedly responsible for every difficulty in Iraq), and observing a tactful silence or near silence about the ugly forces of the Iraqi 'insurgency'. The many left opponents of regime change in Iraq who have been unable to understand the considerations that led others on the Left to support it, dishing out anathema and excommunication, more lately demanding apology or repentance, betray the democratic values they profess.

Vandalism against synagogues and Jewish graveyards and attacks on Jews themselves are on the increase in Europe. 'Anti-Zionism' has now developed to a point where supposed organizations of the Left are willing to entertain openly antisemitic speakers and to form alliances with antisemitic groups. Amongst educated and affluent people are to be found individuals unembarrassed to claim that the Iraq war was fought on behalf of Jewish interests, or to make other 'polite' and subtle allusions to the harmful effect of Jewish influence in international or national politics – remarks of a kind that for more than fifty years after the Holocaust no one would have been able to make without publicly disgracing themselves. We stand against all variants of such bigotry.

The violation of basic human rights standards at Abu Ghraib, at Guantanamo, and by the practice of 'rendition', must be roundly condemned for what it is: a departure from universal principles, for the establishment of which the democratic countries themselves, and in particular the United States of America, bear the greater part of the historical credit. But we reject the double standards by which too many on the Left today treat as the worst violations of human rights those perpetrated by the democracies, while being either silent or more muted about infractions that outstrip these by far. This tendency has reached the point that officials speaking for Amnesty International, an organization which commands enormous, worldwide respect because of its invaluable work over several decades, can now make grotesque public comparison of Guantanamo with the Gulag, can assert that the legislative measures taken by the US and other liberal democracies in the War on Terror constitute a greater attack on human rights principles and values than anything we have seen in the last 50 years, *and* be defended for doing so by certain left and liberal voices.

D. Conclusion

It is vitally important for the future of progressive politics that people of liberal, egalitarian and internationalist outlook should now speak clearly. We must define ourselves against those for whom the entire progressive-democratic agenda has been subordinated to a blanket and simplistic 'anti-imperialism' and/or hostility to the current [George W. Bush] US administration. The values and goals which properly make up that agenda – the values of democracy, human rights, the continuing battle against unjustified privilege and power, solidarity with peoples fighting against tyranny and oppression – are what most enduringly define the shape of any Left worth belonging to.

7

The reductions of the left

(First published in *Dissent*, Winter 2005)

The attacks on New York and Washington on September 11, 2001, lit up the global landscape. Not only in these two cities, but wherever the news and the pictures reached during the first hours after the planes struck – all over the planet, therefore – there were people quickly able to make out features of the contemporary world that they had not previously taken in, or taken the measure of fully, things that challenged their earlier expectations and existing frameworks of understanding.

Not, however, in one quarter. With a section of the Western left, the response was as if everything remained just as it had always been. Leave aside the callousness in much of the left's response toward the human dimension of the tragedy; but in explaining the crime of 9/11 the same thin categories that had been deployed in one conflict after another during a decade and more were instantly pressed into service. Imperialism and blowback – that was pretty much all one needed to understand what had befallen the citizens of Manhattan, the passengers on the planes, and the workers at the Pentagon, and there were accordingly people content to describe the attack as a comeuppance. The crime that so brutally illuminated the contours of the international political landscape thus revealed at the same time a frozen structure of concepts and assumptions. With the aid of it, many on the left shielded themselves from realities they didn't want to see or to assign their proper weight. In what follows I comment on some aspects of this theoretical nexus.

I begin from a short essay by Paul Berman entitled 'A Friendly Drink in Time of War', which appeared in the Winter 2004 issue of *Dissent*. In that essay Berman offers six reasons why many on the left didn't see things his way over the war in Iraq, which he supported. Abbreviating them, and also adding a seventh to the six that he enumerates (it appears toward the end of his argument, though he doesn't include it as an 'official' item with its own number), I set out those reasons: (1) George W. Bush; (2) the United States as being responsible for all the problems of the world; (3) support for anything construable as being anticolonial; (4) cultural relativism; (5) hostility to Israel; (6) a failure to take antisemitism seriously; and (7) lack of any genuine grasp of, or feeling for, the meaning of extreme forms of evil and oppression. As to this last point, Berman writes,

> I always figured that a keen awareness of extreme oppression was the deepest trait of a left-wing heart. Mass graves, three hundred thousand missing Iraqis, a population crushed by thirty-five years of Baathist boots stomping on their faces – that is what fascism means!

I have no quarrel with the claim that these seven themes figured as part of the left advocacy that Berman and others of us have opposed in the debate about the Iraq War. However, looking at things more generally, beyond simply the debate over Iraq, it is worth asking if any of these reasons have priority for the distinctively *socialist* left, some of it of Marxist persuasion or formation – and within which I would reckon cultural-relativist and postmodern tropes to be rather weak.

I suggest that two of them do carry more weight: namely, numbers (2) and (7). One way of supporting this suggestion is to point out that a very large segment of the political constituency I am talking about not only opposed the Iraq War, but also opposed the intervention in Afghanistan before that, and in Kosovo before that, and so on back to the first Gulf War that evicted Saddam Hussein's armies from Kuwait. And Berman's other reasons – (1), and (3) through (6) – did not figure, or did not figure every time, in the previous conflicts I have mentioned. But the United States as the foremost embodiment of global capitalism, on one side, and (speaking loosely) regimes and movements of an utterly ghastly kind politically, on the other-these have been two common poles throughout. Why does the combination lead so many on the left to come down each time on the side they do: morally and politically, in my own view, the wrong side?

One obvious answer – put to me on a previous occasion when I raised this question on my blog – is anti-imperialism. For it is a tradition of the Marxist, and also the broader socialist, left to identify with any 'backward' (or third world, or developing) country in a conflict between it and an imperialist power. I am, of course, familiar with that tradition of identification, and so I am not surprised by the suggested answer to my question. But it is not an answer at the level of analysis I intend. I am interested, rather, in what it might be about these Marxist and other, broadly left, theoretical outlooks (within which anti-imperialism has been a large and proper concern) that so minimizes, if it doesn't completely evacuate, all competing considerations, as to lead the Western left, time after time, to campaign for courses of action that would leave the most hideously repressive regimes in place, whether in the countries they rule or in those they invade; and which seemingly forbids – as in Kosovo or Sierra Leone

– Western interventions to halt ethnic cleansing, mutilation, and widespread murder? Why does the category of 'imperialism' so dominate and exhaust the thinking of a section of the left as to lock it into these regrettable positions?

The question is all the more perplexing to me because of the particular generation of the left to which I belong. I mean the generation formed intellectually and politically during the 1960s, post- and anti-Stalinist in its conception of itself, and which labored strenuously – I mean this literally: it *labored* in its literary output, in dense and prolific works of argumentation, theory, historiography, social and political analysis – to separate itself from the earlier simplifications and reductions of the tradition it came from and that it sought to enrich. This was a generation for whom anti-reductionism was a constant watchword. A reductionist Marxist was something that, even at the height of Marxist intellectual fashion, no one wanted to be. Whether by way of the cultural themes of the Frankfurt School, of Gramscian 'hegemony', Althusserian 'relative autonomy', or the more empirically grounded methods of Anglophone socialist research, an enormous effort was made to establish a complex and multilayered theoretical sensibility, so that henceforth we might be in a position more effectively to grasp the multiple determinations of both the present and the past. It was a generation claiming to know that such determinations, in their range and variety, were intractable to being unified within one simple, all-encompassing story. Much of this effort, to be sure, was not related directly to issues of political strategy, much less of political ethics – an always neglected domain in Marxist writing. It concerned the need for a more advanced *cognitive* apparatus for grasping the complexities of the social world. Still, within this exigency, there was also significant recognition of the importance of democratic and related norms. Not everything was to be seen, henceforth, as reducible without residue to economic causalities and naked class interest.

In affecting the general alignment of most of the socialist left in the conflicts that have preceded and followed the events of September 11, 2001, all this effort that I have tried briefly to characterize might just as well not have taken place. For even if more advanced models of theoretical explanation are now available to the left, it nonetheless seems to suffice in any given international conflict to know that on one side is the United States, and that the United States is a capitalist power that always has designs on the natural and human resources of the rest of the world. If you know this, everything else falls instantly into place; all other levels of analysis, all other considerations, are superfluous. They can either be ignored altogether, or they can be conceded in passing, but as merely secondary and hence ignorable in practice. The political alignments are always defined by the primary determinant – imperialism. But how does this differ from imperialism's being the only thing, with every other social, political, or ideological reality merely epiphenomenal, taking its place and meaning within the whole from the one true cause?

This, in any case, is how the would-be correct left alignment seems perpetually to establish itself. Knowing what the United States is – hegemon of global capitalism – and knowing what it must be up to, you have no need to allow any explanatory or strategic weight to other social, political, legal, or ideological realities. No need to give any decision-making, choice-determining weight to mass murder, or torture, or the fundamental rights of human beings; to the laws of war, the effects of specific political structures and belief systems, or the effects of the operational and moral choices made by movements cast by part of the left in an anti-imperialist role; to the character of the regimes opposed to the United States and its allies, however brutal those regimes might be; to the illegalities and oppressions for which they are responsible, whether at home or beyond their own borders; to genocidal processes actually ongoing and about which something cries out to be done; to the threats posed to democratic societies by movements that have already shown their deadly intent.

If this basic way of establishing the obligatory left alignment – always 'anti-imperialist', at best evasive and at worst apologetic with respect to tyrannical regimes and reactionary social forces on the other side of the conflict from democratic capitalist powers – does not by itself suffice, other supplementary moves are also available. The United States is responsible not only for what it demonstrably does or has done; it is responsible also for all the reactionary forces, whether regimes or movements, opposed to it. It created them; it armed them; it used to support them (even if it no longer does). The United States – or imperialism – is therefore bad not merely in its direct embodiment, but indirectly as well, in the way it reappears within every noxious political reality across the globe. And even if it did not create and/or arm and/or previously support whatever unpleasantness is at issue, that still is not the end of the story. For the U.S. hegemon works its effects in multifarious ways. All bad things lead back to it. There are grievances out there simmering, and they too are its fault. Its global impact makes for grievances, and these grievances are transmuted into regressive ideologies and movements that, even if this section of the left does not unambiguously support them, it contrives to 'understand' in a more or less indulgent way.

There is another route to the same conclusion. Once a conflict breaks out, you can forget about the codes of war or even the most elementary moral norms deriving from centuries of ordinary human experience. Moral responsibility for every wrong that occurs in the conflict resides on the same side. If American soldiers kill civilians or commit atrocities, the United States is to blame. If those against whom the United States is fighting perpetrate similar wrongs, the United States is to blame. This might be because it started the conflict (as with Iraq in 2003); but even if it was itself responding to an act of aggression on U.S. soil (as with Afghanistan), then, well, in some deeper sense, it still started the conflict. Either the grievances at the 'root' of the crime it was responding to are traceable back to it or it should not have responded in so aggressive a manner. In the endless circle of the left-apologetic mind, everything always goes back to the master cause of worldly evil, to its unique North American source.

The first part of an answer, therefore, to the question I posed above – why the category of 'imperialism' should so dominate the thinking of a section of the left that, in one conflict after another, has positioned itself so lamentably vis-à-vis the very ugliest regimes and movements on the planet – is that this section of the left operates a kind of de facto or practical reductionism, all the theoretical sophistications of the Marxism of the last decades notwithstanding.

The second part of the answer – to which I now turn – is a seeming lack of ability, of the imagination, to digest the meaning of the great moral and polit-ical evils of the world and to look at them unflinchingly.

This is a complementary failure. Elsewhere I have argued that Marxism is as familiar as any other intellectual tradition with the realities of human violence and oppression and the more negative traits and potentialities in the makeup of human beings. At the same time, because of its utopian aspiration – which I do not mean in any pejorative sense – because of its progressive and meliorative impulse, there has always been a tendency within this tradition to minimize, or sometimes just deny, the independent force of such negative characteristics. They come to be treated, generically, as the product of class societies and, today, as the product of capitalism. The affinity between this overall intellectual tendency within Marxist and other left thinking, and the practical reductionism I have just described – in which America is identified as the source of all worldly wrongs – should be transparent.

The effect of the tendency, however, is to denature what one is looking at when one looks at the horrors of the world: a massacre of innocents; a woman being beaten in a public place or hanged in a football stadium; a place in which a man can have his ears surgically removed or his tongue cut out, or be broken and destroyed, to be followed by the next such victim, and the next, in a contin-uous sequence of atrocity; or a place in which a parent can be forced to watch her child tortured and murdered in front of her; or a place in which a husband can be forced to watch his wife repeatedly raped; an 'ethnic cleansing' or a genocide in progress, in which entire communities are pulled up by the roots and people are shot or hacked or starved to death by the thousands or the tens of thousands; mass graves opened to yield up their terrible story.

The list, as anyone knows who keeps reading when the overwhelming temp-tation is to look away, could be much extended. The items on it are moral and political realities in their own right. They need to be registered and fully recognized as such. To collapse them too quickly into their putative original causes, to *refer* them immediately, or refer *from* them, to other things that have preceded them is not to give them their due as the specific phenomena they are. The horrors, for those destroyed by them or enduring them, for those whose lives are torn and wrecked and filled with grief by them, are in a double sense reduced by this quick and easy reference back to something else, putatively their real cause or origin.

Furthermore, not all the contributory causes of such grim events are of the type that the section of the left under discussion here likes to invoke – that is, causes arising *elsewhere*, either geographically (in the United States) or societally (in the dynamics of capitalism). Moral and political evils of this order – and I make no apology for calling them that – can and generally do have causes that are more local in a spatial sense; and they are governed or influenced by political, ideological, and moral specificities every bit as real as the capitalist economy. Not everything is systemic, in the sense of being an effect of pressures or tendencies of economic provenance, whether from the global economy or from some more particular region of it. There are independent patterns of coercion and cruelty, both interpersonal and embedded within political structures; forms of authoritarian imposition; types of invasive assault and violence, at the micro-level and at the macro-level, involving large social forces.

It is necessary to recognize the weight and causality of these things, both in trying to understand the world we live in and in critically applying the normative principles that guide our actions. There is a space of political and moral particularity that the reference back to capitalism or imperialism, and the reference sideways to the United States of America, cannot displace. Structures and procedures of authoritarian or dictatorial or out-and-out murderous rule are just what they are, and they differ – in ways that matter as much as anything in the social universe matters – from democratic institutions and procedures and the protections afforded to individual human beings by the rule of law. These differences have their own specific gravity, and it is mystifying why so many people worldwide, whose central values purport to be about the liberation of human beings from oppression, have seemed to give them so little weight, so little practical, choice-determining weight, in how they have aligned themselves politically in recent times.

The Taliban in Afghanistan; Saddam's Iraq; the reduction of a human being by torture; the use of terror randomly to kill innocents and to smite all those by whom they are cherished; mass murder; ethnic cleansing; all the manifold practices of human evil – to look upon these and at once see 'capitalism', 'imperialism', 'America', is not only to show a poverty of moral imagination, it is to reveal a diminished understanding of the human world. A social or political science, or a practical politics, that cannot rise to the level of what has been understood, in *their* own mode, by the great religions – and I say this as a resolute and lifelong atheist – and what has also been understood, in their own mode, by all the great literatures of the world, is a science and a politics that can no longer be taken seriously. It should not be taken seriously by anyone attached to the democratic and egalitarian values that have always been at the heart of the broad socialist tradition.

Two personal stories, before concluding. When the Abu Ghraib scandal broke, a friend of mine, a longtime socialist of mature years and outlook, surprised me by his reaction. It was to express his revulsion, a revulsion widely and rightly felt about the brutalities that U.S. soldiers had perpetrated in that prison, in terms of the sickness, the depravity, of the *system* that had produced them. In saying this, he wasn't talking about the prison administration, or about the military chain of command, or about particular policies adopted by either. He was talking rather, in a wholly familiar way, about the one true and original cause of everything: the *capitalist* system. Well, in the end, no. This way of talking says too little, and it also says too much. Torture is not only about capitalism even when it is partly about capitalism, and sometimes it isn't about capitalism at all. It is late in the day to be having still to point this out.

The second story. Somewhat over a year ago I asked that my name be removed from the list of contributing editors to the *Socialist Register*. It was a departure without either anger or animus on my side or on the side of the two main editors, who both responded in a friendly and regretful spirit; and it was a step I had taken with some regret myself, because I have always held the *Register* in affection and regard, and I still have friends among those who edit and write for it. The step was an inevitable one for me, all the same. In the light of the concerns I have articulated in this essay, I looked at the contents list of the recent (post-9/11) volumes, to find that the *Register* was just not where I am. If one single thing can be cited as summing up the unease I would have felt had I not decided to make the break, it is this passage from the preface to the 2003 volume titled *Fighting Identities*:

> The 'fighting identities' we are concerned with reflect two closely linked global realities. One is the dual role of the American state as both the manager of a world capitalist order (a role it alone can play) and as the embodiment of the American national interest-and an all too often chauvinist identity. The other reality is the way particularist and exclusivist identities are so often a response to something universal, i.e. the pain felt by victims of oppression and exploitation everywhere. Even reactionary fundamentalist identities may be seen as distorted and perverse responses of this kind, in the vacuum created by the defeat of rational and progressive alternatives.

Note the way in which identities seen here in negative terms are simply left as what they are on the American side of the global dualism, but assigned a benign and 'understandable' source on the other side. The U.S. state is simply world capitalism; it is the embodiment of an 'all too often chauvinist' identity. By inference and by contrast, Osama bin Laden, al-Qaeda, and the like – 'reactionary fundamentalist' identities – are for their part a response to the pain induced by oppression and exploitation. That is the normative shape of the world, in essence a moral bipolarity. Except that it isn't – not if the world is the real world, in which the politics of democracy differ importantly, irreducibly, from more regressive types of politics and systems of belief.

One last observation. I have written about the political dispositions of a significant segment of the left, some of it of Marxist persuasion or formation, and some of it not, although the latter also socialist and sharing with the Marxist part the same tendencies to practical reductionism and deficiency of moral imagination that I have here set out. I would suggest also, however, that within the international 'peace' movement, as it flatters itself to be, there is an even wider constituency, not only not Marxist but not recognizably socialist either – liberals, radicals, greens, anarchists, and other progressives of one kind and another – which exhibits variants of the same double tendency I have diagnosed: on the one hand, the practical reductionism by which the wrongs of the world are lightly referred back to their alleged causes, whether in U.S. foreign policy, or economic hardship, or grievance, or whatever; on the other hand, a disinclination or refusal to acknowledge in their full magnitude and moral significance the political evils for which other states, organizations, and movements are responsible.

This wider constituency has not been my subject here, and I will not attempt to account for it at length. I offer merely this conjecture. There is a looser, progressivist, and (so to say) 'sociologizing' variant of the themes I have focused on above, whereby wrongdoing in the world, and much worse than wrongdoing, has nearly always to be seen as somehow redeemable by reference to background social conditions – which may then be taken as alleviating the scale of the wrongs, or the worse-than-wrongs, in question. (I say 'nearly' always, because the forever blameworthy are excluded from this explanatory indulgence.) You only have to attend for a few weeks to the left-liberal press and the traffic on the opinion and letters pages there in order to find this wider constituency, most of it unattached to Marxist doctrine of any kind, yet very attached to the thematic couple that has been the subject of this essay. There is, of course, another way of characterizing its outlook. It is Manichaean: everything bad in the world drains away from one side of it toward the other.

PART II

The longest hatred: antisemitism

8

Alibi antisemitism

(This is the text of a presentation by Norman Geras to the YIVO Conference on Jews and the Left held in May 2012 in New York City, first published in *Fathom*, Issue 2, Spring 2013)

In Marx's essay On the Jewish Question,[*] written in 1844, there are two contrasting sets of themes vis-à-vis the Jews. In Part II of the essay Marx deploys some well-known negative stereotypes, according to which: the mundane basis of Judaism is self-interest, egoism, or, as Marx also calls it, 'an anti-social element'; the worldly religion of the Jew is huckstering; and the Jew's jealous god – 'in face of which no other god may exist' – is money. The emancipation of the Jews is said by him to be equivalent to the emancipation of mankind *from* Judaism. Part I, on the other hand, presents a version of secular democracy in which the Jews, like any religious or other particularistic grouping, may retain their religion and their separate identity consistently with the state itself rising above such particularisms, and rendering these politically irrelevant.

Though Marx himself regards this – political emancipation – as an incomplete form of emancipation, he nonetheless articulates a genuine type of moral universalism: different faiths, ethnicities, peoples, have a right to assert their specific identities and shared beliefs within the free secular order of the democratic state. The distinctions between such groups just cease to have a political bearing. Marx does not extend this argument beyond the single state to the global arena (that not being part of the discursive context), but the correlate at the international level of what he argues in Part I of *On the Jewish Question* is today embodied in the notion of a right of nations to self-determination, as affirmed in Article 1.2 of the United Nations Charter.

The contrasting themes of Marx's essay may be taken as emblematic of the state of affairs obtaining today between Jews and the left. It is not difficult to understand the long affinity there has been between them. Common traditions of opposition to injustice, the commitment within liberal and socialist

---

[*] www.marxists.org/archive/marx/works/1844/jewish-question/index.htm

thought to ideals of equality (whether this is equality under the law or equality in substantive economic terms), opposition to racist and other similar types of prejudice – these things have long served to attract Jews to organisations and movements of the left, and they still do.

Israel as alibi

At the same time, that affinity has now been compromised by the existence of a new climate of antisemitic opinion *within* the left. This climate of opinion affects a section of the left only, and not the whole of it. But it is a substantial section. Its convenient alibi is the state of Israel – by which I mean that Israel is standardly invoked to deflect the charge that there is anything of antisemitism at work. Israel, so the story goes, is a delinquent state and, for many of those who regard it so, a non-legitimate one – colonialist, imperialist, vehicle of oppression and what have you. Similarly, diaspora Jews who defend Israel within their home countries are not seen as the conduit of Jewish interests and/ or opinion in the normal way of any other democratic articulation; they are treated, rather, as a dubious force – the notorious 'Jewish lobby' – as if their organised existence were somehow improper.

These themes pitch those who sponsor them out of a genuine, and into a spurious, type of universalism: one where the Jews are special amongst other groups in being obliged to settle for forms of political freedom in which their identity may not be asserted collectively; Jews must be satisfied, instead, merely with the rights available to them as individuals. I call this a spurious universalism because people's rights to live as they will (subject to the usual constraint of not harming others) is an incomplete right – a truncated and impaired right – if it does not include the freedom to associate with others of their own kind.

To repeat: Israel has been made an alibi for a new climate of antisemitism on the left.

But could it not be, perhaps, that there is no such climate? Could it not be that Israel's critics are just what they say they are, no more and no less: critics of the policies of successive Israeli governments, just in the same way as there are critics of the governments of every country? Well, it *could* be. There has been enough to criticise, goodness knows – from the long occupation of the West Bank and Gaza to the policy of permitting Jewish settlements on Palestinian land. It not only could be, it even in many cases is, since there are both critics and criticisms of Israel which are not antisemitic – such as the two criticisms I just made. Yet, if it both could be and is, it also in many cases is not. Much of the animus directed at Israel today is of a plainly antisemitic character. It relies (just as Marx did in Part II of *On the Jewish Question*) on anti-Jewish stereotypes. This can be shown with near mathematical precision; I endeavour to show it in the rest of what I have to say.

Antisemitism as epiphenomenal

A first form of the Israel alibi for contemporary antisemitism is the impulse to treat such of the antisemitism as there is acknowledged (by whomever) to be – in Europe, in the Arab world – as a pure epiphenomenon of the Israel–Palestine conflict. One instance of this was the statement by film director Ken Loach* in March 2009 that if there was a rise of antisemitism in Europe this was not surprising: 'it is perfectly *understandable*' (my emphasis), he was reported as saying, 'because Israel feeds feelings of antisemitism'. The key word here is 'understandable'. This might just mean 'capable of being understood'; but since more or less everything is capable of being understood, it would be pointless to use the word in that sense about the specific phenomenon of a rise in anti-semitism in Europe. 'Understandable' also means something along the lines of 'excusable' or, at any rate, not an issue to get excited about. To see plainly the way in which Israel acts as an exonerating alibi in this case, one need only imagine Loach, or anyone else on the left, delivering themselves of the opinion that a growth of hostility towards, say, black people, or towards immigrants from South Asia, or from Mexico, was *understandable*.

Another instance of this first form of the Israel alibi is provided by a thesis of Gilbert Achcar's concerning Holocaust-denial in the Arab world. Achcar is a professor at the School of Oriental and African Studies in London and a longtime leftist; he is editor of a volume of essays on *The Legacy of Ernest Mandel*. Holocaust-denial – as I shall merely assert and not argue here – is a prominent trope of contemporary antisemitism; it is indeed continuous with a practice of the Nazi period itself, when camp guards and the like would mock their Jewish victims by telling them that not only were they doomed to die, but also all knowledge of what had happened to them would be erased. They would be forgotten; the world would never know. Achcar accepts that Western Holocaust-denial is an expression of antisemitism. Much Arab Holocaust-denial, on the other hand, he puts down to† such factors as impatience in the Arab world with Western favouritism towards Israel, a suspicion that the Holo-caust has been 'amplified' for pro-Zionist purposes, and exasperation with the cruelty of Israel's treatment of the Palestinians.

Whether or not these explanations are valid, a racist belief does not cease to be one on account of its having context-specific causes. No one on the left would dream of suggesting that a belief that black people were lazy, feckless or simple-minded, was less racist for being held by a certain group of white people on account of motives which eased their way towards that belief. But the Israel alibi is currently exceptional in its legitimating power in this respect.

---

* http://normblog.typepad.com/normblog/2009/03/an-understandable-hatred.html
† http://normblog.typepad.com/normblog/2010/05/antisemitism-as-attitude-and-as-speech.html

No antisemitism without deliberate intent

A second form of the Israel alibi for antisemitism is the plea that antisemitism should not be ascribed to anyone without evidence of active hatred of Jews on their part; without, that is to say, some clear sign of antisemitic *intent*. A well-known case of this second form arose with Caryl Churchill's play 'Seven Jewish Children,'* following upon Israel's invasion of Gaza in 2008–9. This play puts into Jewish mouths the view that Palestinians are 'animals' and that 'they want their children killed to make people sorry for them'; but that there is no need to feel sorry for them; that we – the Jews – are the chosen people and that it is our safety and our children that matter; in sum, that 'I wouldn't care if we wiped them out'. I will not insist here on how this echoes the blood libel; it is enough that Churchill ascribes to the Jews, seeing themselves as chosen, murderous racist attitudes bordering on the genocidal. On the face of it, one would think, this is a clear candidate for antisemitic discourse.

Churchill, however, disavowed that charge when it came from critics. She did so on the grounds of what one might call an innocent mind. No antisemitism had been intended by her. On the one hand, the blood libel analogy had not been part of her thinking[†] when she wrote the play; on the other hand, those speaking the offending lines in it were not meant to be Jews in general,[‡] merely individual Israelis. Churchill is evidently innocent here of any memory of the figure of Shylock in *The Merchant of Venice*, long thought of, despite his being only one character, as putting Jews in a bad light. She is innocent, too, of her own generalising tendencies in naming her play 'Seven *Jewish* Children' and then linking the broad themes of the Jews as victims of genocide and as putative perpetrators of it in their turn.

Contemplate, briefly, the idea of a sociology of racism in which racism was held to be a matter exclusively of mental *attitudes*, of what some given person or group of persons had in their minds and, most particularly, of hatreds explicitly formulated; but not also of a language that embodies negative stereotypes, or of unconscious prejudicial assumptions, or of discriminatory practices, and so forth. For no other kind of racism would such a narrowly-conceived sociology be taken seriously even for a moment.

A much more recent instance of the same thing is Günter Grass's poem 'What Must Be Said'.[§] It imputed to Israel, on the basis of absolutely nothing in the way of evidence, a genocidal ambition against the Iranian people. Grass has been defended[¶] in his turn on the grounds that he is not personally an antisemite – as if this might settle the question of whether or not his poem contained antisemitic tropes.

---

* www.guardian.co.uk/stage/2009/feb/26/caryl-churchill-seven-jewish-children-play-gaza
† www.guardian.co.uk/theguardian/2011/mar/04/antisemitism-feeding-homeless-cctv-hamlet
‡ www.guardian.co.uk/theguardian/2011/mar/08/get-carter-accents-maypoles-spinal-tap
§ www.guardian.co.uk/books/2012/apr/05/gunter-grass-what-must-be-said
¶ www.eurozine.com/articles/2012–04–23–lerman-en.html

Programmatic rhetoric

Grass's poem may serve, also, to introduce a third form of what I am calling alibi antisemitism. For the poem contains a reference to the 'loudmouth' president of Iran – Mahmoud Ahmadinejad – at once Holocaust-denier and lead spokesman for removing Israel from the page of history. Like others for whom this is a central goal, the loudmouth president sometimes has benefit of the consideration that such talk is mere rhetoric, and so not to be treated as in earnest.

And you do not have to go far to find either journalists or activists of the left similarly playing down antisemitic elements within the programmatic objectives of Hamas and Hezbollah: not just their commitment to getting rid of Israel; also openly Jew-hating statements, as for example in the Hamas Charter.[*] This latter document cites 'The Protocols of the Elders of Zion' as authoritative and as establishing a Zionist ambition to dominate the world. It has Jews hiding behind rocks and trees against the threat (which it celebrates) that Jews will in due course be killed.

Leftists and liberals of a would-be pragmatist turn of mind can appear remarkably untroubled[†] by this sort of thing. Either the offending contents of the Hamas Charter are consigned by them to a receding past, or they are said not to represent the thinking of a moderate section of Hamas willing to contemplate a long-term (though not unlimited) truce with Israel. It is never explained[‡] by such pragmatists why, if the anti-Jewish components of the document are a thing of the past, no longer relevant, of merely rhetorical status, they have not been, or cannot now be, amended away.[§]

I shall leave aside here the question of whether or not there are sound tactical reasons for Israel to consider negotiating with Hamas; it is not germane to my present concern. However, and as before, one should try to imagine a person of the left able to adopt so casual and indulgent an attitude to *other* openly racist discourses, able to treat them as merely rhetorical racism – while continuing to be held in respect within the left or liberal political milieu to which he or she belongs. It doesn't happen. Only Israel provides a pretext in that milieu for the mere-rhetoric plea. By some convenient metonymy, people saying 'Jews' may be taken really to mean 'Israel'. And Israel today is fair game for being hated.

A climate of complicity

The fourth and final alibi phenomenon I shall deal with is more oblique. It consists neither of the direct expression of antisemitic themes nor of attempts

---

[*] http://normblog.typepad.com/normblog/2008/05/the-protocols-o.html

[†] www.guardian.co.uk/world/2006/jan/27/comment.mainsection

[‡] http://normblog.typepad.com/normblog/2009/01/twostage-solution.html

[§] http://normblog.typepad.com/normblog/2009/05/as-time-goes-by.html

to explain these away, but rather of turning a blind eye. It is relevant to the case here, all the same, since prejudice makes its way more successfully when there is a certain tolerance of it by others, not actively hostile themselves but indulgent towards those who are.

I will take as my example of this the *Guardian* newspaper today. This once great paper of British liberalism now provides space on its opinion pages for the spokesmen of Hamas,[*] the contents of its programmatic charter notwithstanding; provides space on its letters page for philosophers justifying the murder of Jews;[†] and provides space on its website for people who deploy well-known antisemitic themes[‡] even while professing that they have nothing whatever against Jews. The *Guardian* is, as you would expect, on record as being vigorously opposed to racism: as, for example, when it referred in a leader of November 2011 to 'a message that is not heard often enough … that racism is never acceptable, wherever it takes place'.

Instructive, in the light of that, is to examine how the paper reacted editorially to the killings at a Jewish school in Toulouse in March 2012. On March 20 of this year, before the identity of the killer was known and when it was assumed he was from the French far right, the *Guardian* echoed the sentiment I have just quoted from its November leader, saying that[§] 'the [French] republic will come together in the face of such an assault on its minorities'. While cautioning against speculation about the killer's motives, it nonetheless allowed itself to allude to Sarkozy's lurch to the right, his claims of 'there being too many immigrants in France', and other such expressions of xenophobia. This may be seen as an instance of treating racism as unacceptable 'wherever it takes place'. Two days later, once it was known that the killer was Mohammed Merah, an Islamist jihadi who had said he wanted to avenge the deaths of Palestinian children, a second *Guardian* editorial[¶] endorsed Sarkozy in 'condemn[ing] any attempt to denigrate the French Muslim community by associating it with the mad crimes of a terrorist'; and then added precisely nothing about the kind of ideas which might have been influential in Merah's willingness – not as a Muslim but as an Islamist and jihadi – to slaughter three Jewish children. 'Mad crimes of a terrorist' was all, and not so much as a breath about antisemitism. But the killing of Jewish children, even if to avenge the deaths of Palestinian children, is antisemitism of the most unadulterated kind. Those children were guilty of nothing and were killed by Merah *because* they were Jewish.

A liberal newspaper, committed to racism's never being acceptable anywhere, can find the words to name the poison that is rightwing anti-immigrant xeno-

* www.guardian.co.uk/commentisfree/2011/jan/26/palestinian-cause-betrayed-hamas-initiative
† http://normblog.typepad.com/normblog/2011/01/honderich-the-guardian.html
‡ www.guardian.co.uk/stage/2009/feb/26/caryl-churchill-seven-jewish-children-play-gaza
§ www.guardian.co.uk/world/2012/mar/20/france-republican-ideals-editorial
¶ www.guardian.co.uk/commentisfree/2012/mar/22/toulouse-shooting-nicolas-sarkozy-editorial

phobia, but not the word for hatred of Jews. Incomprehensible – but for that familiar alibi, Israel as cause.

Conclusion

It is a moral scandal that some few decades after the unmeasurable catastrophe that overtook the Jewish people in Europe, these antisemitic themes and ruses are once again respectable; respectable not just down there with the thugs but pervasively also within polite society, and within the perimeters of a self-flattering liberal and left opinion. It is a bleak lesson to all but those unwilling to see. The message of 'never again' has already proved to have been too sanguine. Genocides still occur. We now know, as well, that should a new calamity ever befall the Jewish people, there will be, again, not only the direct architects and executants but also those who collaborate, who collude, who look away and find the words to go with doing so. Some of these, dismayingly, shamefully, will be of the left.

This is not a hopeful conclusion, but it is a necessary one. The best of hope in politics must always be allied to a truthful realism. We need to know what we are up against.

9

Marxists before the Holocaust

(This essay was first published in *New Left Review*, No. 224, July/August 1997)

I shall begin here from an astonishing fact. In December 1938, in an appeal to American Jews, Leon Trotsky in a certain manner predicted the impending Jewish catastrophe. Here is what he wrote:

> It is possible to imagine without difficulty what awaits the Jews at the mere outbreak of the future world war. But even without war the next development of world reaction signifies with certainty the *physical extermination of the Jews*.[1]

This was just a few weeks after Kristallnacht and it was one month before Hitler's famous Reichstag speech of 30 January 1939 in which he 'prophesied' the annihilation of European Jewry in the event of a world war.

I call Trotsky's prediction an astonishing fact. For it is a common and well-grounded theme in the literature of the Holocaust that the disaster was not really predictable. It was outside the range of normal experience and sober political projection or indeed imagination. Even once the tragedy began to unfold, many people found the information on what was being done to the Jews hard to absorb, hard to connect up into a unified picture of comprehensive genocide, hard to believe; and this applied to wide sections of the Jewish population itself. Then, after the event, its enormity has seemed to many difficult to grasp. It has seemed to be in some measure beyond understanding and explanation. We have the evidence of such a reaction from none other than Trotsky's great biographer. Referring to 'the absolute uniqueness of the catastrophe', Isaac Deutscher would later write:

> The fury of Nazism, which was bent on the unconditional extermination of every Jewish man, woman, and child within its reach, passes the comprehension of a historian, who tries to uncover the motives of human behaviour and to discern the interests behind the motives. Who can analyse the motives and the interests behind the enormities of Auschwitz? … [W]e are confronted here by a huge and ominous mystery of the degeneration of the human character that will forever baffle and terrify mankind.[2]

How are we to account for Trotsky's prescience in this matter? Was it perhaps just some sort of stray, dark intuition? Or was it rather a hypothesis founded on the forms of knowledge which he brought to trying to understand the realities of his time? I shall in due course propose as an answer that it was something in between. But I will come to this answer by way of a critical review of Ernest Mandel's thinking on the same subject. This is the main purpose of what I want to present here, though my aim will be as well, through it, to offer some more general reflections on Marxism as a body of theory in relation to the Nazi genocide against the Jews.

I say a critical review of Mandel's thinking on the subject and critical is what it will be; although it will be somewhat less so in relation to his later views as compared with the earlier ones, since there was an internal development and enlargement of these. Still, overall, it will be critical. And I am bound to observe, therefore, that so critical a review may seem out of place on the occasion, devoted as it is to registering and honouring Mandel's achievement.[3] Let me just say three things about this. First, like other participants here I held, and I hold, Mandel's life work in the highest regard, and nothing in what follows affects that. Second, in the proper place I have recorded my own debts to him. In particular, his work helped me to an understanding of something centrally important in the thinking of Rosa Luxemburg, as also in any rounded conception of emancipatory socialist struggle.[4] (I refer by this not only to what he wrote specifically about Rosa Luxemburg but also to his political writings more generally.) Third, Mandel himself, I believe, would not have been happy with anything less: anything less than the frankest appraisal on whatever question, and if frankly critical, then so be it.

An early effort by him to take the measure of the Jewish tragedy is an article of 1946, 'La question juive au lendemain de la deuxième guerre mondiale'. Please keep in mind that it was written by Mandel at the age of 22 or 23, and also (in light of that date, 1946) how much difficulty in general people have had, over several decades, in facing up to the implications of this catastrophe. Mandel begins by evoking the horrors of it, and he then gestures towards the soft of uncomprehending response I have already illustrated with the words of Isaac Deutscher. The human imagination has trouble grasping the significance of the experience, Mandel writes; the misfortune of the Jews seems 'absurd'. The mind 'refuses to admit that material interests could have determined, in cold logic, the extermination of these innumerable defenceless beings'.[5]

This is not, however, the response that Mandel for his part wants to recommend. The fate of the European Jews he firmly situates, as being explicable by it, in the broader context of the mortal crisis of capitalism; and in the context, a product of this crisis, of the other horrors of the Second World War. It is 'capitalism [that is] responsible for their [the Jews'] tragic fate and for the impasse in which the whole of humanity finds itself'.[6] The Nazi genocide against the Jews is also 'contextualized' by the young Mandel by reference to certain actions and attitudes of the Allied powers: the deportation of ethnic Germans from parts of east and central Europe at the end of the war; the callousness of the British towards mass suffering in India, or of the Americans in connection with the use of the atomic bomb at Hiroshima; the responsibility borne by the whole capitalist order, by 'all the governments of the world', in not coming to the aid of the Jewish people. And next to 5 million murdered Jews (the figure Mandel gives), 'one finds the 60 million victims of the imperialist war'. The general spirit of this assessment is captured by formulations like the following:

> The barbarous treatment of the Jews by Hitlerite imperialism has only pushed to paroxysm the barbarism of the habitual methods of imperialism in our epoch.
>
> Far from being isolated from, or opposed to, the destiny of humanity, the Jewish tragedy only announces to other peoples their future fate if the decline of capitalism continues at its present rate.[7]

This early attempt by Mandel to assess the significance of the Shoah is marked, in my opinion, by a triple weakness. It can be described in terms of the three polar oppositions set out below. The destruction of the Jews of Europe:

>   is comparable to other crimes / is singular or unique;
>   is rationally explicable / is beyond comprehension;
>   is the product of capitalism and imperialism / is due to some other combination of factors.

Now, I do not believe any adequate assessment can be made by just embracing either one pole or the other of these three oppositions. A certain (particular) intermediate standpoint is called for in relation to each. The weakness of this initial article by Mandel is that he pretty well does embrace the first pole of each opposition. According to him, the destruction of the Jews of Europe is *rationally explicable* as the *product of imperialist capitalism*, and as such it is manifestly *comparable* to the other barbarisms which this socio-economic formation throws up. That both the specificity of the event and a certain 'elusiveness', such as very many people have felt and expressed about it, are thereby leveled or lost, is perhaps best brought out by this hypothesis towards the end of the essay:

> [I]t is not just possible but probable that an American fascist movement will go beyond, in its technical 'perfection', the brutalities of Nazi antisemitism. If the next decade is not witness to the proletarian revolution in the United States, it will prepare for American Jewry hecatombs that will surpass Auschwitz and Maidanek in horror.[8]

The Holocaust is here turned into a more or less regular type of occurrence of our epoch. Terrible as it may have been, it only anticipates much worse, and this within a decade or two should capitalism survive.

I may as well indicate before proceeding any further that I do not think Ernest Mandel ever made good the three weaknesses I have identified from this early article (and will shortly come back to enlarge upon). Although in the last decade of his life, returning to the same subject, he would elaborate a view of it more qualified and enriched, the same weaknesses in one way or another were to remain.

That they continued at least into the 1960s and 1970s can be marked by drawing attention to a certain absence. In his Introduction of 1969 to the collection of Trotsky's texts *The Struggle Against Fascism in Germany*, Mandel does not even directly mention the Holocaust. The same thing in the relevant chapter (chapter 8) of his *Trotsky*, published in 1979. There are some generic references to 'an advancing barbarism', and to threats to the survival of 'broad human groups' or to 'human civilization' itself. But this is as close as he gets.[9] To be sure, the writings of Trotsky that Mandel here introduces themselves predate the 'Final Solution', so one would not expect the topic to loom enormously large in what he says about them. Even so, Trotsky *before* the event, in some well-known passages to which I shall later return, seems to anticipate the extremes of barbarism that a triumphant National Socialism would portend. Is it not remarkable that twenty-five, and thirty-five, years *after* the event, in full awareness of what one of these extremes turned out to be, Mandel finds no place to mention it directly, much less to discuss it, in presenting Trotsky's ideas about the rise and the victory of Nazism?

What he does present is a general theory of *fascism*: a theory of it centred on the crushing of the workers' movement, and articulated through Marxist concepts of class, capitalist economic crisis, the different political forms and methods of rule of the capitalist state.[10] We may note two particular claims made by Mandel in presenting this theory. First, fascism, he insists, is 'a universal phenomenon that knows no geographical boundaries [and which] struck roots in all imperialist lands'; 'attempts at explanation that chiefly emphasize this or that national peculiarity are wholly inadequate'.[11] While I have on one level, no quarrel with this, it is nevertheless an optic likely to discourage attention towards a certain specificity of German National Socialism and of one of its policies. Second, the superiority of the Marxist method of social analysis, Mandel contends, lies in its total character. It seeks 'to comprehend all aspects of social activity as connected with and structurally coordinated to one another'. This is a thesis put forward also at other places in his writings. But it is not tested here against the difficulties of explaining the 'Final Solution'.[12]

In 1986, coming back to the subject forty years after his first youthful assessment, Mandel tried to meet this test – in his book on the Second World War. Even here the first signs are not propitious. Only three pages are devoted by him to the Holocaust, and the context plainly renders it a subordinate issue. For his discussion of it occurs in a country-by-country survey of *ideology* within the major arenas of the war. The fate of European Jewry figures only as part of this survey. The discussion nevertheless marks a definite development of Mandel's viewpoint as compared with his essay of 1946. No longer is it only 'material interests', capitalist economy and crisis, that are at work. His explanation of the Holocaust now combines a particular form of ideology on the one hand, with features of capitalist modernity on the other. The ideology is racism. This, Mandel argues, is 'congenitally linked to institutionalized colonialism and imperialism', owing to the need with these political and economic formations to dehumanize whole groups of people in order to rationalize and justify oppressing them in extreme ways. It is then a short step from there, from dehumanizing them, to denying such groups the right to life itself. When racist ideology combines with the global irrationality of capitalism and its '"perfect" local rationality' – what Mandel calls also 'the deadly partial rationality of the modern industrial system' – that step, according to him, 'is frequently taken'.

Further, a number of additional factors, political and psychological, are brought in by Mandel to account for the particular result that was the Nazi genocide. Amongst these factors are: a desperado elite holding political power; the *va banque* aggression unleashed by it in conjunction with sectors of big business; a policy of state terrorism with 'an implacable logic of its own'; the passive complicity of thousands of people, civil servants and other executive agents; and 'a fetid substratum of unconscious guilt and shame'.[13] I shall come back to the significance of these other factors. But clearly there has been an inner differentiation and some filling out of Mandel's thinking on this question, as one would expect from a writer of now greater maturity. I find, all the same, that the key problems are unresolved.

First, Mandel offers precious little sense, and certainly no attempt at an elaboration, of the singularity of specificity of the Shoah. On the contrary, the overwhelming weight of his emphasis is, once again, on contextualizing it – on its comparability with other historical phenomena. We are referred by him to 'the mass enslavement and killing of Blacks via the slave trade' and to the extermination of Indians by the *conquistadors*; to the fact that gypsies and 'sections of the Slav people' also figured in the list of the Nazis' victims, as did tens of thousands of ethnic Germans murdered in the T4 (so-called 'euthanasia') programme; to the Japanese atrocities in 'Unit 731' in Manchuria, 'only one rung below Auschwitz'; to the bombing of Hiroshima and Nagasaki, reflecting a contempt for human beings 'not far removed from extreme racism'; and to the fact that antisemitism and other Nazi attitudes were and are widespread beyond Germany.

True, Mandel also writes this: 'the Holocaust – the deliberate and systematic killing of six million men, women and children simply because of their ethnic origin – stands as a unique crime in mankind's sad criminal history'. But that is all he writes. And it is not now clear in what the Holocaust *is* unique, if it is.

I do not want to be misunderstood. I am not suggesting that the Jewish tragedy is not at all, not in any way, comparable to other great horrors and crimes. Of course it is. But there are the respective weights Mandel gives to the two sides of the question: several paragraphs on the comparability of the tragedy; a single, unexplicated sentence on its specificity or uniqueness. This is a much debated and difficult question within a now very extensive literature (though, like many of the other difficult questions there, it is not one much reflected on by Marxists). The historian Yehuda Bauer has proposed in connection with it the metaphor of a huge volcano rising out of a dark, forbidding landscape: the volcano is part of the landscape; but it also stands out against it.[14] Mandel says much about the landscape ('mankind's sad criminal history') and about the Holocaust's being part of this. He says nearly nothing about the Holocaust standing out. Or he says only *that* it stands out, but not how.

Second, Mandel is extremely confident of the power of social and political explanation here. Referring to 'those who have treated Hitler's fanatic anti-semitism leading to the Holocaust as beyond rational explanation', he writes that 'such drastic historical exceptionalism' cannot be sustained – then going on to proffer the explanation I have summarized. Now, again, in order to avoid being misunderstood, let me say that I do not support any radical incomprehensibility thesis. The attempt to destroy the Jews was an event in history, and its preconditions, causes, processes, can and must be investigated with a view to trying to understand them. In this matter more perhaps than any other we need to understand as much as we can, so as to be able to resist as well as we can all further projects of mass murder and appalling cruelty. However, the sort of opinion I have quoted from Isaac Deutscher (and which is shared by many others) expresses the sense, even if sometimes exaggerated, that there is a residue within this historical experience beyond the regular forms of social, political or ideological explanation: a residue which is called by Deutscher baffling, and 'degeneration of the human character', and called by other people other things. Mandel seems to give it no legitimate place. This will become clearer in light of my last critical point.

Which is that, third, for all the greater complexity of his analysis at this later date, the Holocaust is still presented by him as being an effect of *capitalism*; as the product of its global irrationality, its partial (functional) rationality, and the racist ideology generated by its imperialist forms. But this explanation does not suffice to its object, no more than do explanations of the catastrophe as a product of modernity. Faced with either one or the other we may legitimately ask why, in view of the generality of the social condition invoked as primary to the event, *this* has happened so far only once. (The question should not be taken to imply that the structures of capitalism or of modernity do not have any important part in an overall explanation.) In truth, Mandel is obliged for greater completeness to bring in as factors of his own explanation less class-specific and capitalism-specific causes, both motivational and political: such as the servile complicity and lack of critical judgement of tens of thousands of people; unconscious guilt and shame; extreme policy choices with a dynamic of their own; and indeed dehumanization itself, now become a central category and for its part a rather widespread and familiar human disposition. But none of this is recognized by Mandel as having broadened the scope of the analysis to encompass more general, less historically specific themes – perhaps even to the point where a residue of sheer, ungrounded excess may remain.

This failure to recognize the now broader nature of his analysis is highlighted by one startling and cavalier judgement which he allows himself. Having got to the end of his multi-factor exposition of what led to the Jewish catastrophe – not only extreme racism and the irrationality of capitalism, coupled with its functional, industrial rationality, but also widespread complicity, a desperado political elite, its *va banque* [taking a really big risk] policy of aggression, a state terrorism with its own logic, and then an unconscious layer of guilt and shame as well – Mandel comments:

> The Holocaust only comes at the end of this long causal chain. But it can and must be explained through it. Indeed, *those who understood the chain were able to foresee it.* (Emphasis added.)

The reference here is to Trotsky's prediction from which we began, and to me this is a *reductio ad absurdum* of the totalizing ambition of Mandel's approach: attempting to 'recover' the heterogeneity in the explanation by treating everything in it as part of one unified chain, and then imagining that Trotsky's 1938 prediction might really have been based on being able to foresee all the individual links in it *and* their connection. I cannot take the suggestion seriously. Especially not, remembering the context of general unpreparedness and incredulity vis-à-vis the Jewish calamity as it first loomed and then became a reality. Trotsky would have needed to be superhuman to have had this much understanding in advance. I think we have to look, rather, towards a looser kind of foresight on his part, although coming together this, needless to say, with his Marxist knowledge of the grave dangers of capitalist crisis and of the typical conflicts it throws up and the ugly new forms it can breed.

Intimations of what I am getting at in speaking of this looser kind of fore-sight are to be found in observations Ernest Mandel himself made about Trotsky, both earlier and later. Earlier, in this study of him already referred to, Mandel writes that Trotsky understood 'the fact that irrational ideas, moods and yearnings of great force had survived from pre-capitalist times in large parts of bourgeois society'; and that though racism is a typical ideology of the colonial-imperialist epoch it is combined with 'remnants of pre-bourgeois ideology'.[15] Later, in *Trotsky as Alternative* (first published in German in 1992), he repeats this latter point. And he says also that Trotsky saw fascist ideology and rule as involving, at one and the same time, a 'relapse into pre-capitalist reaction and obscurantism' and a late, catching-up form of modernization.[16]

Many of you will be familiar with the better known passages on which Mandel here draws; passages, in particular, from the article of 1933, 'What Is National Socialism?'. In this, Trotsky characterizes Nazi ideology as a reaction against the rationalism and materialism of the last two centuries, and as integrating a pogromist antisemitism into the defence of capitalism against the threat represented by the working class. He goes on to talk of 'the depths of society' having been opened up; of 'inexhaustible reserves … of darkness, ignorance, and savagery'. And he says that what should have been eliminated as excrement from the national organism with 'the normal development' of society 'has now come gushing out from the throat; capitalist society is puking up the undigested barbarism. Such is the physiology of National Socialism'.[17] It is a repugnant image but in its own way also a prophetic one. Undigested barbarism. Its final consequences of a darkness inexhaustible indeed. Trotsky would later, in a manifesto of the Fourth International on the war, describe fascism 'as a chemically pure distillation of the culture of imperialism', with antisemitism a stable element within the racial themes of Nazi propaganda and belief.[18]

Now, in an illuminating analysis of the development of Trotsky's thinking on the Jewish question, Enzo Traverso has presented us with an evolution broadly as follows: from antisemitism being seen by him initially as a feudal survival in the process of dying out, to a later appreciation of its significance as a symptom of capitalist crisis and modernist barbarism. Antisemitism within Nazi ideology, Traverso proposes likewise, was at first viewed by Trotsky as part of an obscurantist reaction to modernity, then later understood as an authentic expression of contemporary capitalism and imperialism.[19] While there is a clear textual basis for this interpretation,[20] nevertheless I think, myself, that in his emphasis on the change in Trotsky's thinking Traverso bypasses the importance of the *combination* (of new and old ideological forms) that some of Mandel's quoted formulas bring out. The continuity – and so susceptibility to such combination – between pre-modern and modern forms may be highlighted in two ways.

Consider, first, the category of dehumanization, become pivotal to Mandel's account. Undoubtedly a development occurs between older forms of Christian antisemitism and the Nazi, racial, variant of it. However, whether the Jews are seen as refusing the truth they themselves had anticipated, as God-killers and in some sort a demonic influence, or are seen rather as beings of a biologically inferior type, they are placed at the margins of, or actually excluded from, the sphere of the fully human and from the reciprocal moral consideration associated with it. Nazi popular attitudes were certainly hybrid here, drawing on long-standing Christian prejudices and linking these with a pseudo-scientific racial theory. More generally, it is hard to believe that just *any* people could have been as murderously dealt with over a whole continent, or as readily abandoned to its torment, rather than this particular people, hated and vilified there for going-on two millennia. The psychological distancing effected by fixing others as in one way or another menacingly alien is at any rate an age-old symbolic mechanism. It has a transhistorical dimension.

Similarly, the content of the category of barbarism as used by Mandel and other Marxists (whether wittingly or not) is of a highly generic kind, and is, I would suggest, essentially anthropological. The category is used to refer loosely to such phenomena as obsessive, unreasoning hatreds, extreme or endemic violence, the enjoyment of cruelty, indifference to great suffering and so forth. None of this is specific to capitalism.

The centrality of such categories to Mandel's understanding of the Holocaust indicates why it is not genuinely containable by an explanation in terms of the socioeconomic and ideological forms of capitalism. I shall come to an elaboration of this point by way of examining his last and most developed attempt to grapple with the issue. I mean the article of 1990, 'Prémisses matérielles, sociales et idéologiques du genocide nazi'. (In discussing it I shall make supplementary reference also to an appendix Mandel wrote for the German edition of his book on the Second World War, published just one year later than this article. What is relevant in the appendix for the most part reproduces the theses of the article. So far as it differs from it in one interesting respect, I shall speak of the difference later, in concluding.) The central strands and weaknesses of Mandel's approach in this article remain basically unchanged. But it represents, all the same, a further development of his thinking, because the residual factors in the explanation have been reinforced. I shall take these two sets of features of the article in turn.

We still find here just a couple of brief phrases on the singularity of the Holocaust. Mandel writes of it as 'a unique event in history up to now', and as involving 'the worst crimes in history'. His reasons for the judgement remain to be clearly spelled out.[21] The 'contextualizing' material, on the other hand, is rather fuller. We are reminded with a multiplicity of references – to slavery in the ancient world, the persecution of witches, the fate of the American Indians, black slavery; and to the murder of gypsies, Poles and Russians during the Second World War – that, whether as victims *tout court* or as victims of the Nazis, the Jews belong to a very much larger company.[22] Who amongst serious people is in need of this reminder?

Then, too, Mandel continues to reject as (without qualification) 'obscurantist' the view that the Holocaust is incomprehensible. I return shortly to a claim he makes in that connection.[23] And the key to his own explanation remains what it was before. The Holocaust is to be understood as 'the most extreme expression to this point of the destructive tendencies present in bourgeois society'.[24] It is the product of a biological racism itself arising from socio-economic practices that require the systematic dehumanization of other peoples; linked, this, to that 'typical combination of partial perfect rationality and global irrationality … characteristic of bourgeois society'; in conditions, generally, of the crisis of imperialism; and conditions, specifically, of a profound social and political crisis in the given (that is, German) national arena.[25]

That all this is to the point is one thing. That it fully captures its intended object is another. It does not. We begin to see why by looking at what Mandel throws in here, sometimes just by the way, as additional factors: factors of a psychological, ethical and experiential nature.

Thus, first, in connection with dehumanizing racist ideologies that rationalize the mistreatment of other human beings, he speaks of a need, consequent upon such mistreatment, for '"neutralizing" bad conscience and the feeling of individual guilt' – but without any further enlargement.[26] Second, in connection with the Nazi policy of extermination having 'begun with the Jews', Mandel gives us a partial cause of this 'the lunatic belief of Hitler and some of his lieutenants in an "international Jewish conspiracy"'.[27] Third, there is a passing reference to the First World War as an event without which Nazism as a mass phenomenon would have been unthinkable. In the aforementioned appendix to the German edition of his book on the Second World War, Mandel deals with the same point at greater length and says that 'the chauvinist enthusiasm [of 1914] … the acceptance of senseless mass killings and boundless destruction constitute the great break in contemporary history. This was the first decisive step towards barbarism …'.[28] Is there not an important insight here? The suggestion may be speculative, but could not this trauma of mass death, this prolonged, unprecedentedly large and useless slaughter, with its scarring effects on the consciousness of a generation, have had some part in preparing the 'moral' ground for the genocide to follow?

However that may be, Mandel addresses himself also, fourth, and perhaps most crucially in this context, to reasons for the Jewish tragedy 'of an ethical order': to do with the complicity and obedience – and whether on account of routine, self-interested calculation or cowardice – of millions of Europeans, ordinary people accepting the authority of the State rather than 'the fundamental rules of ethics'. He concludes in this regard, 'In the face of massive injustice, individual and above all collective resistance and revolt are not only a right but a duty … That is the principal lesson of the Holocaust'.[29]

In touching on such matters Ernest Mandel connects to a wider historiographical, socio-psychological and other literature on the Holocaust, adding to it, to be sure, what Marxism is best-placed to add. He connects there also to another layer of human understandings *as well as* difficulties of understanding. It is doubtful these can be easily recuperated within a crisis-of-capitalism type of explanation as it is Mandel's constant tendency to try to recuperate everything.

For think of it now: bad conscience and guilt. Think, even in terms of quite ordinary experience, of some of the behaviours this can produce. Think of *lunatic* beliefs and what they can produce. Think of mass death and those who take part in the experience of it, and of those who have to cope emotionally with its enduring effects. Think of moral cowardice or merely moral 'slippage', of failure to act against known wrongs and of the many different ways there are of living comfortably with that. We begin to reach into the sub-soil, so to say, of the human psyche. And we are not so far, surely, from Deutscher's 'degeneration of the human character'. But for Deutscher something here was still baffling where for Mandel, seemingly, everything is clear. The former view for many people has appeared to be more persuasive: that, in the excess, the passage to the limit of what the 'Final Solution of the Jewish Question' envisaged, indeed the passage in the execution of it beyond every familiar limit, there was something which eludes historical understanding and social scientific explanation. You can spell out all the conditions, factors, contributory causes; still, these were not bound to produce exactly *that*. By themselves, therefore, they do not altogether explain it.

One especially influential voice has argued to this effect. I refer to Primo Levi. Levi wrote that the commonly accepted explanations did not satisfy him. 'They are reductive; not commensurate with, nor proportionate to, the facts that need explaining ... I cannot avoid the impression of a general atmosphere of uncontrolled madness that seems to me to be unique in history.' For Levi, multi-factor explanations were necessary but they also fell short. He preferred, he said, the humility of those historians who 'confess to *not understanding*', to not understanding *such* a furious hatred. It was, Levi wrote, 'a poison fruit sprung from the deadly trunk of Fascism, but outside of and beyond Fascism itself'.[30]

In his 'Prémisses' essay, Mandel seeks to fend off views of this kind with the argument that they generalize responsibility for evil to humanity at large, in effect accusing everybody and consequently nobody in particular, not Hitler, nor the Nazis, nor their supporters.[31] But to me this is an obvious *non sequitur*, not worth lingering over. That we may not be able to comprehend everything about the calamity visited on the Jews in no way entails that we are then unable to see any difference between the innocent and the guilty.

I come back now to Trotsky's remarkable prediction of 1938 and I ask again: what was its basis? Doubtless his Marxist understanding of the dangers of fascism in general and of German National Socialism in particular had something to do with it. But this on its own could not have sufficed to yield the extremity within the prediction he made. I want to suggest that there was an element of plain intuition here, spun from Trotsky's broader human sensibility in which something was already known about 'uncontrolled madness', deadly hatred and the passing of all limits. Of this broader sensibility one could cite much evidence. It is what made Trotsky the powerful and creative Marxist intellect he was, his many calumniators notwithstanding. But I shall cite only a single relevant piece which I have had occasion to draw attention to once before.[32]

It is an account of a pogrom from his book *1905*, an episode narrated there of the failed Russian revolution of that year. Describing the build-up to the pogrom, Trotsky – Marxist – sketches both its political background and something of the social composition of the mob. Then he writes this: 'the gang rushes through the town, drunk on vodka and the smell of blood'. Drunk *on the smell of blood*. What specifically Marxist category is there for that? Trotsky relates:

Everything is allowed to him [the member of the gang], he is capable of anything, he is the master of property and honour, of life and death ... If he wants to, he can throw an old woman out of a third-floor window together with a grand piano, he can smash a chair against a baby's head, rape a little girl while the entire crowd looks on, hammer a nail into a living human body ... He exterminates whole families, he pours petrol over a house, transforms it into a mass of flames, and if anyone attempts to escape, he finishes him off with a cudgel ... There exist no tortures, figments of a feverish brain maddened by alcohol and fury, at which he need ever stop. He is capable of anything, he dares everything ...

And Trotsky goes on:

The victims, bloodstained, charred, driven frantic, still search for salvation within the nightmare. Some put on the bloodstained clothes of people already dead, lie down in a pile or corpses ... Others fall on their knees before the officers, the policemen, the raider, they stretch out their arms, crawl in the dust, kiss the soldiers' boots, beg for mercy. In reply they hear only drunken laughter. 'You wanted freedom? Here, look, this is it.'

In these last mocking words, Trotsky says, 'is contained the whole infernal morality of the pogrom policy'; and he repeats once again, 'capable of everything'.[33]

Already long before 1938 Trotsky had seen into the depths. He had seen the spirit of limitless excess, the exaltation people can feel in exercising a merciless power over others and the 'total-ness' there can be in a humiliation – both the horror and the joy that is taken in inflicting it, lethal couple in what is already an annihilation. He had seen also one of the more terrifying faces of human freedom, self-consciously turned against its other, better faces. In all of this he had seen part of what there would subsequently be in the Shoah, including the element of an irreducible choice. The preconditions and the surrounding context of this kind of choice can and always must be explored and described. But it remains in the end what it is: underdetermined, a choice.

Whether or not there was in Trotsky's mental processes any direct route running from the memory of his earlier description of a pogrom to predicting in 1938 the physical extermination of the Jews cannot, of course, be known. I simply offer as a hypothesis that it was out of the kind of understanding which that narrative of his betokens, as much as it was out of his Marxist theorizing about capitalism or fascism, and his anticipation of Nazism's ultimate barbarity may have come. What he wrote there in any case foreshadows themes that were to be proposed later by others in thinking about the Shoah itself. I want to mention two of these others.

Saul Friedlander has written of a feeling evident alike within the Nazi leadership and amongst some of its followers, 'of accomplishing something truly, historically, meta-historically, exceptional'; a feeling manifested, for example, in 'the insistence of some of the commanders of the *Einsatzgruppen* [engaged in the mass murder of Jews by shooting] to stay on duty'.[34] Developing the point he has argued that, beyond the undeniable explanatory importance of antisemitic ideology and the dynamics of bureaucracy, there is also 'an independent psychological residue [that] seems to defy the historian'. It concerns, Friedlander says, 'a compelling lust for killing on an immense scale, driven by some kind of extraordinary elation …'. And it is just here, with this elation, that 'our understanding remains blocked on the level of self-awareness':

> The historian can analyse the phenomenon from the 'outside', but … his unease stems from the noncongruence between intellectual probing and the blocking of intuitive comprehension …[35]

Friedlander reads such a feeling of elation in a notorious speech of Himmler's before a gathering of SS officers, at which the Nazi leader praised the magnitude of their accomplishment in the destruction of the Jews. The same thing can be read, repeated, in testimonies from those present at the sites of mass murder.

The elation and the lust for killing. A battalion of German reserve policemen on duty in Poland and drafted into rounding up and shooting Jews is enjoying a visit from an entertainment unit from Berlin. 'The members of this unit had … heard of the pending shooting of the Jews. They asked, indeed even emphatically begged, to be allowed to participate in the execution of the Jews.'[36] Again: 'Members of the Grenzpolizeikommissariat [Frontier Police Authority] were, with a few exceptions, quite happy to take part in shootings of Jews. They had a ball! … Nobody failed to turn up.' 'As usual a few of the new officers became megalomaniacs, they really enter into the role wholeheartedly.' '… after a while we saw numerous soldiers and civilians pouring on to an embankment in front of us, behind which … executions were being carried out at regular intervals.' '… some marines from the naval unit came past … they had heard that Jews were always being shot in the town and … they wanted to see this for themselves … The execution area was visited by scores of German spectators from the Navy and the Reichsbahn (railway).' 'I saw SD personnel weeping because they could not cope mentally with what was going on. Then again I encountered others who kept a score-sheet of how many people they had sent to their death.'[37] Or here, a Norwegian imprisoned at Sachsenhausen describes a group of young Germans let loose with truncheons on hundreds of starving Jews:

> [T]he act of striking intoxicated them and drove them wild … they were living devils, possessed, transported with ecstasy … they went on striking at them as they lay, trod upon them, kicked them, while the blood was streaming from mouths, ears, and wounds. Every time they needed a rest, they turned exultantly to their laughing and smiling comrades, laughed back, and gave the truncheon a limber, playful swing round their heads. Then they flew at it again.[38]

The critic George Steiner, like Friedlander acknowledging the importance of what has been explained of this historical experience by the various disciplines of empirical enquiry, suggests that these have been unable nonetheless to fathom the intensity of the hatreds that were unleashed, or to account for the extreme lengths to which the Nazis were willing to go in pursuit of their murderous objective. In a thesis he concedes to be unprovable, Steiner argues that it might have been as the inventors of monotheism, of 'an infinite … ethically imperative God', that the Jews drew upon themselves all the furies released in the course of the Nazi-led assault against them. Representing what he calls the 'blackmail of perfection', they perhaps incurred a hatred the more intense because of a recognition at some level by their tormentors of the desirability of the ethical demands embodied in the Jewish tradition.[39] The thesis is of a guilt turned outwards, of resentment focused on a people which had thought to make itself the bearer of hope for a better world. It recalls hints we have encountered in Mandel and Trotsky: the former's allusion to bad conscience; the scene narrated by the latter of a freedom not liberating, but cruelly, willfully, destructive. Unprovable as Steiner's thesis may be and in manifest tension even with other more familiar, dehumanizing and demonizing tropes, it is hard, I believe, to refuse it any weight once one has absorbed from the vast chronicle of this catastrophe the sense that is so pervasively present in it of a determination by the perpetrators, a glee almost, in taking advantage of the innocence, vulnerability, persistent hope and propensity to think in terms of what was reasonable, of their targeted victims.

Whatever the sources of the anti-Jewish fury, and they are probably multiple, no one reading at all widely in the testimony and historiography of the Holocaust could fail to notice what both Friedlander and Steiner speak of in their different ways, neither the cruel desires and sense of an unusual elation, nor the emotional charge produced – and maybe required – by the assault upon the innocent. Such features are obscured, however, in a certain body of the theoretical literature by alternative discourses there. One of these is the 'banality of evil' argument, due originally to Hannah Arendt but disseminated very widely since. The other, frequently related to it, is a broader argument about modernity to be found in the work of many different writers.

Both of these arguments register things that are important to understanding the Nazi genocide. In a nutshell, the first draws attention to the general normality of the perpetrators from a psychological point of view: to their kinship with the rest of humankind as, mostly, ordinary people, not monsters and, especially, not animals. The second argument draws attention to the characteristically modern structures and resources, social, organizational and technical, without which an enterprise of this type and scale – gathering and transporting six million people from across the countries of Europe in order to kill them all, and this within a period of less than four years and under a blanket of attempted secrecy – would have *been* much more difficult, if not actually impossible. But despite the pertinence of these arguments, they can come, when given a too unilateral emphasis, to present a picture of rule-governed, bureaucratic murder in which some of the other aspects we have been concerned with, symbolic, emotional and to do with the unfettered 'play' of destructive human capacity and imagination, are all but marginalized. There is something here that is not about modernity; something that is not about capitalism either. It is about humanity.

It is something that Marxists have often been reluctant to face up to but with which – returning now to him – Ernest Mandel ought to have had no trouble. In an essay of 1980 entitled 'Man is the Supreme Being for Man', he wrote of there being anthropological constants. One such constant was expressed in a yearning for freedom and in 'the inextinguishable spark of revolt' against injustice and oppression. But there were also, Mandel recognized, 'deeply embedded in human beings', impulses towards tribalism and destructiveness.[40]

Confronted with the enormities produced by these latter kind of impulses, the better side of human nature that is represented by impulses of the former kind can find itself, it seems, at a loss – as to how to understand. This is what Deutscher and Levi and Friedlander all tell us, each in his own particular accents. It is good that human beings experience the difficulty as widely as they do. Should we ever entirely cease to, we would be entirely lost. This, for its part, is the meaning – an ethical rather than psychological meaning – of the discourse of the *monstrosity* of radical evil.

I want, finally, to note a respect in which, in the pages he appended to the German edition of his book on the Second World War, Mandel found it necessary to express himself more fully than he had ever done before. It was on the issue of the uniqueness of the Jewish calamity. I conclude with some observations arising from a certain change of emphasis about this.

Hitherto, at least after the initial article of 1946, although Mandel characterizes the Holocaust as unique (and not in any trivially individuating sense but in the sense, as we have seen, of uniquely criminal, worst), he does so without spelling out the reasons for his view. The texts we have so far considered oblige us to rely on the briefest of indications to gather what those reasons might be.

Thus, in both *The Meaning of the Second World War* and in his 'Prémisses' essay, he refers to the systematic nature of the killing. Other comments made by him suggest that 'systematic' might unpack into two features commonly cited in debates on this question, features which we may label, for short, *modernity* and *comprehensiveness of intent*. Mandel writes that the perpetrators of earlier massacres were not more humane than the perpetrators of this one; it is just that 'their means and plans... were more limited'. And he writes of the Jews being killed 'simply' on account of their ethnic origin.[41] It is, then, because of the modern methods applied to their murder and because the intention of the Nazis was a total one, to kill them all, that the crime against the European Jews is to be seen as a *novum* morally speaking?

It turns out to be so. Such is what Mandel now puts forward in a more explicit and elaborated way in this German appendix. He begins with a description of the crime as the 'systematic, carefully planned and rapidly industrialized murder of six million people for the 'single reason [of] their supposed descent', and he goes on to present a version of the modernity thesis, a version of it of strong Marxist coloration. This emphasizes, on the one hand, the technical, administrative and division of labour aspects of the genocide, and its dependence on the railways and the chemical and building industries. And it insists on the part played, on the other hand, by 'the "basic moral values" of the ruling class': a pervasive mentality of obedience to the state, patriotism, nationalism and conformity. It was such organizational structures and such attitudes making for passive complicity that were, according to Mandel, decisive; as much as it was fanatical antisemitism and much more than it was any 'moral nihilism'.[42]

Now, there are some difficult and unpleasant questions here about why these features, whether separately or jointly, should distinguish the Holocaust as uniquely bad – questions about the normative comparison of evils that I will have to leave to one side. I intend to address them on another occasion.[43] It is interesting, however, to consider why it should have been just at this juncture, in this particular text, that Mandel endeavoured at last to lay out more fully the view that the Holocaust was unique, where before the weight of his emphasis had been much more upon its comparability with other historical experiences. Naturally, it is hard to be sure about the answer, but I would venture that the literary context is significant: an afterword for a German audience, in the wake of the recent 'Historikerstreit' (the historian's controversy), and dealing with the views of Ernest Nolte and their manifest tendency to apologia.

What follows should only be said bluntly. Within this apologia there is a standpoint bearing a formal resemblance to something I have criticized in Mandel. I mean the energetic contextualization of Nazi crimes by Nolte, even while briefly conceding their singular and unprecedented character: his insistence that they belong to the same history of modern times as the American war in Vietnam, the Vietnamese invasion of Cambodia, the exodus from Vietnam of the boat people – a 'holocaust on the water' – the Cambodian genocide, the repression following on the Iranian revolution, the Soviet invasion of Afghanistan and, above all, the liquidation of the kulaks, and the Gulag. Against that backdrop, Nolte urged that the Third Reich 'should be removed from the isolation in which it still finds itself'.[44] This is what came, in the debate in question, to be called 'relativization' of the Holocaust; and it is what Mandel himself calls it in taking issue with Nolte's views.[45] He (Mandel) continues even now to assert that the Holocaust was an extreme product of tendencies which are historically more general.[46] But he perceives a need, evidently, to balance the assertion with a greater emphasis on the singularity of the fate of the Jews.

On this matter especially, let there be no misunderstanding. I speak of a formal resemblance. But the same moral significance is not to be attached to the two standpoints formally alike: that of a German conservative historian and that of a Jewish Marxist revolutionary. For what motivated their respective emphases was not the same. A national particularism concerned with 'normalizing' Germany's modern historical identity was plainly at work in the first case. And the very opposite was probably at the root of the second, a socialist and in its way Jewish universalism that would not risk belittling the sufferings of others by dwelling too emphatically on the tragedy of the Jews.

It is an old story of socialism, going a long way back. It was represented by a figure of great importance for Mandel, of great importance for him in many respects, but one of these in having voiced the clearest of warnings about capitalist barbarism. From prison during the First World War, Rosa Luxemburg wrote to her friend Mathilde Wurm:

> What do you want with this particular suffering of the Jews? The poor victims on the rubber plantations in Putumayo, the Negroes in Africa with whose bodies the Europeans play a game of catch, are just as near to me. Do you remember the words written on the work of the Great General Staff about Trotha's campaign in the Kalahari desert? 'And the death-rattles, the mad cries of those dying of thirst, faded away into the sublime silence of eternity.' Oh, this 'sublime silence of eternity' in which so many screams have faded away unheard. It rings with me so strongly that I have no special corner of my heart reserved for the ghetto: I am at home wherever in the world there are clouds, birds and human tears.[47]

An old story of socialism and an old story of Jews on the left, and these words of Rosa Luxemburg are excellent ones, not to be forgotten or renounced, especially not today. Still, in the second half of the twentieth century, they are also less than adequate. A Jewish socialist ought to be able to find some special corner of his or her heart for the tragedy of the Jewish people. A universalist ethic shorn of any special concern for the sufferings of one's own would be the less persuasive for such carelessness. Whatever one may think about that, a balance is at any rate called for in estimating the place – comparable *and* unique – of the Shoah.

I take one last precaution to avoid the risk of an imbalance here myself. Writing about the Jewish question, both Mandel and Trotsky argued that there could be no satisfactory resolution of it except through the achievement of socialism.[48] All of the foregoing indicates, I hope, the shortcomings I see in that formula. Nevertheless, it secretes a certain truth as well. If we generalize from the so-called Jewish question to other cases of extreme persecution and oppression, the link which has so often been made by the political tradition of Mandel, Trotsky and Luxemburg, the link between capitalism and barbarism, is not to be lightly shrugged aside. Capitalism is a social and economic order systematically producing for millions of people – and all confident contemporary liberalisms notwithstanding – conditions of extreme want and oppression, in which hatreds are the more likely to accumulate, fester, erupt. It encourages moral attitudes, moreover, that may be described as underwriting a 'contract of mutual indifference': under which people in acute danger or trouble may be simply left there, so far as their situation is considered to be the business of anyone else. Not responsible for all evil, capitalist social relations and values contribute their massive share to it. Socialism represents the hope of another moral universe, one in which, to advert again to Mandel's principal 'lesson of the Holocaust', there might come to be enough people no longer willing to tolerate the morally intolerable that the instances of this could be at last radically reduced. It is to that vision that, balanced or not on any particular question, Mandel devoted his life.

Notes

1 Leon Trotsky, *On the Jewish Question*, New York, 1970, p. 29, emphasis in the original.
2 Isaac Deutscher, 'The Jewish Tragedy and the Historian', in his *The Non-Jewish Jew and other essays*, London, 1968, pp. 163–164. For discussion of the unpredictability of the Holocaust and the initial difficulties of belief, see: Yehuda Bauer, *The Holocaust in Historical Perspective*, Seattle, 1978, pp. 7, 16–22, 81; Jacob Katz, 'Was the Holocaust Predictable?', in Y. Bauer and N. Rotenstreich, eds, *The Holocaust as Historical Experience*, New York, 1981, pp. 23–41; Walter Laqueur, *The Terrible Secret*, London, 1980, pp. 1–10; and Michael Marrus, *The Holocaust in History*, London, 1987, pp. 156–164. Yehuda Bauer goes so far as to say that nobody predicted the Holocaust, whatever may have been claimed to the contrary; that the most that anyone could have envisaged was 'pogroms, economic destruction, hunger, or forced emigration', not 'the mass murder of millions of human beings'. I have no way of knowing whether Bauer is familiar with Trotsky's quoted remarks but, however things may be in general on this score, I do not see how those remarks can be taken in the way Bauer suggests. It is not only that Trotsky puts it so, and emphasizes: the *physical extermination* of the Jews; repeating the point, indeed, a few lines on with the claim that 'not only their political but also their physical fate' is tied to the struggle of the international proletariat. It is also that immediately before making this prediction he speaks of an ever-diminishing space for the Jews on the planet, with the

number of countries that expel them ceaselessly growing, the number willing to accept them always decreasing. In *this* context 'physical extermination of the Jews' is what he sees as logically coming next and what he actually says; and physical extermination of the Jews is what Hitler and his accomplices undertook. Naturally, this is not to say that Trotsky foresaw the specific form of what was to happen.

3 This is the revised text of a paper presented to the conference 'The Contribution of Ernest Mandel to Marxist Theory', held in Amsterdam, 4–6 July 1996. It will be part of a volume of essays about Mandel's work arising from that conference, and has appeared also in *New Left Review*, No. 224 (July/August 1997).

4 See my *The Legacy of Rosa Luxemburg*, London, 1976, p. 119.

5 E. Germain [Mandel], 'La question juive au lendemain de la deuxième guerre mondiale', afterword to A. Lèon, *Conception matèrialiste de la question juive*, Paris, 1946, p. I.

6 Ibid., p. VI.

7 Ibid., pp. I–III.

8 Ibid., p. XI.

9 See the Introduction to Leon Trotsky, *The Struggle Against Fascism in Germany*, New York, 1971, pp. 9, 39; and Ernest Mandel, *Trotsky: A Study in the Dynamic of his Thought*, London, 1979, p. 88.

10 In this connection, see particularly *The Struggle Against Fascism in Germany*, pp. 17–21.

11 Ibid., p. 15.

12 Ibid., pp. 12, 17. And cf. Ernest Mandel, 'Der Mensch ist das Hochste Wesen für den Menschen', in F.J. Raddatz, ed., *Warum Ich Marxist Bin*, Frankfurt, 1980: 'The great intellectual attraction of Marxism lies in its (up till now unique) ability to achieve a rational, all-inclusive and coherent integration of all social sciences'; 'It is … in the final analysis the science of mankind *tout court*'. Quoted from a typescript translation in the author's possession, made by Jurrian Bendien.

13 See Ernest Mandel, *The Meaning of the Second World War*, London, 1986, pp. 90–92. Reference to Mandel's views in the paragraphs following is to these pages until otherwise indicated.

14 *The Holocaust in Historical Perspective*, pp. 37–38.

15 *Trotsky: A Study …*, pp. 89–90.

16 Ernest Mandel, *Trotsky as Alternative*, London, 1995, p. 108.

17 *The Struggle Against Fascism in Germany*, pp. 403–405.

18 *On the Jewish Question*, pp. 30–31 – and cf. p. 20.

19 Enzo Traverso, 'Trotsky et la question juive', *Quatrieme Internationale*, No. 36 (1990), pp. 76–80; and his *Les Marxists et la question juive*, Montreuil, 1990, pp. 155–156, 219–222.

20 See the references given in note 18 above.

21 Ernest Mandel, 'Prémisses matérielles, sociales et idéologiques du génocide nazi', in Y. Thanassekos and H. Wismann, eds, *Révision de l'histoire*, Paris, 1990 (pp. 169–174), sections 1 and 11. All references to this text will be given so, by section number.

22 Ibid., sections 2, 3.

23 Ibid., section 11.

24 Ibid., section 10.

25 See in turn, ibid., sections 1, 6, 5, and 8; and also, on the rationality/irrationality combination, Mandel's appendix ('Zum Historikerstreit') to his *Der Zweite Weltkrieg*, Frankfurt, 1991, at pp. 224–225.

26 'Prémisses', section 1. And cf. 'Zum Historikerstreit', p. 220: 'An investigation of this sort... should by no means rule out consideration of ideological, and mass-psychological as well as individual-psychological, factors of the chain of causation.'

27 'Prémisses', section 3.

28 Ibid., section 5; and 'Zum Historikerstreit', pp. 229–230.

29 'Prémisses', section 7; and cf. 'Zum Historikerstreit', p. 232.

30 Primo Levi, Afterword to *If This Is a Man and The Truce*, London, 1987, pp. 394–396.

31 'Prémisses', section 11.

32 See Norman Geras, 'Literature of Revolution', *New Left Review*, Nos 113–114 (January/April 1979), pp. 25–29; reprinted in my collection *Literature of Revolution*, London, 1986, at pp. 247–250.

33 Leon Trotsky, *1905*, London, 1972, pp. 131–135.

34 See Martin Broszat/Saul Friedlander, 'A Controversy about the Historicization of National Socialism', *Yad Vashem Studies*, 19 (1988), pp. 28–29.

35 Saul Friedlander, 'The "Final Solution": On the Unease in Historical Interpretation', in Peter Hayes, ed., *Lessons and Legacies: The Meaning of the Holocaust in a Changing World*, Evanston, 1991, pp. 23–35, at pp. 25, 30–31. The essay is reprinted, slightly modified, in Friedlander's *Memory, History, and the Extermination of the Jews of Europe*, Bloomington, 1993, pp. 102–116.

36 Christopher R. Browning, *Ordinary Men: Reserve Police Battalion 101 and the Final Solution in Poland*, New York, 1993, p. 112.

37 Ernst Klee, Willi Dressen and Volker Riess, eds, *'Those were the Days': The Holocaust through the Eyes of the Perpetrators and Bystanders*, London, 1991, pp. 76, 89, 118, 127, 129.

38 Odd Nansen, *From Day to Day*, New York, 1949, p. 438.

39 George Steiner, 'The Long Life of Metaphor: An Approach to the "Shoah"', in Berel Lang, ed., *Writing and the Holocaust*, New York, 1988, pp. 154–171, at pp. 161–166. The article is reprinted from *Encounter*, 68 (February 1987), pp. 55–61.

40 See the reference given in note 12 above.

41 *The Meaning of the Second World War*, p. 92; 'Prémisses', section 2. And see also, with respect to the comprehensiveness of intent, *Trotsky as Alternative*, p. 155, note 25.

42 'Zum Historikerstreit', pp. 209, 222–223.

43 There is also the explanatory question already once mooted. Mandel is unable to account even for the unique features of the event as he identifies these, since neither the structures nor the mentalities he focuses on seem to suffice, given their pervasiveness in the modern world, to the extremity of what occurred. He is aware of the problem, for he sets himself to trying to respond to it: to explaining what it was that produced the specific outcome from these more general tendencies. (See ibid., pp. 240–243.) But his response – in terms of the failure of the German bourgeois revolution, the rapid growth of German industry and the ambitions of German imperialism for a redivision of existing spheres of influence – seems to me to fall

far short of the thing it purports to address. None of these causes speaks directly to the aim of *wiping out a people*.

44 Ernst Nolte, 'Between Historical Myth and Revisionism?' and 'A Past That Will Not Pass Away', *Yad Vashem Studies*, No. 19 (1988), pp. 49–63 and 65–73. Also in J. Knowlton and T. Cates (translators), *Forever in the Shadow of Hitler?*, Atlantic Highlands, 1993, pp. 1–15 and 18–23.

45 'Zum Historikerstreit', p. 209.

46 Ibid., pp. 239, 242, 245.

47 Stephen Eric Bronner, ed., *The Letters of Rosa Luxemburg*, Boulder, 1978, pp. 179–180.

48 See Trotsky, *On the Jewish Question*, pp. 18–22, 28–29; Germain [Mandel], 'La question juive au lendemain de la deuxième guerre mondiale', p. XII; and Ernest Germain, 'A Biographical Sketch of Abram Leon', in Abram Leon, *The Jewish Question: A Marxist Interpretation*, New York, 1970, p. 17.

10

Marx and antisemitism

(This article was first published on 'Normblog', 13 May 2009)

I've never understood the inclination of certain Marxists, as well as others who admire aspects of Marx's work, to deny the antisemitic material there is in his essay *On the Jewish Question*. Michael Ezra cites the work in a post at the blog "Harry's Place" discussing whether Marx was an anti-Semite. Michael refers also to an opinion of Gertrude Himmelfarb's to the effect that Marx expressed views there that 'were part of the classic repertoire of antisemitism'. This is plainly and undeniably so.

It is true that the central theme of *On the Jewish Question* is one supportive of the political rights of Jews. Bruno Bauer, against whom Marx was polemicizing in that essay, had argued that the political emancipation of the Jews, their availing themselves of political and civil rights within the democratic state, was incompatible with their Jewish *particularism*; remaining Jewish they could not be true citizens. Against this, Marx counter-argued that political emancipation, so far from being incompatible with religious particularisms, presupposes them. The democratic state gives everyone the right to their own beliefs and to practise their religion.

None of this, however, can obscure the themes which Marx deploys in the second part of his essay. Here is a key passage from it:

> For us, the question of the Jew's capacity for emancipation becomes the question: What particular *social* element has to be overcome in order to abolish Judaism? For the present-day Jew's capacity for emancipation is the relation of Judaism to the emancipation of the modern world. This relation necessarily results from the special position of Judaism in the contemporary enslaved world.
>
> Let us consider the actual, worldly Jew – not the *Sabbath Jew*, as Bauer does, but the *everyday Jew*.
>
> Let us not look for the secret of the Jew in his religion, but let us look for the secret of his religion in the real Jew.
>
> What is the secular basis of Judaism? *Practical* need, *self-interest*. What is the worldly religion of the Jew? *Huckstering*. What is his worldly God? *Money*.

> Very well then! Emancipation from *huckstering* and *money*, consequently from practical, real Judaism, would be the self-emancipation of our time.

Further on:

> Money is the jealous god of Israel, in face of which no other god may exist.

And further on again:

> Contempt for theory, art, history, and for man as an end in himself, which is contained in an abstract form in the Jewish religion, is the real, conscious standpoint, the virtue of the man of money.

It is fruitless to pretend that these sentiments are expressed merely ironically when there is no clear supporting evidence that they are to be read in that way rather than straightforwardly. Supporting evidence points in the opposite direction. Marx and Engels exchanged standard antisemitic remarks from time to time. Marx once wrote to Engels of Ferdinand Lassalle:

> The Jewish nigger Lassalle who, I'm glad to say, is leaving at the end of this week, has happily lost another 5,000 talers in an ill-judged speculation. The chap would sooner throw money down the drain than lend it to a 'friend', even though his interest and capital were guaranteed. In this he bases himself on the view that he ought to live the life of a Jewish baron, or Jew created a baron (no doubt by the countess).

Engels wrote to Marx of someone else:

> As a Jew he simply cannot stop cheating …

The only reason for not facing up to these things is to protect Marx's reputation as a thinker. But this is not a good reason, because it's no protection; what's there is there. Better to admire Marx for whatever in his work is really worthy of admiration.

PART III

The responsibility to protect

11

The duty to bring aid

(This chapter is an extract from *The Contract of Mutual Indifference: Political Philosophy after the Holocaust*, Verso, London, 1998)

There is an aspect of the unconditional in the duty to come to the help of people in danger. This has about it the pull of an irresistible demand. A sense of its unconditionality suffuses the literature of catastrophe; it breaks forth there again and again. Let us look for it first in what may appear the least likely of places: among those whom one might think not in a good position to help, or not in any position to.

In Zygmunt Bauman's book, the story is cited of a Polish family that offered to hide a Jewish friend during the German occupation but declined to take in his three sisters, more obviously Jewish in speech and appearance than he was. But the friend would not be saved alone. The writer here, who learned of this episode from another member of the family, reports:

> Had the decision of my family been different, there were nine chances to one that we would all be shot. The probability that our friend and his sisters would survive in those conditions was perhaps smaller still. And yet the person telling me this family drama and repeating 'What could we do, there was nothing we could do!', did not look me in the eyes. He sensed I felt a lie, though all the facts were true.[1]

Speaking of circumstances even more directly threatening than these, one Dora Rosenboim names the emotion which was this man's in being unable to look his interlocutor in the eyes. According to Rosenboim's testimony, in a village near Lodz in 1942, during the Purim festival, the Gestapo ordered ten young Jews hanged by the Jewish police, with the rest of the community forced out of their houses to watch.

> Many women fainted seeing the terrible and horrible sight, how ten of our brothers were writhing on the gallows. Our faces were ashamed and our hearts ached, but we could not help ourselves.[2]

Prisoners at Auschwitz were also forced to be present at hangings. Primo Levi tells of one of these; and of his feeling afterwards of being 'oppressed by shame.'[3] And it is Levi who, as not uncommonly in this domain, has put that feeling into the form of a more general and troubling wisdom for his readers. I shall quote him at length since what he has to say about shame bears upon our theme.

Levi writes of the moment of liberation for himself and some other prisoners left behind at the evacuation of Auschwitz. He describes how the Russian soldiers coming upon him and his group seemed overtaken by 'a confused restraint' at the sight before them.

> It was the same shame which we knew so well, which submerged us after the selections, and every time we had to witness or undergo an outrage: the shame that the Germans never knew, the shame which the just man experiences when confronted by a crime committed by another, and he feels remorse because of its existence, because of its having been irrevocably introduced into the world of existing things and because his will has proven nonexistent or feeble and was incapable of putting up a good defence.[4]

The act of witnessing. It is perhaps only an accident of expression but Dora Rosenboim says: our *faces* were ashamed. That is where it is, in the face. Primary point of interchange between the world and the self. To see such a thing. To have to face it. And to be unable to look another in the eyes. Seeing, a mode of and common metaphor for knowing. Averting one's face, a way not to know. This has, consequently, more sources than one. Not only the inability to bear what you might see should you carry on looking, but another avoidance as well: shame. The shame of seeing and not acting. And whatever the conditions and the risks – although, to be sure, the greater the risks, the less 'genuine' the cause for shame, as we are bound on some level also to feel. But is it not conversely then, too? And the shame proper to humanity incalculable?

Levi in fact goes on to speak of such 'another vaster shame, the shame of the world'. Invoking John Donne, he speaks about those who, like the majority of Germans under Hitler, 'delud[ed] themselves that not seeing was a way of not knowing, and that not knowing relieved them of their share of complicity ...'.

> But we were denied the screen of willed ignorance ... we were not able not to see. The ocean of pain, past and present, surrounded us... It was useless to close one's eyes or turn one's back to it, because it was all around, in every direction, all the way to the horizon. It was not possible for us, nor did we want, to become islands; the just among us, neither more nor less numerous than in any other human group, felt remorse, shame and pain for the misdeeds that others and not they had committed, and in which they felt involved, because they sensed that what had happened around them in their presence, and in them, was irrevocable. It would never again be able to be cleansed; it would prove that man, the human species – we, in short – were potentially able to construct an infinite enormity of pain; and that pain is the only force that is created from nothing, without cost and without effort. It is enough not to see, not to listen, not to act.[5]

Such is the moral economy of bystanding. Simply by omission you contribute your share to producing an enormity of suffering. The direct responsibility, of course, will lie with others; with the authors of the misdeeds or, as the case may be as well, with those upholding and enforcing conditions of grave oppression or wretchedness. Yet there is, so Levi suggests, a responsibility on all of those who know, even the most threatened of them. Its affective correlate (amongst the just) is shame.

In some more extensive reflections whose parallel with Levi's has been noted before,[6] the German philosopher Karl Jaspers put forward a similar idea. Writing just after the war on the subject of German guilt, Jaspers proposed a fourfold schema: of, in turn, criminal, political, moral and metaphysical guilt. It is the last pair that is of particular interest in the present context, but I briefly summarize the schema as a whole.

Criminal guilt, in Jaspers' schema, relates to acts of violating unequivocal laws and susceptible of objective proof, it is established through formal proceedings under the jurisdiction of a court, and it is subject to punishment as determined by the court. Political guilt arises from the fact that everyone 'is co-responsible for the way he is governed' and has therefore to bear the consequences of deeds of state; this may involve liability for reparations following on defeat in war. Moral guilt arises because we are, as individuals, responsible for our actions, including the execution of orders. The proper forum of moral guilt is the individual's own conscience and the opinion of others, and it may lead to 'penance and renewal'.[7]

Note, however, the limit which Jaspers deems appropriate to this type of guilt. It rightly applies where there has been inaction in face of the crimes of others, but only up to a certain point. He writes:

> [E]ach one of us is guilty insofar as he remained inactive ... Impotence excuses; no moral law demands a spectacular death ... But passivity knows itself morally guilty of every failure, every neglect to act whenever possible, to shield the imperilled, to relieve wrong, to countervail. Impotent submission always left a margin of activity which, though not without risk, could still be cautiously effective ... Blindness for the misfortune of others, lack of imagination of the heart, inner indifference toward the witnessed evil – that is moral guilt.[8]

The thought would seem to be that if we can act to make a difference for the better ('to relieve ... to countervail') without definite risk to our own lives, then we ought to do so, or else we are morally guilty. But though we should be willing to take some risks – Jaspers does not specify how great – we are not obliged, under this third form within his schema, to incur a plain mortal danger. 'Morally we have a duty to dare, not a duty to choose certain doom.'[9]

It is otherwise with the fourth form, with metaphysical guilt. Here we are obliged absolutely. Whatever the risks, we owe our support to people under threat:

There exists a solidarity among men as human beings that makes each co-responsible for every wrong and every injustice in the world, especially for crimes committed in his presence or with his knowledge. If I fail to do whatever I can to prevent them, I too am guilty. If I was present at the murder of others without risking my life to prevent it, I feel guilty in a way not adequately conceivable either legally, politically, or morally. That I live after such a thing has happened weighs upon me as indelible guilt.

And Jaspers writes also:

Metaphysical guilt is the lack of absolute solidarity with the human being as such – an indelible claim beyond morally meaningful duty. This solidarity is violated by my presence at a wrong or a crime. It is not enough that I cautiously risk my life to prevent it; if it happens, and if I was there, and if I survive where the other is killed, I know from a voice within myself: I am guilty of being still alive.[10]

The boundary here between moral and metaphysical guilt is not altogether distinct: a consequence of Jaspers' suggestion that the taking of some risk to help others in jeopardy may reasonably be expected as part of a person's moral duty, but not the taking of too great and definite a one. It is in the nature of this idea, the idea of 'cautiously' risking, that to attempt a precise quantification of what, in general, would be a reasonable risk is unlikely to be fruitful. I want, though, to comment on another area of apparent uncertainty. This comes out of Jaspers' presentation of the concept of metaphysical guilt itself – the responsibility to help whatever the risks – and it concerns how close to the individual a given crime or injustice has to be for such a responsibility to be thought applicable.

In the first of the two passages cited above, Jaspers speaks of crimes committed in a person's presence or 'with his knowledge'. In the second passage, he speaks, seemingly more restrictively, just of 'my presence at a wrong or a crime'; and he says, 'if it happens, and if I was there ...'. But I take it that by presence in this context he does indeed mean, as well as direct physical presence at a given site of crime, also something less proximate that that. I take it so not only for consistency with the first passage, but because in what immediately follows the second passage in his text, Jaspers goes on to quote from an address he gave in August 1945, and the view he puts forward there about German guilt looks as if it should be taken in this broader way. It looks as if it is meant to refer to a sizeable public: to all who knew about the persecution of the Jews of Germany and were close enough that they could have opposed it; and not merely to those who happened to be on a particular street at a particular time. This is what Jaspers says:

Thousands in Germany sought, or at least found death in battling the regime, most of them anonymously. We survivors did not seek it. We did not go into the streets when our Jewish friends were led away; we did not scream until we too were destroyed. We preferred to stay alive, on the feeble, if logical, ground that our death could not have helped anyone. We are guilty of being alive.[11]

One last point here. Jaspers characterizes metaphysical guilt as being 'before God'.[12] I assume, however, that there is a secular, non-theistic equivalent for it. For Jaspers himself more than once associates metaphysical guilt with the feeling of shame,[13] and in one of the passages I have quoted he writes also of knowing of it 'from a voice within myself'. But if shame and this kind of inner voice do for some people have their basis in a belief in God, neither requires it, as the moral outlook and sensibilities of large numbers of other people attest. That Primo Levi, without appealing to or drawing support from any religious faith, could write of a reaction to injustice so evidently similar to the one Jaspers describes, attests equally that there are other human impulses behind it.

Whatever the impulse behind it, whatever the basis in personal conviction or metaphysical belief, we have testimony of another sort to show that a moral sentiment similar to the one discussed by Levi and Jaspers was also felt in a positive manner, so to say, felt as a motive for acting to help others in danger. The testimony I refer to is from the 'Righteous among the Nations' as they are sometimes known, those who, often at great risk to themselves, came to the rescue of Jews in Nazi Europe. Such people may describe their motives for what they did in different ways. But a core element persists across the differences: the idea of a pressing, an unavoidable imperative to help. One Polish woman formulates it in terms of a fundamental human duty: 'What I did was everybody's duty. Saving the one whose life is in jeopardy is a simple human duty.'[14] A Dutch rescuer expresses the same thing as an obligation of justice: 'You could do nothing else ... It was obvious. When you see injustice done you do something against it.'[15] Another says simply, 'I got such satisfaction from helping out, from keeping people safe ...' and another, 'I had feelings in my heart that I had to help.'[16] The idea was frequently expressed in religious terms. A minister in the Dutch Reformed Church in Friesland preached to his congregation: 'By staying idle at a time when we are the last resort for innocent people condemned to die, we blaspheme against God's commandment against killing.' The same man, it is relevant to note, also spoke of the 'tacit contract' that makes each of us his brother's keeper, a contract without which everyone is vulnerable.[17] Testimony of this kind exists in some quantity. Suffice, for our purposes, to say that the small sample of it I have given is typical, evidence of a shared moral sense amongst the rescuers that in the circumstances under consideration they could do no other than they did.

The question I want to address now is this. How far may we take the example of these rescuers as the image, or anticipation, of an alternative* possible ethical landscape? Can one envisage a moral culture so transformed as to give real practical force to the sense of responsibility for the safety of others that Levi and Jaspers discuss under the headings of shame and moral and metaphysical guilt, and that the rescuers articulate as having compelled them? Could one feasibly entertain the vision of a global human community in which an obligation to come to the assistance of others in danger or distress was widely felt as amongst the most powerful of imperatives, moving people to action when the risk of acting were small to non-existent, making a serious demand on their consciences – on their day-to-day practical deliberations – even when the risks were greater than that, and making of shame something more than a 'metaphysical' shadow, more than a *post hoc* individual sentiment following failure to act; making of shame, and of the foretaste of it, an effective, mobilizing norm of social life?

Only by way of such a moral culture, one that would be at least *very much* informed by this sense of a generalized obligation for the security and well-being of others, could we escape the darkness of the conclusion of the contract of mutual indifference. This is a moral darkness in which it is widely treated, lived, as being acceptable that large numbers of human beings are regularly overtaken by disaster and indeed subjected to it. The familiarity of the conjunction – disaster for some comfortably lived with by others – the unexceptional character of its occurrence, no more brightens it up, morally speaking, than does the fact that slavery has been taken for granted as a mode of human coexistence brighten that up. '*Very much* informed' here may be thought to be rather too indeterminate, but it is determinate enough for the broad mapping of the terrain being undertaken. I try to make it a little more determinate in due course.

A legal and moral culture of rights and obligations largely structured around the notion that one should refrain from harming others, but that helping or not helping them is a matter of individual inclination, is plainly inadequate. It is not demanding enough given the extent of the evils that are our subject. Following the usage of Laurence Thomas in discussion of these same issues, I shall call this kind of legal and moral culture a liberal one. The characterization is narrowing, obviously. Refraining from harm does not exhaust the scope or the varieties of liberalism. I choose to take as paradigmatic a liberalism of negative duties only, duties of non-interference, where more positive duties as well, duties of active intervention and supportive material provision, can be accommodated within a liberal outlook and liberal institutional practices. But the narrowing characterization will do. It captures accurately enough what has been a prominent, and probably the dominant, moral culture for most of the duration of most of the societies known as liberal. In particular, in these societies practical indifference to the calamities and sufferings of others is taken to be a legitimate mode of personal conduct. Living side by side with them, not regarding them as one's own responsibility – to try to mitigate or to seek to end – is not widely seen as a form of moral depravity. It may be said against this that liberal cultures not only permit, they also leave space to encourage, empathy, benevolence, charity; and that it is consistent with a structure of mostly negative rights and duties to admire and praise those who go beyond what is required of them, in order to help others, as being better people. It remains, however, that this is extra to what is either demanded or expected of anyone in the general run of things, and that the threshold, correspondingly, of moral turpitude or serious wrong-doing is for its part set demandingly high: high enough that people who do nothing, or nothing much, by way of this extra are not judged to have crossed it. As Laurence Thomas writes, 'being a morally decent person would seem to be compatible with allowing others to suffer great harm'. As he also says, we do not tend to think of those who stood by to the destruction of the Jews, in the way we think of the actual perpetrators, as wicked: 'Is it not revealing ... that those who could tolerate so much evil can pass for being morally decent individuals? This consideration alone would suggest that our view of the morally decent stands in need of serious upgrading'.[18]

A liberal culture underwrites moral indifference. It makes much room for the bystander to suffering. And this is perhaps not so surprising. For the principal economic formation historically associated with liberalism, defended by liberals – whether confidently or apologetically – today as much as ever, is one in which it has been the norm for the wealth and comfort of some to be obtained through the hardship and poverty of others, and to stand right alongside these. It is a whole mode of collective existence. Not only an economy. A world, a culture, a set of everyday practices. But if it is of no concern within this ensemble, no practical, life-transforming concern, that others may dwell within reach of us in some form of wretchedness, then to all intents and purposes the judgement is that their sufferings are of little consequence. Those who *live* such a judgement upon others are perhaps not at all that likely to come to the aid of people in danger or emergency. And, as I have already argued, via the contract of mutual indifference even the more minimal of liberal rights are then also nullified.

An alternative ethical landscape to this may be given various names. One of them during the last two centuries has been socialism. I do not mean that the thought of socialism *as* ethical alternative has always or necessarily been primary to the conception of socialism amongst its adherents. I mean only that this has usually been part of the conception: embedded in it at some level, either consciously or unconsciously, an idea of mutual concern and mutual help. Some such idea is a stark moral necessity. It is a necessity against the darkness of the contract of mutual indifference. And so far as this necessity is indeed projected under the heading of socialism, the latter should not be visualized as a realm of altogether spontaneous harmony and goodness. It would have to be a moral and political order in the familiar sense. It would have to be a rule-governed, normative system, constraining its members as well as benefiting them, curbing evils amongst them as well as encouraging and generating goods, requiring duties as well as upholding and protecting rights.[19] Amongst these duties would be the duty of aid. A serious-minded view of socialism today, no less than any other meliorative conception – be it of justice or rights, moral or political progress – is dependent for its consistency and realism on the centrality of the imperative of mutual care.

Of course, this affirmation of a necessary mutuality may be expressed also in a less politically specific idiom. To cite just one example from the Holocaust literature itself, at the end of her remarkable book about Franz Stangl (commandant at Sobibor and then Treblinka) Gitta Sereny places a short reflective epilogue in which she proposes that the inner core of our being, 'the very essence of the human person', is our capacity for responsible decision. But since it is profoundly dependent on our freedom to grow, to grow within family, community, nations and 'human society as a whole', this essential human capacity, Sereny says, 'is evidence of our interdependence and of our responsibility for each other'.[20]

The thought is brief and wholly general. It was also stated more famously by Kant in exemplifying the categorical imperative, stated by him explicitly as involving the obligation to render aid. Kant considers the possibility of a man proposing as a maxim for himself what is in effect a principle of mutual non-assistance ('I will not take anything from him or even envy him; but to his welfare or to his assistance in time of need I have no desire to contribute'); and he then goes on to say:

> although it is possible that a universal law of nature according to that maxim could exist, it is nevertheless impossible to will that such a principle should hold everywhere as a law of nature. For a will which resolved this would conflict with itself, since instances can often arise in which he would need the love and sympathy of others, and in which he would have robbed himself, by such a law of nature springing from his own will, of all hope of the aid he desires.[21]

I disagree that this is, in truth, impossible to will. One can will things that conflict with one's needs; the more especially if they are not present needs, and even recognizing the possibility that they could become one's needs. But in any case, though the thought is not expressed by either of them in overtly contractual terms, we may note the generic similarity between Sereny's and Kant's arguments here and that of the Dutch rescuer lately quoted, for whom we are all of us our brother's keepers by way of a tacit contract, or else we are all vulnerable. Kant himself in fact puts forward the same thing in contractual terms elsewhere. He does so in relation to states and not individuals, but the logic of a common vulnerability is no different. In the essay on 'Perpetual Peace' Kant speaks of the necessity 'of establish[ing] a federation of peoples in accordance with the idea of an original social contract'. This is 'so that states will protect one another against external aggression ...'[22]

No matter if the idea is or is not formulated in contractual terms, the main difficulty with it, which we must now face, concerns how extensive the obligation to help others may be held to be. This question can itself be divided into two. How extensive is the obligation in a physical, or geographical, sense? How far, that is, does it reach, for any individual person, across the world's population? Second, how demanding is it, how demanding in the way of the costs to be incurred, or of the time and the risks to be taken, in meeting it? My answer to these two questions will be as follows: that, with due allowance made for considerations of practicality, the obligation is unlimited in the first, the geographical sense, and that it is limited in the second, the burdening sense, although not *that* limited relative to currently prevailing practices. In whichever sense, the obligation is in principle very extensive. I shall elaborate on these preliminary indications in the terms of a dictum which Dostoyevsky puts into the mouths of two of his characters, namely, the Elder Zosima and his brother Markel, in *The Brothers Karamazov*.

The dictum: 'each one of us is indubitably guilty in respect of all creatures and all things upon the earth ... each for all people and for each person on this earth'; again, 'each of us is guilty before all for everyone and everything'.[23] This resembles Jaspers' metaphysical guilt except for being stated in a more absolute way. But regardless of its metaphysical significance in the mind of its author, I present it as expressing well enough the spatial scope of individual obligation in face of the suffering of others, provided that certain obvious limitations on what is possible for any single person are taken into account. There will be such limitations as a result – at least – of what the particular individual knows about or can get to know about; of what he can reach, whether literally or through the agencies of others; and of what he can feasibly do or contribute, given anything or everything else he may be doing in the same sort of helping line. Still, in principle, if he does know, and he can reach, and he can act or contribute towards making a beneficial difference, there is no better reason for him to attend to the suffering of others in this place rather than that one. There is no stronger claim on him just *qua* human being – I say nothing yet of more special claims – that he should respond to this person's suffering or violation rather than to that person's. If, at any rate, our shared humanity as moral agents, or our shared vulnerability or common capacity to suffer, is sufficient to establish between us bonds of mutual obligation, it is not clear why, other than by reasons of practicality, those bonds should stop at some regional or national boundary. In this general theoretical sense our responsibility for all of humankind and our guilt for the ills befalling others are universal and unlimited.

However, it is different with respect to the amount of help any single person's duties can be thought to encompass. Here there must be a limit, or so I shall argue. No one can be guilty for everything. Nor can they even for that small fraction of the world's ills which it would entirely consume their own lives to put right. Within what is intended as a general moral code, we should not be drawn into a moral absolutism, permit ourselves a standard fit only for saints. This is for metaphysical and anthropological reasons, and it is also for reasons of straightforward humanity in the ethical sense. I take these three kinds of reasons in turn.

First, the note of unconditionality which there is in the feeling of shame or guilt at being an unprotesting (even if impotent) witness to evil, represents the demand of the moral realm against the harms of the world. By the harms of the world I mean both its brute realities, beyond all intention, and its deliberately inflicted brutalities. As *absolute*, however, the moral realm cannot be realized. That is a discourse of would-be perfection, of a moral purity uncorrupted by mundane facts, when the facts are never pure but are 'spoiled' by necessity and the shortcomings of the real. The note of unconditionality in the moral realm can only ever be at best an idea towards which to aspire and to move. For some this is the idea of God, or it is within the idea of God; for others it is a secular ideal. But that is as much as it can be: a criterion, a direction, a measure of hope. It could not just *become*, without limitation, the humanly lived world.

Second, the project of a moral culture so changed as to have spread far and wide a compelling sense of obligation for the security and well-being of others, is a tall enough order as things are without addition of the requirement for a population of perfectly moral beings, of the kind who would be capable of giving unqualified priority to their duties to others. Such a demandingly utopian ethic flies in the face of well-known facts about human weakness and the partiality of individuals towards their own interests, not to speak of any dispositions worse than that. I shall not repeat myself here, but the historical experience at the basis of this whole discussion is sufficient caution in itself against the idea of human perfectibility.[24] A perfectibility in the matter of the dutiful will is not exempt from the caution.

Third, the notion of an absolute, all-encompassing moral demand on the individual in the face of great evil or emergency, life-saving as it may be intended to be, is also life-consuming. It is life-consuming in one way where it requires of anyone that they risk death for the safety of another; and it is life-consuming in a different way where it requires of them that they give up everything of their time, their experience of living, the very stuff of their own personal existence, to saving or improving the lives of others. Pressed to such extremity this is itself an inhumane demand. And it is an unjust one. For to allow the individual no claim at all on her own life vis-à-vis the lives of other people amounts to saying that she must be sacrificed for them. If I may link the considerations of humanity and justice being urged here with the metaphysical one that went before: it is just an irresolvable tension within mundane reality that, to be met, certain urgent moral claims can require life-consuming sacrifices on the part of those who would go to meet them; in this manner amongst others, the unconditionally moral vies with the impure facts of life.

It may be noted, moreover, that if the wisdom of the survivors does include the strongest of counsel concerning the perilous slope of moral indifference, of standing inactively by to other people's tragedies, it includes another precept as well, with which that counsel has to be placed in some balance, Micheline Maurel, who spent two years imprisoned at Neubrandenburg, a subsidiary of the women's camp at Ravensbrück, gave one clear formulation of this precept: after some lines of Ronsard, 'May you be happy! If you only knew how much one can regret all that was left undone ...' Or, delivered as a message from the doomed on behalf of the dead themselves:

> What did we ask of the living when we were like the dead? To think of us? To pray for us? Yes, a little, in the beginning. But mainly to do all they could to send us material to help, and then, when they had done all they could, oh, above all, to enjoy life to the fullest! We so often cried out to them, 'Be happy, be happy! ...'[25]

It is a recognition of everyone's own needs of living, even alongside the desperate call on them of the needs of others.

One can, though, set the level of an obligation to bring aid rather too low, and I want to consider this contrasting impulse by turning to the work of another who has written on the same issue. I mean Tzvetan Todorov, in his book *Facing the Extreme*. The book has much in it that is of value. It has, in particular, a salutary meditation (somewhat in the manner of Terrence Des Pres' earlier study, *The Survivor*) on the tenacity of ordinary virtue, the persistence of good 'even in the most desperate circumstances'[26] – a matter to which I shall shortly return. Todorov offers, also, pertinent reflections on the ubiquity and the dangers of moral indifference, and he points to the element of denial, of affecting not to know, that it contains. He writes:

> The misfortune of others, it seems, leaves us cold if in order to alleviate it we have to sacrifice our own comfort ... Acts of injustice take place all around us every day and we do not intervene to stop them ... We have grown used to seeing extreme poverty all around us and not thinking about it. The reasons are always the same: I didn't know, and even if I had, I couldn't have done anything about it. We, too, know about deliberate blindness and fatalism, and here totalitarianism reveals what democracy leaves in the shadows – that at the end of the path of indifference and conformity lies the concentration camp.[27]

Todorov proposes along the way an interesting, if speculative, connected hypothesis about Primo Levi's inner path towards suicide (assuming this is indeed what Levi's death was). The hypothesis is that his expectations may have been too high: thinking that after Auschwitz 'all must prefer truth to comfort and be willing to help one another' eventually led Levi to despair, because humanity had not improved but refused to learn the lesson of the catastrophe.[28] What practical conclusion, then, does Todorov himself derive from the observation about indifference and blindness just quoted?

> Must we each, in consequence, take upon ourselves all the suffering in the world, ceasing to sleep peacefully so long as there remains somewhere ... even

the slightest trace of injustice? ... Of course not. Such a task is beyond human strength ... Only the saint can live in perfect truth, renouncing all comfort and consolation. We can, however, set ourselves a more modest and accessible goal: in peacetime, to care about those close to us, but in times of trouble, to find within ourselves the strength to expand this intimate circle beyond its usual limits and recognize as our own even those whose faces we do not know.[29]

The conclusion falls back behind Todorov's own argument. In peacetime: as though this were an apt description of the general condition of humankind, and not a retreat into that very haven of mental comfort which the relatively comfortable make for themselves *in* blindness, declining to see the miseries of others. In times of trouble: but Todorov says it, acts of injustice and extreme poverty are all around us. How much trouble do we need? Expansion of the intimate circle notwithstanding, these look rather too much like formulas for the world as it already is. The claims of the intimate circle are real and important enough. Yet the movement from intimacy, and to faces we do not know, still carries the ring of a certain local confinement. For there are the people as well whose faces we never encounter, but whom we have ample means of knowing *about*. As those other formulas – of Levi, Jaspers and Dostoyevsky – remind us, their claims too, in trouble, unheeded, are a cause for shame.

So where to draw this particular line? Where, between the intimate circle merely and a crushing guilt for everything?

Well, perhaps it might be, here, that 'the way down is the way up'.[30] Perhaps on the very bottom, in that humanly-contrived hell whose legacy and images press so hard against the effort to hold on today to a hope of progressive moral direction, we can find something useful on this question. Todorov himself, in a passage I can only read as being in tension with that other, more confined judgement of his, emphasizes how 'even under the most adverse circumstances imaginable, when men and women are faint with hunger, numb with cold, exhausted, beaten, and humiliated, they still go on performing simple acts of kindness', and he argues that it is up to those of us living 'peaceful lives' to recognize and confirm such acts of dignity and care as representing 'one of the supreme achievements of the human race'; he speaks of a 'code of ordinary moral values and virtues ... commensurate with our times' based upon this recognition.[31] Terrance Des Pres before him had drawn attention to the same thing: to the 'innumerable small acts of human-ness', an 'unsuppressible urge toward decency and care', even within the concentrationary universe.[32] And the two of them have not been alone; they highlight what is a recurring theme within this literature, in direct survivor testimony and the secondary, discursive literature alike.

One should not simplify or seek false and easy comforts there. The general climate in the camps was of a desperate battle for survival. It was one in which self-interest had to be fundamental and much prisoner behaviour was of an openly, sometimes brutally, egocentric kind. Primo Levi, on the very first page of his famous memoir of Auschwitz, refers to 'the doctrine I was … to learn so hurriedly in the Lager: that man is bound to pursue his own ends by all possible means, while he who errs but once pays dearly'.[33] But while Levi fairly summarizes in this the spirit of vigilant and remorseless struggle on their own behalf that was necessary for those imprisoned in the camps just to keep going from one day to the next, nevertheless there is an exaggeration in what he says if it is taken literally. The generality of prisoners did not pursue their ends by all possible means and nor does Levi's account show that they did. In their relations to one another they observed – even there – some moral norms and limits.

Anna Pawelczynska, a sociologist and also a former prisoner at Auschwitz, has produced a valuable study on this subject, and her overall conclusion is relevant to our present concern. According to Pawelczynska, when 'evaluated from the standpoint of the highest moral principles … all prisoners succumbed to savagery'. Since sticking to high principle in that environment was usually fatal, there was an unavoidable adaptation of and reduction in the prisoners' values, whatever the basis of these, secular or religious. Pawelczynska gives some examples. The commandment not to steal became, for many, a rule against stealing in ways harmful to one's fellow prisoners. The ideal of equality gave way to the aspiration 'to fill the higher places in a structure of inequality [i.e. the prisoner hierarchy] with persons who would protect, not murder, their fellow man'. More generally, for prisoners fighting to keep a part of their values intact, the maxim 'Love your neighbour as yourself' turned into something like 'Do not harm your neighbour and, if at all possible, save him'. This was, says Pawelczynska, a 'basic norm', widely practised, despite the inescapable diminution in values. It is one, she adds, 'the observance of which is everywhere indispensable'.[34] The general tenor of it, as it so happens, is consistent with a remark attributed to another woman at Auschwitz, Ena Weiss; who, according to our source for the remark, did as much as anyone to help others in the camp, using her position as a doctor there to save many lives. 'Ena Weiss … once defined her attitude thus, in sarcastic rejection of fulsome flattery and at the same time with brutal frankness: "How did I keep alive in Auschwitz? My principle is: myself first, second and third. Then nothing. Then myself again – and then all the others."'[35]

Now, it may seem strange to invoke, of all things, this milieu, its values so radically pared down, in trying to think about the possibility of an improved, a more humane, moral landscape. However, reduced and impoverished as in so many respects it obviously was, there is a normative core in what we have before us that will withstand comparison with the fuller and more cultured ways of better times and places. For consider. First, second, third and again, oneself, and then all the others. Not to harm and, if at all possible, to save. These two principles might equally be written thus. First, second, third and again, oneself, *but* then all the others. Not to harm *but also*, if at all possible, to save.

The elements so combined, it may be said, will lead to practical contradictions, and in many circumstances they will. Fighting for his failing health, say, a person may not have energy left over for others. Or, supporting a loved one in grave trouble, he may have little or no time for anyone else. In grief, distress or other inner turmoil, you or I may not be able to find the emotional resources with which to go beyond not harming people, towards saving, or even helping, them. There is no difficulty in imagining endless variations of circumstance that will block the harmonious fulfilment of the above two precepts. Think how much easier it is for all that, and for how many people – how much easier than in the concentration and death camps of the Third Reich – to put oneself first, second and so forth, and still have something left over, a surplus, as it were, available for the needs of other people in peril, emergency or dire hardship.

More than this, in any event, cannot be expected or required. It cannot be expected or required in what is proposed for a general moral code. That is not to say that more will never be given. We know that it sometimes is, even up to the willing sacrifice of life or of a large part of a lifetime. But while more may be given, it cannot be morally demanded, and this for the same kind of reasons as we are able to call on in support of what can be demanded. I shall enumerate these reasons in the mode, once more, 'first, second, third and again, oneself'. First, if the lives to be saved through a given individual's other-regarding efforts are of worth *to* be saved, so is that individual's own life. Second, except as being at least somewhat robust, she is hampered in living her life as she would, and is of no use then, anyway, as a potential helper to other people. Third, she will have those whom she cherishes – children, parents or other members of her family, friends, lovers: her intimate circle – and no world in which the obligations to such others must be simply overridden in favour of the needs of strangers seems likely to be morally supportable, let alone attractive. Again, as the tragedy or misfortune which she seeks by her efforts to relieve will be due in part to a portion of the happiness or fulfilment denied to those whose tragedy or misfortune it is, so she herself has a claim on a portion of the same things. Each human being, in short, may legitimately give priority to the preservation of their own life and health, to their vital commitments to the people they love, and to securing some reasonable portion of what they want their life to be *for*. More cannot be expected of them than these priorities allow.

But nor should any less be, either. And this leads – not for everybody, or for everybody all the time, but for many people a lot of the time – to an extensive duty of aid and support, much more extensive a one than is commonly observed as things are. It will be hard to quantify the extent of it with any great precision. Nevertheless, I shall take it that the general idea of such a duty of aid to others, once a person's own basic needs of life and living are met, is clear enough in a rough and ready way, as are the beneficial consequences that would come from its widespread recognition and observance. There is a predictable objection that will be made here but I shall decline to meet it on its own terms. It is an objection on behalf of the selfish and the greedy, or else by those given to intellectual play in such matters, that the basic life concerns which I have just enumerated will *always* be able to be expanded to exhaust a person's time, energy and resources and leave nothing available for the crises of others, because under the rubric of happiness or fulfilment (and, *mutatis mutandis*, of commitments to loved ones) anyone will be able to put anything whatsoever they want: as many possessions and diversions, as much comfort, as costly a project or projects as they care to name. It could be argued against this that, as stated, the concern in question was for some reasonable, not exorbitant, portion of happiness or fulfilment; a point which might then be defended under a conception of broad moral and social equality. Important as the task is, I shall not be detained by it, however. I leave this to other capable intelligences whose work it already is. I prefer for my part simply to say that, if the objection is thought to hold, then so too, with it, will the contract of mutual indifference. Either our claims upon the pursuit of fulfilment leave room, in principle, for attending to the needs of endangered others, or they do not. If they do not, other people's similar claims do not have to do so either. We are then, all of us, alone. No one is obligated to bring, and people are not entitled to expect, help in emergency. There is no obligation to those who, in Saul Bellow's words, have been marked for death. Upheld, the objection will make good a moral universe in which even genocide (to say nothing of torture, famine and all the rest) goes through.

Our duty to bring aid is, as things presently are when much aid is needed, a very demanding one. Even in the absence of great precision, it seems possible to assert with confidence that there is in the lives of many people a significant quantum of time and effort, income, wealth, not devoted to the fundamental life concerns I have outlined, but given over rather to the pursuit of less pressing conveniences and enjoyments. These are of a sort, and they are permitted an extent, that it would be hard to make a compelling case for putting before the needs of others in extremity. I mean an open, public and unashamed case, laying out clearly side by side the nature and extent of the conveniences and enjoyments on the one hand, and the extremity on the other, and affirming the acceptability of their coexistence without remedy. Yet there is a paradox with respect to the duty of aid. The paradox is that this duty is the more demanding on any given individual the less widely it is acknowledged and acted upon. In existing conditions where, for structural, ideological, psychological and other reasons, people have difficulty in bringing themselves to do as much as they might in the way of fulfilling the duty, even when they do feel a sense of their responsibility in this regard, the amount there is to be done is enormous. Under different economic, social and cultural conditions where – one has to hope it may be possible – the same responsibility was much more taken for granted, entrenched within the value system as normal and routine, seen as necessary for fending off what had come to be unthinkable (that those in grave trouble might be left without help), what there was to be done overall might be brought within more feasible limits. More being expected of everyone, and more being given by more of them, less would in practice be required of each person.

The paradox takes us back to a very old question. It may be formulated so. How, if people are not already inclined to behave in the way envisaged, can one realistically conceive a path towards the state of affairs in which they will have become inclined to behave in that way? I do not have an answer to this question; no more than anyone else does, so far as I know. It remains the problem it has always been. But there is an observation about it I want to make in concluding the present section, so as to forestall a misunderstanding that could arise from what has been the central preoccupation of this essay.

My focus on the moral logic, first, of the contract of mutual indifference, and then, as alternative to it, of the proposed idea of mandatory care, should not be taken as intended either to solve or to substitute for the problem of agency as it is sometimes called: the problem of the forces for and the ways of progressive change. This problem is as crucial as it ever was. It is a *political* one in the broadest sense: that of seeking the social constituency, the means and the strategies, that might succeed in moving us towards the alternative moral universe in view. It is the task, as well, of attempting to sketch the politics and economics, the institutional basis, of that alternative. This is, patently, a very large agenda in itself, and it is in no way made redundant by pursuing separately, as I have, the question of an alternative social ethics. On the contrary, the very idea of a humanity that would be more regularly moved to act by compassion and a lively sense of responsibility for the welfare and safety of the rest of their kind – and one can throw in the well-being of animals also, since a world in which cruelty to other species continued on anything like its present appalling scale could not be the world of such a humanity – is scarcely thinkable without the robust democratic political institutions and the egalitarian economic and social relations that would be apt to those more caring dispositions and promote them. The imperative of mutual care not only does not exhaust the agenda of progressive change, it does not even stand alone in its own function; it would need the support of an enabling, encouraging institutional environment.

At the same time, there are points to be made in the opposite direction. In the first place, those who argue – and this is more or less standard on the political left – that it is agency and politics, rather than ethics, that we must attend in attacking the great social evils that have been under discussion here, do not themselves escape the difficulty faced by the radical moral philosopher. For if the latter has a gap to bridge between current bystander inaction and a putatively greater willingness to render aid in some future, happier condition, then so too does the sponsor of political agency have that gap to bridge. He has it to bridge in explaining what it is that will mobilize the prospective agents of change to become *in fact* agents of it, when they are drawn from the same human constituency as are those whom the moral philosopher has within her field of vision. The notion that 'interest', whether class or some other type of interest, will just do the trick in this domain where moral considerations will not, is not very convincing. On its own, self-interest, even if this is the interest of a group, offers an improbable route towards a state of things in which sympathetic care and support for others will have come to occupy a much more prominent place. Furthermore, self- or group interest and the interest in a juster, more compassionate world are the less likely to coincide the further away are the supposed agents of change from the achievement of that world. And they *are* a long way away from it, whoever they may be thought to be. For these reasons the moral argument, though not free-standing, is also not redundant. An ethic of mutual concern and care has to inform any worthwhile politics of justice, or equality, or socialism, as much as the politics and economics of a different kind of society would be needed to underpin and envelop the widespread practice of that ethic.

In the second place, the robust political and other institutions of a democratic society, indispensable as they are, cannot supplant the pervasive activity of mutual aid I have projected as alternative to the contract of mutual indifference. The thought may be opposed to this that the democratic polity itself can do the work of the imperative of mutual care. The state, that is, might be put forward, in this context, as the institutional representative of a contract amongst the citizens by means of which they ward off their common vulnerability; as bearer of the responsibility for coming to the help of those under assault or in other serious trouble. However, it is as well to remember that states are not always reliable in these matters. They themselves err, offend, violate, break down. Even apart from the extreme horrors they can bring about or stand by to, there are the more 'elementary' miscarriages of justice they habitually accommodate. As it is, how many citizens of democratic states exert themselves over these? Unless we do, what moral basis do we have for supposing others should ever exert themselves on our behalf? Someone sits in a cell robbed of years of their life. And if, in response to this, we do nothing? Genuinely just and robust institutions would require the support of a dense network of relations of multilateral aid.

In a nutshell, although the social ethic of mutual care is indeed not self-sufficient, it has its own specific autonomy. If the politics of utopia, or of progressive change – and whether conceived as socialist or conceived otherwise – must not be collapsed into the morality of it, nor can the morality be collapsed into the politics. There is no reduction in one direction. And there is no reduction in the other direction, either.

Conceived as socialist. It used to be said that socialism was a historical necessity. It is not that. However, it stood and it stands, in its own way, for a moral necessity. That moral necessity is mutual human support and aid, the universal responsibility for the safety and well-being of others. Without the commitment we are vulnerable individually to anything that may happen or be done to us, and we sit collectively on the edge of a moral abyss. For we are, by way of the contract of mutual indifference, morally entitled to nothing at all. Today, after the unparalleled calamity of the Holocaust, political theories which do not pay the most direct regard to the primary human duty to bring aid are wanting. The more so, are any theories which deny it.

Notes

[Editors' note: The endnotes below have been renumbered for this volume; in the original text, they run from 72 to 106.]

1 Cited in Zygmunt Bauman, *Modernity and the Holocaust*, Polity Press, 1991, pp. 201–202.
2 See Martin Gilbert, *The Holocaust: The Jewish Tragedy*, Fontana, 1987, p. 299.
3 Primo Levi, *If This Is a Man and The Truce*, Abacus, 1987, pp. 154–156.
4 See Primo Levi, *The Drowned and the Saved*, Abacus, 1989, p. 54. Levi is here quoting a passage from his own earlier memoir of liberation. See *If This Is a Man and The Truce*, p. 188.
5 *The Drowned and the Saved*, pp. 65–66.
6 See Terence Des Pres, *The Survivor: An Anatomy of a Life*, Oxford University Press, 1976, p. 43.
7 Karl Jaspers, *The Question of German Guilt*, New York, 1947, pp. 31–32, 36.
8 Ibid., pp. 69–70.
9 Ibid., p. 71.
10 Ibid., pp. 32, 71.
11 Ibid., p. 72.
12 Ibid., pp. 32, 72.
13 Ibid., pp. 33, 72.
14 Cited in Nechama Tec, *When Light Pierced the Darkness*, Oxford University Press, 1986, p. 165.
15 Cited in Gay Block and ,Malka Drucker, *Rescuers: Portraits of Moral Courage in the Holocaust*, Holmes and Meier 1992, p. 67.
16 Ibid., pp. 46, 226.
17 Cited in Andre Stein, *Quiet Heroes: True Stories of the Rescue of Jews by Christians in Nazi-occupied Holland*, University of Toronto Press, 1988, pp. 93, 95.
18 Laurence Thomas, 'Liberalism and the Holocaust', in Rosenberg and Myers, *Echoes from the Holocaust*, pp. 109–110. See also Thomas's *Vessels of Evil: American Slavery*

and the Holocaust, Philadelphia, 1993, chapter 3.

19 I have offered argument to this effect in my 'Socialist Hope in the Shadow of Catastrophe', reprinted here below. [Editors' note: i.e. in *The Contract of Mutual Indifference*.]

20 Gitta Sereny, *Into That Darkness*, London, 1991, p. 367.

21 Immanuel Kant, *Foundations of the Metaphysics of Morals*, Indianapolis and New York, 1959, p. 41.

22 See 'Perpetual Peace: A Philosophical Sketch', in Hans Reiss, ed., *Kant: Political Writings*, Cambridge, 1991, p. 165.

23 Fyodor Dostoyevsky, *The Brothers Karamazov*, London, 1993, transl. D. McDuff, pp. 186, 332.

24 See, again, my 'Socialist Hope in the Shadow of Catastrophe' below.

25 Micheline Maurel, *Ravensbrück*, Digit, London, 1958, pp. 92, 158–159.

26 Tzvetan Todorov, *Facing the Extreme: Moral Life in the Concentration Camps*, New York, 1996, p. 139.

27 Ibid., pp. 252–253

28 Ibid., pp. 267–271.

29 Ibid., p. 253. And cf. pp. 256–257, 295.

30 Des Pres, *The Survivor*, p. 21.

31 Todorov, *Facing the Extreme*, p. 291.

32 Des Pres, *The Survivor*, pp. 142, 153.

33 *If This Is a Man and The Truce*, p. 19.

34 Anna Pawelczynska, *Values and Violence in Auschwitz: A Sociological Analysis*, Berkeley, 1979, pp. 137–144.

35 Ella Lingens-Reiner, as cited in Des Pres, *The Survivor*, p. 153.

12

Humanitarian intervention

(This chapter is extracted from *Crimes against Humanity: Birth of a Concept*, Manchester University Press, Manchester, 2011)

We have seen in the preceding chapters[*] that the concept of crimes against humanity implies a limit to state sovereignty. It is natural, therefore, that discussion of the concept, and especially of its beginnings, should make reference to an earlier tradition within international law to which that same limit is germane – I mean the tradition of humanitarian intervention. In fact, the principle of humanitarian intervention stands not only at the origin of the offence of crimes against humanity, but also on the other side of its arriving at maturity, so to say, in the Rome Statute of the International Criminal Court. For if that principle was invoked at Nuremberg, official birthplace of the newly defined offence, as providing a relevant precedent, it has remained, up to the time of writing and in a world now grown used to acts being named and indeed prosecuted as crimes against humanity, a focus of controversy.

I have, earlier, made reference to the assertion by the Chief Prosecutor for the UK at Nuremberg that there is a limit upon the omnipotence of the state vis-à-vis the individual human being, and to his connecting this limit with a 'right of humanitarian intervention by war'.[1] The lineage from that putative right to the new offence of crimes against humanity was mentioned more than once during the post-Second World War trials. One tribunal located the roots of the concept of crimes against humanity in earlier humanitarian interventions undertaken in response to religious persecution. Referring to the same normative precedents, another noted that the Nuremberg Charter 'merely develops a preexisting principle'.[2] It is a pedigree now regularly noted in the literature.[3] This is, perhaps, sufficient justification for a discussion of the principle of humanitarian intervention in a book about the concept of crimes against humanity. However, further justification, if such is needed, is to be had from the fact that contemporary disputes about the rights and wrongs of humanitarian intervention raise similar issues to those we have been examining in connection with the central topic of this book.

---

* Editors' note: i.e. of Geras's *Crimes against Humanity*.

Definitions of the principle of humanitarian intervention generally combine four elements. A humanitarian intervention (a) involves the use of military force (b) by one state on the territory of another (c) in order to protect people in danger of grave harm (d) when the state within the jurisdiction of which they reside cannot or will not do so.[4]

Is there a *right* of humanitarian intervention, so defined? The issue is moot. There is, however, some agreement that humanitarian intervention was lawful under customary international law at least prior to the creation of the United Nations. According to one scholar, 'weighty authorities' supported that conclusion.[5] It was generally accepted, says another, for six hundred years.[6] A third writes:

> [W]hile divergences certainly existed as to the *circumstances* in which resort could be had to the institution of humanitarian intervention, as well as to the *manner* in which such operations were to be conducted, the *principle* itself was widely, if not unanimously, accepted as an integral part of customary international law.[7]

The creation of the United Nations is thought by many to have altered the legal situation. Article 2, Paragraph 4 of the Charter of the new organization laid down that 'All Members shall refrain in their international relations from the threat or use of force against the territorial integrity or political independence of any state, or in any other manner inconsistent with the Purposes of the United Nations'. Much legal opinion takes this clause as being absolutely prohibitive of interventionist action by states other than in self-defence or within the framework of UN authorization. But some commentators, drawing on the same clause from the UN Charter, have argued in support of the right in question. They have done so on the basis that, first, a genuine humanitarian intervention need not in fact be inconsistent with the purposes of the United Nations, since these purposes include the defence of human rights; and, second, that properly conducted, such an intervention does not have to threaten the territorial integrity or political independence of the state on whose territory it is made, because the intervention can and should be followed by the withdrawal of foreign forces once its protective aims have been achieved. An additional point is that, given the UN's failures in crisis situations in which interventionist action to protect populations under threat might have been expected from it, some writers have wanted to reach back to the time before the organization was created, to the customary international law doctrine of humanitarian intervention, as being still applicable in extreme cases, the Charter's prohibition on the use of force notwithstanding.[8]

For my part, I shall propose a short way with this issue. There *is* a right of humanitarian intervention. For the implication of holding the contrary is that crimes against humanity may be committed on a mass scale, violating the most fundamental human rights and all the peremptory norms of international law;

and, other means (diplomatic or economic) failing to stop such atrocities, no coercive action may be taken to do so nonetheless. That cannot be a norm of civilized law, nor therefore part of the emergent law of the world – just in the same way that it cannot be a legitimate norm of a domestic legal system that some people may freely murder others and no attempt may be made by authoritative bodies to prevent and punish these acts of murder. To assert that it cannot be is not to import into a system of positive law normative considerations standing outside it. That is to say, my point here is not to counterpose to a body of law as it exists some alternative conception – of the law as it should be. I appeal, rather, to a set of norms that are *already* embodied in international law, as a way of challenging the interpretation of Article 2, Paragraph 4 of the UN Charter according to which it absolutely prohibits humanitarian intervention by the member states.

Crimes against humanity are themselves, non-controversially, crimes under international law. As we saw in the last chapter, the doctrine of *jus cogens* as supreme law encompasses a number of peremptory norms binding on every state and from which no state may derogate in any circumstances, including circumstances of war. The question of humanitarian intervention is posed when crimes of just this sort – crimes against humanity, crimes according to *jus cogens* norms – are being widely committed in a given country. That the international body which itself has the task of overseeing and protecting human rights across the globe should at one and the same time fail in enforcing their protection and be accepted as the reason against any effective intervention for that purpose by law-abiding states is a proposition too bizarre to be countenanced.

In Chapter 3 I considered whether the definition of crimes against humanity should include a scale threshold or not, and I presented arguments on both sides of the question. By contrast with that discussion, a threshold of scale is in the present context – for the case of humanitarian intervention – generally taken for granted, and I shall not challenge this. Legitimate intervention for humanitarian ends and involving extensive use of military force may only be considered as an option, so it is generally thought, in grave and urgent cases, and gravity and urgency are judged in terms of scale. Michael Walzer, for example, specifies conditions in which 'the violation of human rights within a set of boundaries is so terrible that it makes talk of community or self-determination … seem cynical and irrelevant'. Yogesh Tyagi says that the 'basis for a humanitarian intervention lies in the absence of a minimum moral order in the whole or a part of a state, [a situation] which is inconsistent with fundamental humanitarian norms'.[9] It is right that there should be a scale threshold here, because the consequences of possible war, such as the use of military force opens up, are often unpredictable and they can sometimes be calamitous. '[M]ilitary intervention', as Terry Nardin writes, 'is an uncertain remedy, which has great costs of its own'.[10]

I want to raise two questions, all the same, pertaining to the existence of a scale threshold for humanitarian intervention. The first of them will test whether such a threshold is relevant in every instance, and suggest that sometimes, for atypical cases, it may not be. The second question will ask whether, even in the case that a scale threshold is relevant, it needs to be set as high as it conventionally is. I raise this second question without trying to resolve it; I do so in order to show why, here as well as in defining what crimes against humanity are, the setting of a threshold is not unproblematic.

If a threshold of scale is widely held to be necessary in laying down the conditions for legitimate intervention, it should nevertheless be noted that this is not entailed by the bare definition of what a humanitarian intervention is. Nothing about the *scope* of the harm to be remedied follows from the definition itself. To repeat what I have said above, according to the latter, a humanitarian intervention (a) involves the use of military force (b) by one state on the territory of another (c) in order to protect people in danger of grave harm (d) when the state within the jurisdiction of which they reside cannot or will not do so. If we understand humanitarian intervention in this meaning, one state might send a small military unit into the territory of another to accomplish some quite limited task – as the Israelis did in Uganda in 1976, in the raid on Entebbe, to free airline passengers being held hostage there.[11] Tailoring the case to the concerns of this book, one might equally imagine a small force being sent into one country from another, with the purpose of rescuing a group of people from a notorious torture facility in which they were being brutalized, and of destroying it. As far as I can see, such an action would fit the definition of humanitarian intervention given above, and yet, being a small-scale operation, might not incur the uncertainties and dangers of all-out war. We may therefore ask why a threshold of scale is always needed, why the harms to be intervened against must be widespread as well as terrible before a humanitarian intervention may justifiably be contemplated. At least in more limited cases of this kind, can the scale threshold not be set aside?

I leave the question hanging. I do so on the grounds that though such cases are certainly possible, they are not the standard case or the most pressing. The paradigm for humanitarian intervention is usually taken to be a military mobilization by one state on to the territory of another that is extensive enough to create the risk of serious warfare and major social dislocation. And it is the dangers that war and social dislocation bring with them that then justify the threshold of scale. Humanitarian intervention in the more standard case, in other words, is thought to demand that national sovereignty should not be violated except *in extremis*, because the human costs of war can themselves be so great. The threshold question applies, consequently, to humanitarian intervention not as I initially defined it but under a restriction of the sort 'and (e) when the intervention is on a large enough scale to create the risk of war'.

My second question is, now, what should the threshold be which gives us the meaning of *in extremis*? 'Humanitarian crisis' has become the accepted formula, but how bad must a bad human-rights situation be to count as a humanitarian crisis? One view, which was at the centre of recent political controversy over the Iraq war, is that the situation must involve mass death or the imminent danger of it – killing if not of genocidal scope, then at any rate on a very large scale: massacre, or widespread death through famine, or the prospect of such. Might it be that this sets the bar too high? For it tolerates, before legitimating any external intervention, a level of state lawlessness falling so far short of what the standards of international humanitarian law lay down as to make a mockery of their intended constraining function. If the threshold for humanitarian intervention is set by humanitarian crisis in the meaning I have given, it would follow that, for instance, the sovereignty of a regime that had just carried out a genocide – had just *finished* carrying it out but was no longer doing so – had to be respected. It would follow, similarly, that the sovereignty of a regime which over an extended period was murdering and torturing large numbers of people but never on a scale one could describe as either genocidal or such as to precipitate a general humanitarian crisis in the country concerned, likewise had to be respected; or that the sovereignty of a regime that presided over people starving to death through its own misrule had also to be respected. A system of international law that accommodates such things must surely be accounted gravely deficient.

To this it may be counter-argued that the threshold under discussion applies only to humanitarian *military* intervention; the perpetrators of state crimes may still be brought to justice after the event. The point is an important one. Dispensing justice is a necessary part of an effective international juridical system. But that does not address the issue of prevention, and prevention should also be part of an effective system of law, at least ideally. Punishing the perpetrators after the event does not change the fact that, left standing, regimes of the kind just described would remain accepted actors within the system of states.

Can an alternative threshold to that of immediate or imminent humanitarian crisis be proposed? I do not pretend this is easy, but the difficulty is not a result of any eccentricity of analysis or approach on my part; it is integral to the issue itself. Here, in any case, is what I tentatively put forward by way of a lower, but still determinate and demanding, threshold for humanitarian intervention. It would be reached in two sets of circumstances: (a) when a state is on the point of committing (or permitting), or is actually committing (or permitting), or has recently committed (or permitted) massacres and other atrocities against its own population of genocidal, or tendentially genocidal, scope; or (b) when, even short of this, a state commits, supports or overlooks murders, tortures and other extreme brutalities or deprivations such as to result in a regular flow of thousands of victims.

Whether or not a threshold for humanitarian intervention so defined is more defensible than that of full-blown humanitarian crisis as more commonly conceived I shall leave open here – only repeating that, unless it is, we must conclude that international law in its current state prohibits forcible intervention even against regimes of extreme criminality, when judged by the very standards of international law itself. Perhaps, though, the risks and the costs of war being so high, this deficiency of the international legal system is to be regarded as a cost that is the more bearable one – more bearable for the global community at any rate, if not for the victims of such criminal regimes.

That there is a right of humanitarian intervention does not mean that every intervention for which this right is invoked is a justified one. There are a number of requirements standardly held to constrain the would-be intervening power or coalition of powers. Amongst these requirements are: (i) the exhaustion of other possible remedies, such as diplomatic and/or economic pressure; (ii) a good prospect of the intervention being successful; (iii) a readiness to withdraw expeditiously when the humanitarian purpose has been accomplished; and (iv) proportionality of the military means to the situation with which they are designed to deal. It is, on the other hand, *not* a requirement that the intervening power or powers should have no national interest at stake in carrying out its or their intervention. Few countries would willingly put their soldiers at risk and incur great economic expense if it were. The most that can be required is that (v) there be a genuine humanitarian purpose at work and that it be central in guiding the conduct of the intervention. In practice, whether a humanitarian intervention has been legitimate is often judged *post hoc* by its results.[12]

Nonetheless, with these stipulations in place and a persuasive specification of the threshold of scale, humanitarian intervention, I contend, is not illegal; there is a right of it under international law. This contention is supported by two additional considerations: the international law on genocide in force since 1948; and the more recent doctrine of a responsibility to protect.

As to the first, where genocide is under way or imminently threatened intervention is, arguably, not just a right, it is a duty. Article 1 of the UN Genocide Convention commits the Contracting Parties to confirming genocide as 'a crime under international law which they undertake to prevent and to punish'. But if this is a duty, it must also be in some sort a right, since the international community cannot be obliged to undertake what it is not permissible for it to undertake. Here it may be said that, since the duty is a collective one – of the nations, precisely, united – so, correspondingly, must the right be a collective one too, and only a collective one. I return to the point in a moment. The other additional consideration, the doctrine of a responsibility to protect, was affirmed by the UN General Assembly in September 2005 through its adoption of the 'World Summit Outcome' resolution. Contained at 139 therein is the following paragraph:

In this context, we are prepared to take collective action, in a timely and decisive manner, through the Security Council, in accordance with the Charter, including Chapter VII, on a case-by-case basis and in cooperation with relevant regional organizations as appropriate, should peaceful means be inadequate and national authorities are manifestly failing to protect their populations from genocide, war crimes, ethnic cleansing and crimes against humanity.[13]

The 'timely and decisive' appears clear enough. However, the collective nature of the undertaking is here spelled out explicitly, and unfortunately this requirement can run counter to the commitment to timeliness and decisiveness; indeed, it can run counter to there being any military intervention at all, even in spite of the fact that peaceful means may have proved inadequate and national authorities have failed to protect their populations from the adversities enumerated or, worse still, have been responsible for them themselves.

In these circumstances, a right of humanitarian intervention must devolve to the constituent nations of the UN.[14] The right to intervene on humanitarian grounds, although it should ideally go through the UN Security Council, the preferred avenue wherever possible, cannot be so constrained without exception. It cannot for the simple reason that a situation may arise in which, under the law of nations by which that body is bound, an intervention is justified and urgent, but will not be authorized by the Security Council even so, this for political rather than juridical reasons. We know that that can happen; one or other of the veto-wielding countries may block any resolution for a UN-authorized intervention, not out of any concern pertaining to the criteria of legitimate intervention, but for no better reason than interests of state. From the fact, however, that a duty is a collective one it does not follow that the rights associated with it must also be, invariably, collective. It only follows that they may be. Thus, members of a university department can have a self-imposed duty to spend some of the department's funds on books for their students, but only as and when authorized by a meeting of the Departmental Resources Committee. The right associated with the duty may not be exercised except with the authority of the collective. A people, on the other hand, having a right of resistance against tyranny, cannot 'monopolize' this right by reserving its exercise to collectively authenticated institutions purporting to act for the people as a whole. If an individual under attack by the tyrant or his agents sees fit and is able to resist, without in her turn committing a crime in doing so, then that is her right quite properly. Similarly, if she should come to the aid of someone else under attack from the same quarter.

The member nations of the body that has taken on the commitment to a responsibility to protect are severally and separately authors of this commitment and they cannot reasonably be considered bound by the delinquency – for that is what it is – of which the collective body, the UN, is guilty when it fails to respond effectively to genocide or crimes against humanity on a large scale.

This is somewhat comparable to Locke's thesis, in *The Second Treatise of Civil Government*, that in the state of nature:

> the execution of the law of nature is ... put into every man's hands, whereby every one has a right to punish the transgressors of that law to such a degree as may hinder its violation; for the law of nature would, as all other laws that concern men in this world, be in vain, if there were no body that in the state of nature had a power to execute that law, and thereby preserve the innocent and restrain offenders.[15]

It is only somewhat comparable, because the international order is not a state of nature, there being a body charged with seeing to the execution of the system of (international humanitarian) law in force. When, however, it fails to do this, and there is a state of ongoing lawlessness somewhere, very costly in human life, the agents of a humanitarian intervention will not be acting illegally or without right in undertaking an intervention, provided this meets the criteria by which such an intervention is accounted just.

To this it may be suggested that such a right is open to abuse. But so is any right; so is any normative principle. And the same can be said, in truth, of the stipulation that military intervention for humanitarian ends may only take place if there is authorization by the UN Security Council; since when one of the veto-wielding members of the council exercises its veto for reasons of national interest and nothing more, this is precisely an abuse of its decision-influencing power, which should be subject to the humanitarian issues at stake in the situation and not, for example, to its commercial interests in the country or the region concerned. Jean-Pierre Fonteyn quotes an early proponent of humanitarian intervention as having said on this score, 'It is a big mistake, in general, to stop short of recognition of an inherently just principle, because of the possibility of non-genuine invocation.'[16]

In sum, there is a right of humanitarian intervention, because to insist otherwise is to make international law in certain circumstances the guarantor of gross criminality, as measured by the very norms of international law itself. This right is constrained by a scale threshold, such that in standard cases humanitarian intervention should not be undertaken except *in extremis* – though there is room for argument over exactly how high the threshold should be. According to some authorities humanitarian intervention may not take place outside the framework of the United Nations, but this viewpoint cannot be sustained consistently with preserving the moral authority of international law so long as decision- making by the UN Security Council allows manifestly political interests to deflect what an impartial application of the law itself demands. The collective commitment of the international community, under the UN rubric, to protect against genocide and crimes against humanity on a mass scale translates into a right of the member nations, whether singly or a few of them in concert, to intervene when human rights are under grave and widespread assault and the collectivity itself – the UN – fails in its duty to do so.

Notes

1 See Chapter 1, pp. 2–3, and Chapter 3, p. 90.
2 Beth Van Schaack, 'The Definition of Crimes Against Humanity: Resolving the Incoherence', *Columbia Journal of Transnational Law*, Vol. 37 (1999), 787–850, at pp. 848–849.
3 See, for example, Steven R. Ratner and Jason S. Abrams, *Accountability for Human Rights Atrocities in International Law: Beyond the Nuremberg Legacy*, Oxford University Press, Oxford, 2001, p. 46; David Matas, 'Prosecuting Crimes Against Humanity: The Lessons of World War I', *Fordham International Law Journal*, Vol. 13 (1989–90), 86–104, at p. 103; and Georges Levasseur, 'Les crimes contre l'humanité et le problème de leur prescription', *Journal du Droit International*, Vol. 93 (1966), 259–284, at p. 271.
4 See, for example, Malvina Halberstam, 'The Legality of Humanitarian Intervention', *Cardozo Journal of International and Comparative Law*, Vol. 3 (1995), 1–8, at p. 1; Jean-Pierre L. Fonteyne, 'The Customary International Law Doctrine of Humanitarian Intervention: Its Current Validity Under the U.N. Charter', *California Western International Law Journal*, Vol. 4 (1974), 203–270, at pp. 204 n.3, 205; Van Schaack, 'The Definition of Crimes Against Humanity', pp. 847–848; Michael J. Bazyler, 'Reexamining the Doctrine of Humanitarian Intervention in Light of the Atrocities in Kampuchea and Ethiopia', *Stanford Journal of International Law*, Vol. 23 (1987), 547–619, at pp. 547–548.
5 Halberstam, 'The Legality of Humanitarian Intervention', p. 3.
6 Bazyler, 'Reexamining the Doctrine of Humanitarian Intervention', p. 573.
7 Fonteyne, 'The Customary International Law Doctrine of Humanitarian Intervention', p. 235.
8 Halberstam, 'The Legality of Humanitarian Intervention', pp. 3–4; Bazyler, 'Reexamining the Doctrine of Humanitarian Intervention', pp. 548, 574–581; and Fonteyne, 'The Customary International Law Doctrine of Humanitarian Intervention', pp. 242–245, 253–258.
9 Michael Walzer, *Just and Unjust Wars: A Moral Argument with Historical Illustrations*, Allen Lane, London, 1978, p. 90; Yogesh K. Tyagi, 'The Concept of Humanitarian Intervention Revisited', *Michigan Journal of International Law*, Vol. 16 (1995), 883–910, at p. 884.
10 Terry Nardin, 'The Moral Basis of Humanitarian Intervention', *Ethics and International Affairs*, Vol. 16 (2002), 57–70, at p. 69.
11 Halberstam mentions this action; see 'The Legality of Humanitarian Intervention', p. 2.
12 For discussion of these points, see Bazyler, 'Reexamining the Doctrine of Humanitarian Intervention', pp. 597–607; Fonteyne, 'The Customary International Law Doctrine of Humanitarian Intervention', pp. 258–268; Halberstam, 'The Legality of Humanitarian Intervention', pp. 2, 8; Nardin, 'The Moral Basis of Humanitarian Intervention', p. 69; and Tyagi, 'The Concept of Humanitarian Intervention Revisited', pp. 889–890.
13 UN General Assembly Resolution, '2005 World Summit Outcome', Downloaded December 2009 at http://unpan1.un.org/intradoc/groups/ public/documents/UN/ UNPAN021752.pdf

14 Cf. Halberstam, 'The Legality of Humanitarian Intervention', p. 6: 'The legality of humanitarian intervention should not be subject to the veto power of any one state.'

15 John Locke, *Second Treatise of Civil Government*, chapter 2.

16 Fonteyne, 'The Customary International Law Doctrine of Humanitarian Intervention', p. 269; and see also Halberstam, 'The Legality of Humanitarian Intervention', p. 7.

13

The war in Iraq

(This article was first published on 'Normblog', 29 July 2003*)

I want to say something about support for democratic values and basic human rights. We on the left just have it in our bloodstream, do we not, that we are committed to democratic values. And while, for reasons I can't go into here, there are some on the left a bit more reserved about using the language of basic human rights, nonetheless for many of us it was this moral reality, and more especially its negation, that played a part in drawing us in: to protest and work against a world in which people could just be used for the purposes of others, be exploited and super-exploited, worked maybe to an early death, in any case across a life of hardship; or be brutalized for organizing to fight to change their situation, be 'disappeared', or tortured, or massacred, by regimes upholding an order of inequality – sometimes desperate inequality – and privilege. In our bloodstream.

However, there is also a certain historical past of the left referred to loosely under the name 'Stalinism', and which forms a massive blot on this commitment and these values, on the great tradition we belong to. I am of the generation – roughly 1960s-vintage, post-Stalinist left – educated in the Trotskyist critique of that whole experience, and in the new expansion and flourishing of an open, multi-faceted and pluralist Marxism; educated in the movement against the war in Vietnam, the protests against Pinochet's murderous coup in Chile and against the role of the US in both episodes and in more of the same kind. Of a generation that believed that, even though the Western left still bore some signs of continuity with the Stalinist past, this was a dying, an increasingly marginal strand, and that we had put its errors largely behind us. But I fear now it is not so. The same kinds of error – excuses and evasions and out-and-out apologia for political structures, practices or movements no

---

* Editors' note: as Geras explained on 'Normblog': 'This is an amended and slightly enlarged version of part of a talk given to the Workers' Liberty summer school in London on 21 June under the title "After the Holocaust: Mutual Indifference and Moral Solidarity". To be fair to those who invited me, I should point out that, although the views I expressed in this part of the talk met with a perfectly civil reception, they plainly weren't shared by most of the audience.'

socialist should have a word to say for – are still with us. They afflict many even without any trace of a Stalinist past or a Stalinist political formation.

I obviously don't have the time or space here to rehearse all of the relevant arguments. I will confine myself to sketching some important features of the broad picture as I see it.

September 11

On September 11 2001 there was, in New York, a massacre of innocents. There's no other acceptable way of putting this: some 3000 people (and, as anyone can figure, it could have been many more) struck down by an act of mass murder without any possible justification, an act of gross moral criminality. What was the left's response? In fact, this goes well beyond the left if what is meant by that is people and organizations of *socialist* persuasion. It included a wide sector of liberal opinion as well. Still, I shall just speak here, for short, of the left. The response on the part of much of it was excuse and apologia.

At best you might get some lip service paid to the events of September 11 having been, well, you know, unfortunate – the preliminary 'yes' before the soon-to-follow 'but' (or, as Christopher Hitchens has called it, 'throat-clearing'). And then you'd get all the stuff about root causes, deep grievances, the role of US foreign policy in creating these; and a subtext, or indeed text, whose meaning was America's comeuppance. This was not a discourse worthy of a democratically-committed or principled left, and the would-be defence of it by its proponents, that they were merely trying to explain and not to excuse what happened, was itself a pathetic excuse. If any of the root-cause and griev-ance themes truly had been able to account for what happened on September 11, you'd have a hard time understanding why, say, the Chileans after that earlier September 11 (I mean of 1973), or other movements fighting against oppression and injustice, have not resorted to the random mass murder of civilians.

Why this miserable response? In a nutshell, it was a displacement of the left's most fundamental values by a misguided strategic choice, namely, opposition to the US, come what may. This dictated the apologetic mumbling about the mass murder of US citizens, and it dictated that the US must be opposed in what it was about to do in hitting back at al-Qaida and its Taliban hosts in Afghanistan. (A more extended statement of my views on this subject is to be found in my answer to the question about Michael Walzer in 'Marxism, the Holocaust and September 11th'.)

The liberation of Iraq

Something similar has now been repeated over the war in Iraq. I could just about have 'got inside' the view – it wasn't my view – that the war to remove Saddam Hussein's regime should not be supported. Neither Washington

nor Baghdad – maybe. But *opposition* to the war – the marching, the peti-
tion-signing, the oh-so-knowing derision of George Bush and so forth – meant
one thing very clearly. Had this campaign succeeded in its goal and actually
prevented the war it was opposed to, the life of the Baathist regime would
have been prolonged, with all that that entailed: years more (how many years
more?) of the rape rooms, the torture chambers, the children's jails, and the
mass graves recently uncovered.

This was the result which hundreds of thousands of people marched to
secure. Well, speaking for myself, comrades, there I draw the line. Not one step.

Let me now just focus on a couple of dimensions of this issue.

Humanitarian intervention

First, there is a long tradition in the literature of international law that,
although national sovereignty is an important consideration in world affairs, it
is not sacrosanct. If a government treats its own people with terrible brutality,
massacring them and such like, there is a right of humanitarian intervention by
outside powers. The introduction of the offence of crimes against humanity at
the Nuremberg Trial after the Second World War implied a similar constraint
on the sovereign authority of states. There are limits upon them. They cannot
just brutalize their own nationals with impunity, violate their fundamental
human rights.

Is there then, today, a right of humanitarian intervention under international
law? The question is disputed. Some authorities argue that the UN Charter rules
it out absolutely. War is only permissible in self-defence. However, others see
a contradiction between this reading of the Charter and the Charter's underwriting of binding human rights norms. Partly because the matter is disputed,
I will not here base myself on a legal right of humanitarian intervention. I will
simply say that, irrespective of the state of international law, in extreme enough
circumstances there is a *moral* right of humanitarian intervention. This is why
what the Vietnamese did in Cambodia to remove Pol Pot should have been
supported at the time, the state of international law notwithstanding, and
ditto for the removal of Idi Amin by the Tanzanians. Likewise, with regard to
Saddam Hussein's regime in Iraq: it was a case crying out for support for an
intervention to bring the regime finally to an end.

Just think for a moment about the argument that this recent war was illegal.
That something is illegal does not itself carry moral weight unless legality as
such carries moral weight, and legality carries moral weight only conditionally.
It depends on the particular law in question, on the system of law of which it
is a part, and on the kind of social and ethical order it upholds. An international law – and an international system – according to which a government
is free to go on raping, murdering and torturing its own nationals to the tune

of tens upon tens, upon more tens, of thousands of deaths without anything being done to stop it, so much the worse for this as law. It is law that needs to be criticized, opposed, and changed. It needs to be moved forward – which happens in this domain by precedent and custom as well as by transnational treaty and convention. I am fully aware in saying this that the present [George W. Bush] US administration has made itself an obstacle in various ways to the development of a more robust and comprehensive framework of international law. But the thing cuts both ways. The war to depose Saddam Hussein and his criminal regime was not of a piece with that. It didn't have to be opposed by all the forces that did in fact oppose it. It could, on the contrary, have been supported – by France and Germany and Russia and the UN; and by a mass democratic movement of global civil society. Just think about that. Just think about the kind of precedent *it* would have set for other genocidal, or even just lavishly murderous, dictatorships – instead of all those processions of shame across the world's cities, and whose success would have meant the continued abandonment of the Iraqi people.

It is, in any event, such realities – the brutalizing and murder by the Baathist regime of its own nationals to the tune of tens upon tens, upon more tens, of thousands of deaths – that the recent war has brought to an end. It should have been supported for this reason, irrespective of the reasons (concerning WMD) that George Bush and Tony Blair put up front themselves; though it is disingenuous of the war's critics to speak now as if the humanitarian case for war formed no part of the public rationale of the Coalition, since it was clearly articulated by both Bush and Blair more than once.

Here is one approximate measure of the barbarities of the Baathist regime I have just referred to. It comes not from the Pentagon, or anyone in the Bush administration, or from Tony Blair or those around him. It comes from Human Rights Watch.* According to Human Rights Watch, during 23 years of Saddam's rule some 290,000 Iraqis disappeared into the regime's deadly maw, the majority of these reckoned to be now dead. Rounding this number down by as much as 60,000 to compensate for the 'thought to be', that is 230,000. It is 10,000 a year. It is 200 people every week. And I'll refrain from embellishing with details, which you should all know, as to exactly how a lot of these people died.

Had the opposition to the war succeeded this is what it would have postponed – and postponed indefinitely – bringing to an end. This is how almost the whole international left expressed its moral solidarity with the Iraqi people. Worse still, some sections of the left seemed none too bothered about making common cause with, marching alongside, fundamentalist religious bigots and known racists; and there were also those who dismissed Iraqi voices in support of the war as coming from American stooges – a disgraceful lie.

---

* www.hrw.org/backgrounder/mena/iraq1217bg.htm#1

Good and bad consequences

Second, let's now model this abstractly. You have a course of action with mixed consequences, both good consequences and bad consequences. To decide sensibly you obviously have to weigh the good against the bad. Imagine someone advising, with respect to some decision you have to make, 'Let's only think about the good consequences'; or 'Let's merely concentrate on the bad consequences'. You what?! It's a no-brainer, as the expression now is. But from beginning to end something pretty much like this has been the approach of the war's opponents. I offer a few examples.

(a) The crassest are the statements by supposedly mature people – one of these the Labour politician Clare Short,* another the novelist Julian Barnes[†] – that this war was not worth the loss of a single life. Not one, hey? So much for the victims of the rape rooms and the industrial shredders, for the children tortured and murdered in front of their parents, and for those parents. So much for those Human Rights Watch estimates and for the future flow of the regime's victims had it been left in place.

(b) More generally, since the fall of Baghdad critics of the war have been pointing (many of them, with relish) at everything that has gone, or remains, wrong in Iraq: the looting, the lack of civil order, the continuing violence and shootings, the patchy electricity supply, the failure to find weapons of mass destruction. Is this fair enough? Yes and no. Yes, because it has to be part of any balanced assessment. But also no if it isn't set against the fact, the massive fact, of the end of a regime of torture, oppression and murder, of everything that has *stopped* happening since the regime fell. And typically it isn't set against this massive fact. This fact is passed over or tucked away,[‡] because to acknowledge it fully and make a balanced assessment won't come out right for the war's critics. It just won't stack up – this, this and, yes, also this, but against the end of *all that* – in the way they'd like it to.

(c) Or else your anti-war interlocutor will freely concede that of course, we all agree it is a good that that monster and his henchmen no longer govern Iraq; but it is too stupid a point to dwell upon, for it doesn't touch on the issue dividing us, support or not for the war (on grounds of WMD, international law, US foreign policy, the kitchen sink). Er, yes it does. No one is entitled simply to help themselves to the 'of course, we all agree' neutralization of what was and remains an absolutely crucial consideration in favour of the war. They have properly to integrate it into an overall, and conscientiously-weighted, balance sheet of both good and bad consequences.

(d) The same ploy from a different angle. Since the fall of Baghdad there

* www.telegraph.co.uk news / /main.jhtml?xml=%2Fnews%2F2003%2F04%2F16%2Fwshort16. xml&secureRefresh=true&_requestid=35171

† www.guardian.co.uk/g2/story/0,3604,934300,00.html

‡ www.guardian.co.uk/comment/story/0,3604,980363,00.html

have been voices – both Iraqi voices and those of Western critics of the war[*] –
calling for the immediate departure from Iraq of American and British forces.
One can certainly discuss this as a proposition. Would it be better for Iraq
and its people or worse, such an immediate or early withdrawal? Personally, I
doubt that it would be better. Indeed, it would likely spell disaster of one kind
or another. From more than one survey of Iraqi opinion I've seen, it is the view
also of many Iraqis that there should be no withdrawal for the time being, until
the consolidation of an Iraqi administration. But note, anyway, that the call for
a prompt withdrawal is not a call to restore the Baathist regime to power. No,
it just starts from where things are now, with the regime gone. That is to say,
it starts from a better starting point than would otherwise have been in place.
And this is a good (but not properly acknowledged) achieved by American
and British arms.

(e) If you can't eliminate the inconvenient side of the balance, denature it.
The liberation of Iraq from Saddam's tyranny *can't* have been a good, because
of those who effected it and of their obviously bad foreign policy record:
Vietnam, Chile, Nicaragua and the rest. It can't therefore have been a liberation.
Even allowing the premise to go unchallenged – which in point of fact I don't,
since recent US and British foreign policy also has achievements to its credit:
evicting the Iraqis from Kuwait, intervening in Kosovo, intervening in Sierra
Leone, getting rid of the Taliban regime in Afghanistan – it is a plain fallacy.
A person with a bad record is capable of doing good. There were some antisemitic rescuers of Jews during the Holocaust. This argumentative move just
fixes the nature of the act via a presumption about those who are responsible
for it, sparing one the necessity of examining the act for what it actually brings
about and of assessing this in its own right. It's a bit like saying that because the
guy who returned me the expensive book he'd borrowed has previously stolen
things from others ... you can fill in the rest yourself, and yes, it's silly.

(f) Last and worst here. If the balance doesn't come out how you want it to,
you hope for things to change so that the balance will adjust in your favour.
In the case under consideration, this is a perilous moral and political impulse.
When the war began a division of opinion was soon evident amongst its opponents, between those who wanted a speedy outcome – in other words, a victory
for the coalition forces, for that is all a speedy outcome could realistically have
meant – and those who did not. These latter preferred that the Coalition forces
should suffer reverses, get bogged down, and you know the story: stalemate,
quagmire, Stalingrad scenario in Baghdad, and so forth, leading to a US and
British withdrawal. But what these critics of the war thereby wished for was a
spectacular triumph for the regime in Baghdad, since that is what a withdrawal
would have been. So much for solidarity with the victims of oppression, for
commitment to democratic values and basic human rights.

---

[*] www.guardian.co.uk/comment/story/0,3604,980363,00.html

Similarly today, with all those who seem so to relish every new difficulty, every set-back for US forces: what they align themselves with is a future of prolonged hardship and suffering for the Iraqi people, whether via an actual rather than imagined quagmire, a ruinous civil war, or the return (out of either) of some new and ghastly political tyranny; rather than a rapid stabilization and democratization of the country, promising its inhabitants an early prospect of national normalization. That is caring more to have been right than for a decent outcome for the people of this long unfortunate country.

Conclusion

Such impulses have displayed themselves very widely across left and liberal opinion in recent months. Why? For some, because what the US government and its allies do, whatever they do, has to be opposed – and opposed however thuggish and benighted the forces which this threatens to put your anti-war critic into close company with. For some, because of an uncontrollable animus towards George Bush and his administration. For some, because of a one-eyed perspective on international legality and its relation to issues of international justice and morality. Whatever the case or the combination, it has produced a calamitous compromise of the core values of socialism, or liberalism or both, on the part of thousands of people who claim attachment to them. You have to go back to the apologias for, and fellow-travelling with, the crimes of Stalinism to find as shameful a moral failure of liberal and left opinion as in the wrong-headed – and too often, in the circumstances, sickeningly smug – opposition to the freeing of the Iraqi people from one of the foulest regimes on the planet.

14

On justifying military intervention in Syria

(This article was originally published on 'Normblog', 27 August 2013)

The signs are now clear that Washington[*] and other Western powers,[†] including Britain, are considering military action against Syria on account of the regime's apparent use of chemical weapons against Syrian civilians.[‡] Would such action be justified? In the debate about this at least three types of issue are centrally involved: (1) whether there is a basis in international law for military intervention; (2) whether it is likely to do any good; and (3) whether it might be merited in any case on retributive grounds.

(1) My own view on whether there is a basis in international law for humanitarian intervention in situations of this kind is that there is. As I have already stated[§] this view at some length, I will be brief on the present occasion. There is not only a right, there is a duty, of humanitarian intervention when a government is committing mass atrocities against a civilian population. This can be established by reference both to customary international law and to the doctrine of A Responsibility to Protect, underwritten by the UN. The question, in particular, of whether a UN resolution mandating intervention is required can be quickly answered – no – for a reason given by Louis Charbonneau in 'The U.N. Security Council is not the sole or unique custodian about what is legal and what is legitimate'. To put the same thing another way: a system of law that would countenance mass atrocity without any remedy simply because the interests of a veto-wielding power at the UN blocks remedial action is morally unacceptable, indeed intolerable; and so where the UN itself becomes delinquent by not upholding some of its own most fundamental principles, the UN

---

* www.washingtonpost.com/world/national-security/kerry-obama-determined-to-hold-syria-accountable-for-using-chemical-weapons/2013/08/26/599450c2–0e70–11e3–8cdd-bcdc09410972_story.html

† www.independent.co.uk/voices/comment/is-the-west-prepared-to-cross-the-rubicon-over-syria-probably-8784438.html

‡ Editors' note: this article was written three days before the House of Commons voted against military intervention in Syria, a decisive moment in Western acquiescence to the Assad regime.

§ Editors' note: in 'Is There a Right of Humanitarian Intervention?'.

not only may, it *should*, be defied by member states willing to give those principles more respect.

(2) However, integral to the doctrines of humanitarian intervention and R2P [that is, the 'Responsibility to Protect] alike is the requirement that a prospective military intervention should have a reasonable chance of success. Intervention is not to be contemplated without regard to the likely consequences. In the present case, this is, in my view, the most difficult of the three issues to resolve. Would military intervention against Syria now do any good? That depends, of course, on what its objectives are: whether to influence the overall outcome of the civil war in that country; or merely to weaken the regime's military capabilities; or to deter it from further gas attacks on the Syrian people; etc. I don't propose to offer answers on each different conception of possible objectives. Indeed I don't know that I can. My earlier uncertainties* over Syria have not dissipated. But, in any case, one should note that intervention may be justified *even if* the overall balance of consequences is not beneficial.

(3) For intervention may be undertaken on retributive grounds, to punish a regime that so blatantly flouts the norms of international humanitarian law and the principles of all civilized morality. It may be regarded as morally unthinkable that such a regime should be able to commit gross crimes against humanity with impunity – without being made to suffer any significant penalty. In this situation military intervention is undertaken as a reprisal[†] for the crimes committed.

How one weighs the force of (3) against that of (2) in a case where there may be negative consequences I am unsure. But it is these considerations rather than UN authorization or lack of it that should take precedence.

---

* Editors' note: expressed in 'In defence of Uncertainty (over Syria)', posted on 'Normblog', 28 May 2013.

† www.theguardian.com/world/2013/aug/26/united-nations-mandate-airstrikes-syria

15

Burying humanitarian intervention

(This article was first published on 'Normblog', 24 March 2010)

An article by Mark Mazower for the journal *World Affairs* may seem, at first, to strike an odd note. It characterizes the concept of humanitarian intervention as 'dying if not dead' and links this judgement with the hypothesis of a 'new era of pragmatism ... in the making' that sounds as though it might have the author's approval. For me there is a jarring element in that coupling. Humanitarian intervention is an option that is available when the assumed protections of state sovereignty have failed those supposed to be protected by it, when the authority of the state itself – of some particular state – is turned against them as an instrument of violation, criminality, mass murder or, at the limit, genocide. How could it be a matter for applause that the doctrine of humanitarian intervention should be now dying or dead? Perhaps the opening note struck by Mazower is not really as it sounded to me.

Sad to say, however, it is. Though he grants that the ideal of 'human solidarity in international affairs' is a noble if complicated one, by the end of the piece, Mazower's approval of the demise of humanitarian interventionism has been made explicit. There's a 'new realism', he says, that is welcome; again, the 'new maturity in international relations' is to be viewed positively. His reasons for thinking so are, in short, that 'the way leaders treat their people is not the only problem that counts in international affairs'.

One is bound to accept the truth of this, of course – it *isn't* the only problem that counts in international affairs. Still, the fact that assaults by a state on its own citizens are one of the more terrible fates that can befall people, a fate that usually leaves them with nowhere to turn, and the related fact that in certain circumstances humanitarian intervention is the only recourse, the only means of rescue – these two facts leave me puzzled over why Mazower should see fit so to talk down the importance of the problem in question: of 'the way leaders treat their people'; more particularly, of how to deal with situations in which governments commit crimes against humanity on a mass scale. 'Maturity' isn't the word I would choose to describe the attitude Mazower for his part is welcoming.

He can do it the more easily, however, because when you examine what *other* considerations he thinks should be acknowledged as counting in international affairs, you find that he introduces as being extraneous to the doctrine of humanitarian intervention considerations that have in fact been an integral part of it in pretty well all standard versions. Thus, first of all, sovereignty. Humanitarian intervention has never been considered legitimate as a merely lightminded setting aside of the principle of sovereignty. Because that principle is recognized as itself a fundamental protection of the interests of the citizens of a state, it is only in circumstances of egregious rights violations, violations on a mass scale, that humanitarian intervention has generally been considered justified; only, in other words, beyond a certain threshold. Read any standard account of this concept in the international law literature, and you will see that that is so. But Mazower writes as if sovereignty is an issue lying outside the expiring concept of humanitarian intervention, one which the new maturity of outlook has now to include.

Likewise, with the sequel to intervention. Since it is an elementary truth that an intervention that fails or makes things worse will not effect a rescue of those in need of one, accounts of the principle of humanitarian intervention invariably emphasize that unless there is a good prospect of success, intervention cannot be justified. But Mazower writes as if part of the new and welcome 'pragmatism', 'realism', 'maturity', is the wisdom 'that without willing the means, intervention leads to political and moral failure'. He tells us that interventionism may itself threaten peace and stability, as if the restrictions built in to the doctrine of humanitarian intervention weren't there from the beginning precisely on account of that recognition.

Apart from this tendency of his to want to supplement a putatively deficient concept with components that have long been part of it, Mazower also invokes the shadow of imperial ambition to cast doubt on the validity of the universal principles in light of which humanitarian intervention is justified (when it is). Yet these principles are not – or not just – the principles of the West. They are embodied in international conventions and legal instruments designed to protect all peoples from their own governments, as well as from the depredations of external enemies and invaders. At the end of World War II, after the horrors of Nazism, establishing these principles in international law was held to be a task of some priority and urgency. That it should now be thought immature to uphold a doctrine in which they are taken seriously is a remarkable testimony to the way in which a wide cohort of today's liberal intelligentsia has been knocked sideways by current political animosities it is unable to control.

PART IV

Normblog: the best of

Introduction to Normblog

Ben Cohen and Eve Garrard

When Norman Geras launched Normblog in 2003, the medium that came to be known as 'blogging' was still in its infancy. Over the course of a decade, Normblog became one of the top-tier blogs, attracting thousands of readers to its daily posts. Meticulously constructed arguments about politics and international affairs were accompanied by musings on literature, cricket and jazz, profiles of fellow bloggers, and occasional, deeply personal reflections about work, life and the family he loved. Sadly, the flow of words stopped with Geras's untimely death in October 2013.

Geras wrote at a furious pace, building his readership through methods old (word of mouth) and new (social media platforms like Facebook and Twitter). Thus did his voice hold firm as the global blogging surge transformed the nature of political debate in the democratic world, while simultaneously handing authoritarian regimes one more excuse to engage in brutal censorship.

It was Sam Peckinpah's movie *The Wild Bunch* that provided Normblog with the opening line of its first entry: 'Let's go'. That set the tone for a different and refreshing insight into Geras's thoughts and ideas. In the thousands of posts that followed, due attention was paid to the thinkers and writers who inspired Geras, from Leon Trotsky to Primo Levi, but his style was distinctly non-academic. Jargon was scarce, direct and uncomplicated argument was the rule. On any given day, Normblog readers might start with a piece about Jane Austen, his favourite novelist, move to a critique of the western left's attitude to the former Iraqi tyrant Saddam Hussein and end with an encomium to the legendary Manchester United midfielder Paul Scholes, the footballer he most admired. Ad hominem attacks on political opponents were happily absent, as Geras demonstrated time and again that political conflicts could be won without descending into the grammatically compromised insults that characterized so much of the blogosphere.

The selection of Normblog posts republished here was chosen by a range of different people who knew Norm, either on a personal basis or through his blog posts and other writings. In this section, readers will find plenty of politics and plenty of reminders that there is a world beyond politics. Why Norman

Geras blogged, and what he valued most about blogging, is best expressed in his own words. For that reason, this section begins at the end, with a post written shortly before he died in 2013 and entitled 'A normblog decade'.

A normblog decade

Today is the tenth anniversary of normblog; it began on 28 July 2003 with a simple 'Let's go' (in the immortal words of Sam Peckinpah). To mark the occasion I offer a brief fact and/or observation for each of the ten years.

1. Since my 70th birthday falls late next month, I have now been blogging more or less daily for a seventh of my life, and I have to say I find this astonishing. It would be different if I were only 14. But a seventh of my life at my age! And when blogging still seems a bit like something that's just happened. Anyway, ten years ago I had not the slightest inkling of what I was getting into from a temporal point of view.

2. It's the writing. Maybe I should have been a diarist, though I have never had that inclination; but the main reason I blog and have kept at blogging is that I enjoy the process of putting together an argument or just setting out something that I hope will be of interest to others. That is what motivates me here.

3. Since I started this blog, there have been 15,045 posts – which is 125 per month and some 4 per day on average.

4. The best thing for me about blogging, no question, is the many new friends I've made through doing it. This is internet friends and face-to-friends both. I know people in Australia, in North America, why, even in London, whom I would not have known but for the correspondence that first grew up between us because of my blog, often leading to later personal meetings. I value these friendships enormously. The tale that people who spend too much time on their computers are made lonely by it is one-sided at best.

5. The Euston Manifesto was the main political outcome of my blogging and that is something I'm happy about. I don't mean to claim sole ownership of it. It was produced for a loose grouping of people and there were other inputs than mine, though I was the principal author. But my participation in the group that produced it and what I wrote of the actual text would not have happened had I not been writing regularly for normblog, and in that way my blogging was a precondition. There are, of course, shortcomings in the document; but all in all, and for the time when it was produced, I'm reasonably proud of it.

6. I am grateful to those who have supported normblog over the years, friendly readers, whether regular or occasional – people who email me with pertinent comment, leaving aside the small number amongst these who don't know how to disagree without being unpleasant about it. It is a mark of the general point I'm making here how little of my email correspondence has been of this unpleasant, and how much of it of the other, kind.

7. The total number of visits to normblog over the whole ten years has been slightly in excess of 5,797,000 – on average nearly 1,600 a day.

8. I'm also grateful to people who have contributed to normblog in various ways: by sending me links, by sending helpful comments, by writing guest posts, by contributing to the series I have run: the Writer's Choice series, the memories of cricket, the normblog profiles. And by taking part in my occasional normblog polls.

9. The pleasure of writing (registered at 2 above) has its negative counterpart in the pressure to find something to blog about on 'slow' days: days when the news agenda is rebarbative to one's inclinations, and when Google News and Twitter and Facebook all fail to yield something you want to hook on to. Gee, I *hate* it when that happens. But happen it does and I suppose must now and again, otherwise I'd just be an automaton and then where would I be?

10. Last night, and I think for the first time ever, I actually dreamt a conceptual argument. The dream had other features, with the weirdness that dreams often display. I was at a conference and a friend I was talking to was two different (real) people I have known, now one, now the other. I was annoyed because I still had a question I wanted to raise and the chair had let the session run down and start to break up even though there were still 15 scheduled minutes unused. An item of clothing of mine was – how shall I put it? – not properly in position, and in a way that would normally have embarrassed me but because of my irritation, didn't. Yet, in among all this, my shape-shifter friend set out a conceptual argument (about the transformation problem in Marx, if you must know) that I have never thought while I was awake and that was new to me. I wonder if ten years of blogging can do this to a person: get you dreaming conceptually in search of something to use later on the blog.

Too much Holocaust

The *New York Review* of Books of February 14, 2008 carries an article of more than 4,000 words by Tony Judt, adapted from a lecture he gave in Bremen last year on being awarded the Hannah Arendt prize. Arendt's *Eichmann in Jerusalem* is a work that no serious student of the fate of European Jewry under the Nazis can bypass, and it is therefore entirely appropriate that Judt should centre these reflections of his – entitled 'The "Problem of Evil" in Postwar Europe' – on the ways in which the Shoah or Holocaust (I use the two expressions interchangeably) is remembered and written about today. The general tenor of what he has to say on the subject is regrettable, however. Because Tony Judt's is a name that is respected in the academic world and beyond, I take the space I need here to subject his essay to critical scrutiny.

After a period of relative inattention in the years following the Second World War, the Shoah was increasingly taken up from some time after the 1960s, Judt says, until it became a universal reference point – in films, television, books, specialist studies, memoirs, school curricula. So it remains today. Now that it is so generally emphasized, is everything all right? Judt's immediate answer is that he isn't sure. But by the time he has spelled out the sources of his uncertainty, the burden of the argument has become clear and it is that he thinks that things are *not* all right. He goes through five difficulties he has with the amount of attention now given to the Holocaust. In what follows I summarize these, recording at the same time the difficulties I have with his difficulties.

1. Judt's first difficulty arises from the fact that the way the so-called Final Solution is remembered in Western Europe is not in harmony with the memories of the Second World War in Eastern Europe. Why – he reports people asking there – the sensitivity to the mass murder of the Jews? What was so distinctive about it? What about the non-Jewish victims? And the victims, also, of Stalinism? That these other victims, whether of Nazism or Stalinism, are worth every bit of historical and memorial attention they get, and if this is not enough, then more attention still, is not a point I would dispute. But beyond that, I'm puzzled why this East European perspective should pose any difficulty for Tony Judt. For the question why people should be so sensitive about the destruction of European Jewry is not a good one, and the irritation behind it is not an impulse worthy of respect. These are responses based either on ignorance or on something worse than ignorance and which Judt himself has identified a few paragraphs earlier in his piece in talking of 'the powerful incentive [there was] in many places to forget what had happened, to draw a veil over the worst horrors'. These places include Eastern Europe for the obvious reason that there were East Europeans who colluded with the persecution of the Jews, with expropriation of Jewish property, deportation and all the rest of it.

Why so much attention should be aroused by the mass murder of any very large number of people – in this case millions, but the same would apply were it 'only' tens of thousands – is not the kind of question that should be indulged. It is hard to imagine Judt or any other morally serious person asking, for example, why people should be so focused on what happened in Rwanda in 1994 when there have been victims aplenty in other parts of Africa; or on what is happening in Darfur now, when the people of Zimbabwe or DR Congo are also suffering. To draw attention to these other victims and to say that there isn't enough of it, where there isn't, is perfectly proper. To ask why people should be so sensitive to what happened in Rwanda or is happening in Darfur, or to ask what is so very distinctive about the killing in one or other of those two places, would be morally obtuse. Killing of this magnitude doesn't have to be distinctive to justify anyone's attention; it just has to be what it is – the mass murder of human beings.

So it is hard to fathom why Tony Judt, or we West Europeans, should consider that we have a difficulty here. That some East Europeans have a different view from many West Europeans isn't a compelling reason for thinking so. The difficulty is rather theirs who frown upon the impulse of others to remember a major historical crime. Let us defer, therefore, coming to any conclusive judgement about the meaning of Tony Judt's first difficulty.

2. His second difficulty is a historiographical one: now that 'we are encouraged to think about those sufferings [i.e. of the Jews] all the time', there is a danger that historians, reading the perspective of the present back into the past, may inflate the place the Holocaust actually had at the time in the meanings, the preoccupations, the experiences, of those who lived through the war. But if we think like this, think that the Second World War was *about* the Holocaust, we will not teach 'good history', Judt says. He's right. Again, however, I don't see that this is a difficulty of general scope, rather than just a necessary concern in the training of historians and history teachers. It is practically a law of nature that in any widely populated field of human endeavour there will be mediocre and indifferent productions alongside the examples of excellence or merely competence. Where novelists are many, some novels will be poor; where poetry abounds, some of it will not serve to decorate everyone's day. Just so, if there is much written, spoken and taught about the tragedy of European Jewry and its place in the war that was its backdrop, then some of that will be of better quality and some of it of worse; there will be examples of poor history. So what? The better can be relied on to make its way in the world and outlast the not so good. Judt himself allows that in '*moral* terms' (his emphasis) it is proper that the central issue of the war should now be Auschwitz. If on this account we get some poor history, that is simply an inevitable product of the moral focus that is a proper one according to Judt himself. Unless, that is, he thinks that, its moral centrality notwithstanding, there is just *too much* attention being given to the Shoah today. But we need a reason, in that case, for thinking that this much attention is too much. And we don't yet have it. Could it be that Judt's difficulties are not themselves reasons supporting that conclusion but are rather inferences from the *preconception* that this much attention is too much attention – so that what Judt's essay gives us are not parts adding up to a reasoned whole, but instead an originary meaning essential to the whole and which bathes the individual parts in its illumination?

3. Judt's third difficulty has to do with the word 'evil'. I quote him at length on this:

> Modern secular society has long been uncomfortable with the idea of 'evil'. We prefer more rationalistic and legal definitions of good and bad, right and wrong, crime and punishment. But in recent years the word has crept slowly back into moral and even political discourse... However, now that the concept of 'evil' has reentered our public language we don't know what to do with it. We have become confused.
>
> On the one hand the Nazi extermination of the Jews is presented as a singular crime, an evil never matched before or since, an example and a warning: 'Nie Wieder! Never again!' But on the other hand we invoke that same ('unique') evil today for many different and far from unique purposes. In recent years politicians, historians, and journalists have used the term 'evil' to describe mass murder and genocidal outcomes everywhere: from Cambodia to Rwanda, from Turkey to Serbia, from Bosnia to Chechnya, from the Congo to Sudan. Hitler himself is frequently conjured up to denote the 'evil' nature and intentions of modern dictators: we are told there are 'Hitlers' everywhere, from North Korea to Iraq, from Syria to Iran. And we are all familiar with President George W. Bush's 'axis of evil', a self-serving abuse of the term which has contributed greatly to the cynicism it now elicits.
>
> Moreover, if Hitler, Auschwitz, and the genocide of the Jews incarnated a unique evil, why are we constantly warned that they and their like could happen anywhere, or are about to happen again?

Given Judt's concern about our becoming confused, he couldn't have given better evidence of it than the number of his own confusions collected in these paragraphs.

First, while the Holocaust doubtless plays its part in generating references to human evil, I don't think anyone could plausibly maintain that there is a shortage of alternative sources. From other mass atrocities of historical notoriety, through smaller-scale acts of political murder and torture, to ghastly individual crimes in the private sphere, the word 'evil' has plenty to keep it on the lips of humankind. Why the Holocaust should be lumbered with special responsibility here isn't clear. The idea, just to entertain it for a moment, that if the Holocaust hadn't happened modern conversation would be freer of the idea of evil is merely quaint.

Second, look at the list of items that Judt compiles to show the profligacy with which public discussion has recourse to the word 'evil'. This list includes: Cambodia, Rwanda, Bosnia, Chechnya, the Congo, Sudan, Saddam's Iraq and North Korea. God Almighty (if I may allow myself an imprecation sustained by the beliefs of others). To speak the word 'evil' in any of these cases doesn't seem the least bit exorbitant. Of course, if that word exhausts your verbal or intellectual tool-kit, you won't have much of an understanding of any of the events or political patterns that stand behind these names. But why it should be a difficulty or a worry to anyone that, for example, genocide is spoken of as evil, or an evil, is entirely mysterious.

It may be noted, in passing, while we're on the subject of naming evils, that one name that has got in on the act here is that of George W. Bush. Talk about a universal reference: rather like the Holocaust for evil, Bush's name has today become the embodiment of much badness for Western liberal intellectuals, so it is perhaps no surprise that he is now attached to showing the difficulties that can arise from ... remembering the destruction of the European Jews.

Third, Judt sees it as problematic that the Holocaust should be considered by some as both a unique evil and a repeatable one. He is aware that the claim that the Holocaust is unique is controversial, because he has earlier gestured towards the view that there is an answer to the question why the Shoah is distinctive, without saying what that answer is. I have for my own part argued in my essay 'In a Class of Its Own?' at length, as well as in my post 'The Memory of the Offence', of September 20, 2005 more briefly, that there may indeed be a morally significant sense in which the Holocaust was unique, but that if it is, this is not because of any particularity of Jewish victimhood or suffering; it is rather to do with the nature of the Nazi crime. However that may be, the problem Judt makes of the idea of Holocaust singularity is only testimony to his own confusion. An event can be at once unprecedented, and therefore unique to date, and repeatable. Even apart from this, one can perfectly well believe both that the genocide against the Jews had some morally singular features and that it stands as a warning for the future – this not because of its singularity, but just as a genocide, i.e., because of what it shares with other genocides. That, I venture to suggest, is what the vast majority of those who emphasize the Shoah as a warning do in fact believe.

Fourth, as an additional sign of the omnipresence in contemporary usage of the idea of evil, Judt goes on to say, immediately after the passage I have quoted above:

Every time someone smears antisemitic graffiti on a synagogue wall in France we are warned that 'the unique evil' is with us once more, that it is 1938 all over again. We are losing the capacity to distinguish between the normal sins and follies of mankind – stupidity, prejudice, opportunism, demagogy, and fanaticism – and genuine evil.

I shall come back to the theme of antisemitism shortly. But this verges on argument by clowning. Antisemitic incidents are to be taken seriously where they occur for a simple reason: antisemitism is a form of racist prejudice and racism is a serious matter, a poison in the body politic, in the places where it is secreted or reveals itself. But there is also a specific history of the form of racism that is antisemitism, a history the final fruit of which was Auschwitz and Treblinka. There may be some amongst those who invoke these horrors who really do think that it is always 1938, or 1942. But most of them don't think so – no more than people who remind us of the history of lynching in the US think that drawing the noose as a racist symbol in 2007 actually throws the country back to the 1890s when 'a black person was lynched almost every other day'. These are potent historical reminders of what racism has produced and they have their place in moral and political argument. They are not meant to equate antisemitic graffiti with the gas chambers except in the minds of a few know-nothings.

4. Much the same may be said about Judt's fourth difficulty – a concern he has about 'tunnel vision' or, as he also puts this, 'invest[ing] all our emotional and moral energies into just one problem'. What problem is that? Why, anti-semitism. Judt writes:

> [A]nti-Semitism, like terrorism, is *not* the only evil in the world and must *not* be an excuse to ignore other crimes and other suffering. The danger of abstracting 'terrorism' or antisemitism from their contexts – of setting them upon a pedestal as the greatest threat to Western civilization, or democracy, or 'our way of life,' and targeting their exponents for an indefinite war – is that we shall overlook the many other challenges of the age.

I leave aside terrorism; that is not my topic here. But the suspicion I voiced earlier about Judt's not working from (good) reasons to a conclusion, but rather from a founding preconception towards confecting some (bad) reasons, is really confirmed by these remarkable statements. I don't know what audience or set of interlocutors he has imagined for himself, but if there are people who believe that antisemitism is the only evil in the world and the greatest threat to Western civilization, I doubt there would have been many of them listening to his lecture on Hannah Arendt, I doubt there are many (relatively speaking) in the world at large, and a man of Judt's intellectual capacities and reputation could do with addressing himself to listeners of a higher calibre than he has fashioned with this fourth difficulty of his.

5. Judt's final difficulty, as it had to be in view of what has gone before, is the relation of the Holocaust to arguments about Israel and the Palestinians. It has several components, some of which have already been foreshadowed in what has gone before. (a) Judt deplores the way the Holocaust is invoked to deflect criticism of Israel by the suggestion that such criticism is a stimulus to antisemitism or just is antisemitism without further ado. (b) In fact, the reverse is true, he says: it is the taboo on criticism of Israel and a too intense focus on the Holocaust that are stimulants to cynicism and antisemitism. (c) Relative to other minority groups in the US and Europe, the Jews are not especially stigmatized, threatened or excluded; they are successful, and prominent in many spheres. (d) The Holocaust may 'lose its universal resonance' if it is too closely attached to the defence of a single country; as things are, if you ask outside the West, ask amongst Africans and Asians, what lessons there are from the Shoah, the responses 'are not very reassuring'.

What is striking about these arguments of Judt's is their unqualified, their completely one-sided, character. It is true that the Jewish tragedy in Europe is sometimes misused to justify or excuse Israeli policies that should not be defended. But to say this without noting that there is *also* antisemitic hostility to Israel, in the Arab world and in the West, some of it perfectly overt and some of it more discreet, is to pretend that antisemitism is a smaller problem than it is. To lament such misuses of the Holocaust without mentioning the misuses in the opposite direction that equate Israel with the spirit and the methods of the Nazis is to see with only one eye. The same goes for writing as if the most serious sources of antisemitism might be arguments used by defenders of Israel or an over-emphasis on the Shoah. Really? This is a centuries-old hatred, and yet here we find ourselves in a situation where it is defence of the Jewish state and memory of the genocide against the Jews that are the stimulants of antisemitism; these, at any rate, are Tony Judt's sources of choice.

Judt does not see fit even to notice what many others have perceived as a real trend during the last decade, a resurgence of antisemitism. But attacks on Jews have been on the increase in many countries. To take only the example of Britain, you might think it was of some significance that the Jewish community is 'forced to provide a permanent system of guards and surveillance for its schools, religious centres, and communal institutions'.

And then Judt reprises, with his fifth difficulty, the theme already announced with the first of them: namely, that outside of the West awareness of the Holocaust and responses to the question of what lessons should be drawn from it would not reassure us. And this is our difficulty, not theirs. Why? Can you imagine something similar transposed on to another major ethnic experience of suffering? Being told that because, say, in Sweden or Ukraine, there wasn't much of an awareness of, or there was a cynical disregard for, the experience of New World slavery, this suggested we shouldn't go on making too much of the victims of that terrible institution and the trade in human beings that went with it? I don't think so.

A few words now in conclusion. Is there too much about the Holocaust – too much writing, too much memorializing, too much reference? The whole weight of what Judt has to say pushes towards the conclusion that there is, though without his providing, as I have tried to show, a single compelling argument for this. But my own answer to the question is: no, there is not too much. I offer a moral and a political argument in support of that answer.

Morally – humanly – if you were to spend an hour of every day during a lifetime remembering, learning, lamenting, teaching what was done to the victims of the Nazi genocide you could not encompass all the cruelty and all the pain of those years. We do better to take note of Primo Levi's poem 'Shema':

> Consider that this has been:
> I commend these words to you.
> Engrave them on your hearts
> When you are in your house, when you walk on your way,
> When you go to bed, when you rise.
> Repeat them to your children.

This is true not because of what happened to those *Jews*, but because of what happened to those *people*; and it is therefore likewise true, exactly true, for the other millions of victims of other genocides – in Turkey, in Cambodia, in Rwanda, in Darfur, wherever.

As I have argued in the past, there is not too much attention given to the Holocaust or any other genocide, there is too little. Think only of the energy and attention that is being given, in the US and globally, to the American presidential election; or think of a major sporting event like the football World Cup; and then think how it might be, politically, if there were a planetary consciousness, a world-wide human rights movement, so cognizant of the worst crimes of the past, not turned away from them towards easier preoccupations, that people marched and agitated in their tens and hundreds of thousands whenever there was a genocide in process or threatening, demanded that the governments of the world and the institutions of world governance would treat these situations as urgent. Can Tony Judt, or anyone, be confident that this would not make the world a better place?

But Judt has all these difficulties with Holocaust remembrance, and he has them by way of honouring Hannah Arendt – Hannah Arendt who suggested in *Eichmann in Jerusalem* the possibility that 'mankind in its entirety ... might have been grievously hurt and endangered' by the crime of exterminating whole ethnic groups. It is hard to imagine a more unworthy tribute to her.

Six theses on the death of Margaret Thatcher

I hadn't thought of writing anything about this, but over the last couple of days others have shown themselves interested in what I might have to say – as if normblog were a national newspaper, which it isn't. I have, in the past, made it plain that I was no fan of the late Mrs Thatcher, though with one area of exception. What I feel impelled to say by some of the press and internet discussion of the last few days, however, is pretty much independent of all that.

(1) In a civilized society people owe a duty of respect to the dying, the recently deceased and the bereaved. It is a simple duty of humanity. Each of us faces his or her own death sooner or later, and routine as this is, it is also – each time – a minor tragedy: a whole life, a whole inner world, gone. Whatever differences we may have with another person, whatever dislikes, we should be able to see the irreparable loss involved and mark it appropriately. There may be exceptions to this norm – for mass murderers and the like – but they are few, and should not include democratically elected politicians within one's own community, however much they may have been hated by their opponents.

(2) This duty of respect does not extend to having to speak respectfully or uncritically of a recently deceased individual's political or other public *record*. Why should it? A person's death is typically the time when his or her life is written about and assessed most actively. Some of the assessments are positive and no one asks that these should be toned down or made neutral. There is, equally, no reason for negative, or disparaging, even damning, judgements of the same record to be avoided. It is a political or other *reputation* and *legacy* that is being judged, and it would be 'stacking the deck' of public discussion to regard the expression of positive viewpoints about the life of the deceased as legitimate but critical opinions as out of order.

(3) To publicly rejoice at the death of a democratic political opponent, talk of dancing on her grave, hold street parties for the occasion, and so forth, is contemptible. It says more about the morality inspiring those who engage in such activities than it does about the object of them. Consider that one day it will be you who are dying, and whatever you have done or failed to do in your life, you will deserve the love of those who feel it for you and something better than cruel glee from those who don't.

(4) For, notice that Margaret Thatcher was not still prime minister on the day she died. Her death wasn't instrumental in ending her period of power. So joy in seeing the back of her in *that* sense doesn't come into it. The day she stepped down as PM is already more than two decades behind us – a day on which many, including me, were delighted to see her go. But the power she wielded and what she wielded it for can't possibly justify the rejoicing now.

(5) And notice, too, that Thatcher's political legacy, the continuing influence

of what she did in office, is not altered one way or another by her death. It will continue to make its way in the world, as also to be opposed there, for a good while yet. The expression of public enjoyment has no possible justification, therefore, on these grounds either.

(6) No, when Margaret Thatcher died she was an old and ill woman, with people around her who cared about her. To take pleasure at *this* is an inhumanity that does no credit to those who so indulge themselves. They forget the simplest and most enduring of human truths for an ugly temporary pleasure.

A right denied to millions

Education is neither eastern nor western. Education is education and it's the right of every human being.

So says Malala Yousafzai, who was shot by the Taliban a year ago for campaigning for female education and who now advises British girls not to take their schooling for granted. Writing in the *Daily Telegraph* of October 6, 2013 David Blair highlights how bad the problem is in Pakistan, and for boys as well as girls:

> No one can doubt her courage, nor the inhumanity of her obscurantist tormen-
> tors. Yet it would be too easy to blame the Taliban for the lack of female education
> in Pakistan.
>
> Instead, Malala is only the most vivid symbol of a deep-rooted problem that
> existed long before the birth of the Taliban – and affects areas of Pakistan which
> its gunmen have never reached. In the process, the lives of millions of boys are
> blighted, just as surely as girls.

The problem can be simply stated. Pakistan has neglected to build a public education system worthy of the name. No single leader or political movement can be singled out for blame: this is a calamitous national failure built up over generations.

Today, only 67 per cent of Pakistani girls and 81 per cent of boys go to primary school, according to the United Nations. That may not sound disastrous, until you remember that neighbouring India achieves close to 100 per cent for both genders, and even Uganda and Zambia manage more than 90 per cent.

When it comes to secondary education, the situation is far worse, with Pakistan's enrolment rate plummeting to 38 per cent for boys – and only 29 per cent for girls. Again, the poorest countries in Africa do significantly better, typically achieving around 50 per cent.

Then consider the fact that Pakistan's population exceeds 180 million, of whom almost half are children under the age of 18. If a big majority have no chance to go to secondary school – and a significant minority cannot even gain a primary education – then tens of millions of children are missing out.

Hymning Hizbollah

Here is journalist John Pilger on *The Guardian*'s 'Comment is Free' section singing the praises of Hizbollah:

> The resistance to rapacious power, to epic crimes of invasion (which the Nuremberg judges called the 'paramount' crime) is humanity at its noblest; yet the paradox warns us that no resistance is pretty; that each adds its own form of violence in order to expel an invader (such as the civilians killed by Hizbollah rockets); and this has applied to heroic partisans in Europe and heroic Kurds and those faceless, despised Iraqis who have succeeded in pinning down the American homicidal machine in their country.

I won't dwell here on the judgement, breathtaking though it is, that Hizbollah or the Iraqi insurgency represent 'humanity at its noblest'. Nor on the lame excuse which is its companion, namely, that 'no resistance is pretty' – as if this could obliterate all distinctions between ways and ways of fighting. What I want to focus on is that Pilger can write something like this without uttering a single word about the fact that Hizbollah's attitude to Jews is frankly and straightforwardly racist, with its leader Sheikh Hassan Nasrallah on record as having said:

> if they (Jews) all gather in Israel, it will save us the trouble of going after them worldwide.

One might think this a detail that was relevant to any assessment of the organization by a veteran journalist of the left. But it seems not. Antisemitism is, perhaps, just a bit of that understandable lack of prettiness.

On the same day in the *Guardian*, Jonathan Steele said:

> Lebanon has a government of national unity in which Hizbollah has two ministers. Being anti-Syrian is not the same as being anti-Hizbollah, and the election winners from the March 14 movement, which developed after the car-bomb murder of the former prime minister Rafik Hariri, wisely recognised that the party is an authentic part of Lebanese society. It was better to have it in the government rather than outside.

Demonising Hizbollah as terrorists or Iranian and Syrian agents confuses the picture.

OK, so it's more restrained than Pilger's encomium, and if Hizbollah is a force to be reckoned with, then there's nothing wrong with saying so. But if recognizing its 'authenticity' is what you're doing, and recommending against 'demonization', then don't the goals of the organization vis-à-vis Israel merit attention, and the hostility to Jews likewise? Forget it.

These are only the views of two journalists, of course, but the two of them express those views in the major newspaper of British left-liberalism and on its website, one openly commending an antisemitic organization, the other calling on us not to judge it too harshly. And this has now become entirely *normal*. No one is surprised, let alone shocked, by it. Hey, it may not be my opinion exactly, but it's a point of view and unremarkable; it falls within the range of respectable political opinion. Neither writer even sees a need to explain himself on the matter of Hizbollah's antisemitism. Nobody will feel that they here place themselves, so to say, beyond the pale. Not a bit of it. Hizbollah may hate Jews but... 'humanity at its noblest', or at any rate not to be 'demonized'.

It's just another day at the office. Let free comment follow – in which you can bet there'll be a proportion of commenters cheering.

My Australia

Growing up in Southern Rhodesia, as it then was, I early developed a double relationship to Australia as a cricketing nation. For me the country bore two emotional signs rather than one. Rhodesia was part of South Africa for purposes of international cricket, and so South Africa had my primary allegiance. In the era of Jackie McGlew, Roy McLean and (above all) Hugh Tayfield, it was the Springboks I wanted to see victorious. At the time I first became interested in the game – 1954 or 1955 as near as I can pin it down – South Africa had not long ago returned from a triumphant series in Australia under the leadership of Jack Cheetham, and the book in which that triumph was recounted by him (*Caught by the Springboks*) was like the foundational myth of my cricket consciousness: a tale of great deeds that had put my team on the cricketing map. The series, in fact, was drawn, South Africa levelling it at 2–2 in the fifth and final Test at Melbourne; but so unfancied had they been at the start of the tour that even a drawn series was considered a triumph.

This was against an Australian side that included Neil Harvey – who made four centuries, including one double hundred, and averaged 92.66 for the series – Miller and Lindwall, Arthur Morris and the young Richie Benaud. The result secured by the Springboks was not to be sneezed at, therefore, and like all such successes, particularly in the eyes of boyhood, it contained its heroic elements. McLean saying to his captain as he went out to bat in the final innings at Melbourne, with 104 runs still needed, 'Don't worry Pop, I'll get them for you' – this was part of that founding myth by which my initial loyalties were shaped. Australia were opponents, and powerful opponents. Merely to draw a series with them was a major achievement.

The next contest between the two countries would only reinforce this sense of keen opposition. In the southern summer of 1957–8, South Africa faced Ian Craig's Australians and were soundly beaten by them. But that is to characterize it too clinically. In terms of its impact on me at the time, the blow was a hefty one. I was at the Wanderers in Johannesburg for the whole of the fourth Test of that series, a game in which Benaud scored an exact 100 and took nine wickets. I remember well how his innings ended. No sooner had he got to his century than he let rip, as if wanting to hit the ball right out of the ground. But he only succeeded in hitting it straight up in the air. At the time I thought no cricket ball could ever have been struck as high, and it seemed a long time coming back down. Russell Endean, one of the most reliable of catchers, caught it. Anyway, this was just one year after I'd watched the Springboks beat Peter May's team in the corresponding Test of the 1956–7 series between South Africa and England. On that earlier occasion I had had my first taste of cricketing elation, especially since the victory was clinched by my boyhood hero 'Toey' Tayfield taking nine for 113 in England's second innings. Dozing in the back of the car on the drive back from Johannesburg to Bulawayo, I experienced that warm, happy glow each time I awoke, when a feeling of something really good having happened creeps back to the front of one's mind. And now, only 12 months later, Australia went to lunch on the last day of the fourth Test, with South Africa's second innings just completed and the scores level, needing the undemanding total of one run in order to win both the game and the series. Crushed. And by (in my perception) a hard bunch – men who wouldn't give you a bloody thing you hadn't forced out of them. Just as my witnessing the wonderful victory against May's side the year before had been a first for me, so South Africa's humbling a year later was my introduction to the unanswerable taste of defeat.

And yet, and yet. Even in this simple matter and for a youngster of four-teen, the world is a more complicated place than can be accommodated by any single-value schema. For reasons that must remain obscure at a distance of more than 50 years, seeing Australia as tough and unyielding opponents went together for me with supporting them passionately when the Ashes were at stake. Why? I can't say for sure that I know. How, after all, are these things determined? In my own case, induction into the world of cricket and crick-eting allegiance wasn't guided by anyone else, any mentor with preferences of his own to impart. I became interested in the game, began to follow it and to read about it; and somehow I found myself supporting Australia against the Poms. I *think* it may have been because, like us, Aussies were 'colonials' and this was an issue of elementary solidarity against the Mother Country. To risk an analogy from a different sphere, my dual (or combined) stance in the matter was like wanting to win against political opponents at home, while being at one with them in any fight against anti-democratic forces ranged against the democracy which you and these same domestic opponents share. For me England in this story, I'm sorry to say, constituted an anti-democratic force; they were the bad guys. At the time in question, they prevailed by and large against both South Africa and Australia (a point to which I shall soon return). South Africa might scrap with Australia, no quarter given, but in the England cricket team the two countries faced a common enemy – an enemy, what is more, displaying a touch of imperial presumption and even snootiness towards us rough colonials.

Or maybe it was just that among the cricket books I received as Bar Mitzvah presents there were two by A.G. Moyes – *Australian Bowlers* (1953) and *Australian Batsmen* (1954) – that appealed to me. The line drawing on the dust jacket of *Australian Bowlers* showing J.M. Gregory in action is still Proustian for me; and the plates, within, of Clarrie Grimmett and Bill O'Reilly chimed in with my ambitions at the time – utterly hopeless, it must be said – to become a spin bowler to be feared; though off-breaks (very slow ones) were my speciality, and not wrist spin. Maybe it was because of Bradman, whose batting pre-eminence brooked no contradiction and of whom I was even then in awe. Or maybe it was because when Ian Craig's Australians – yes, the very same ones, but before the Test series had begun – played at Queen's Ground in Bulawayo and I approached the enclosure in which they were sitting, in the hope of getting autographs, Richie Benaud not only gave me his own but also took the trouble to ensure that his team-mates obliged. I could hardly believe my luck. Richie signed the book over a picture of himself taking a catch at gulley to dismiss Colin Cowdrey in the Lord's Test of 1956, and then passed it on to other members of the team also pictured, who obliged at his urging. I have those autographs still: as well as Benaud, Jim Burke, Ken Mackay, Peter Burge, Ian Craig, Alan Davidson and more, all in my rather worn copy of *The Picture Post Book of the Tests 1956* by Denzil Batchelor. Who knows? The exact aetiology of my ranked loyalties is lost in the mists, even for me.

In any case, the fact that England had lately been beating Australia (in 1954–5 thanks to Tyson and Statham, in 1956 thanks to Laker) as well as South Africa (in the English summer of 1955) became the basis of another 'duality' in my attitude to Australian cricket. I have mentioned this once before, in the book I wrote with my friend Ian Holliday about the 1997 Ashes series. But it has lately struck me in a new light and so I come back to it again. Bradman himself; his 'Invincibles' of 1948; other legends of Australian cricket, like Bill O'Reilly and the aforesaid Miller and Lindwall; and that thumping of the Springboks in 1957–8 to which I have referred: these had all lodged in my mind an image of Australia at cricket as being beyond merely tough, and tending towards the mighty. Guys who looked, some of them, like they'd just walked in from the outback – sunburned, grizzled, giving not an inch, ready to grind opponents down; and recently capable, whether in the person or with the aid of their most prolific batting genius, of building individual and team totals that would put the game out of sight of whatever opposition they were playing. Alongside this impressive cricketing might, however, or at any rate alternating with it, there was, as I saw it, an extreme fragility that could suddenly overtake Australia and plunge it into debacle. Here, the influence of 1954–5 and 1956 on a young mind should not be underestimated. The country of Bradman first blown away by the pace of Frank Tyson, and then conceding 19 of 20 wickets in a single match to the offspin of Jim Laker. Horrors and ignominy; defeat upon defeat. The 4–0 victory to Benaud's Australians in the series that followed these two in 1958–9, though celebrated by me with much relief and as being a return to the proper order of things, did not altogether erase from my consciousness this image of Australian fragility, rubbing shoulders there with that other image, of Australian might.

In the 1960s I followed the game more intermittently than I had during the second half of the 1950s. I never lost interest in Test cricket, and certain events from the 60s still caught my attention: among them, the tied Test at

Brisbane in 1961; Bobby Simpson's triple century at Old Trafford in 1964 and the general shape of that drawn game, all but exhausted by two first innings of over 600; above all, Gary Sobers's West Indian side in England in 1966, when I was present for a famous match-saving partnership between him and David Holford at Lord's. But mostly my mind was not on cricket, it was on more serious things. The main reason for this, I believe, is that the milieu into which I settled as an undergraduate after arriving in England in the autumn of 1962, with the interests of many of my friends centred, like my own, on philosophy and politics, was not especially receptive to fervour about either sport in general or cricket in particular. On the left – my political home – this was much more the case than it is today; serious-minded people wouldn't waste their time, as it were, on a mere game. It could well have been this that dampened my earlier enthusiasm. However it may be, by the end of the decade I was more distant from matters of cricket and not especially focused on South Africa's exit from international competition (though I did, for political reasons, support its exclusion, while simultaneously regretting the effect of this in depriving Test cricket of supreme talents like those of Graeme Pollock and Barry Richards). My passion for the game had become more or less dormant.

It began to reawaken in the mid-1970s, first on account of Lillee and Thommo, then – decisively – with the visit to England of Clive Lloyd's West Indians in 1976 and the Centenary Test at the MCG in March 1977. When Greg Chappell's side toured England in the northern summer of the same year, I returned to watching Test cricket in the flesh, and have never since tired of it. It is, for me, one of the great glories, whatever its level of importance in the larger scheme of human affairs. But woe – the Australians that year were not at all of the mighty sort; they were, rather, of the fragile. Symbolic in this regard was the second Test at Old Trafford, where I spent the first four days (only missing the fifth because of an editorial meeting I had to attend in London); a game in which, second time up, Greg Chappell played a wonderful innings of 112 while the rest of his team could muster no more than 90 runs between the whole lot of them. I remember both his flawlessly elegant on-drive and the look of dismay he once or twice allowed himself as yet another Australian batsman feebly perished. Some to-ing and fro-ing in the years that followed ensured that Australia didn't go entirely without success against England – they won in 1979–80 when the Ashes were not in contention, and again in 1982–3 – but the latter part of the 1970s and most of the 1980s made up a wretched period for an Australia supporter. Australia were trounced 5–1 in 1978–9 as most of their best cricketers chose to play for Kerry Packer; put to the sword by Botham in 1981, a summer, for me, of cricketing misery (on the day of Botham's famous Headingley innings I was in Liverpool listening on a transistor radio and couldn't believe how he just batted on and on, blasting away); stuffed again in 1985; and stuffed once more in 1986–7. What an ordeal.

Strange to relate, however, it was in this very period that my Australian allegiance solidified into the primary sporting preoccupation it has become, and even reversed the ranking of loyalties that had prevailed during my childhood and early adult years. I began to back Australia against all comers and this would include, on their return to official cricket, South Africa. Why it happened, don't ask me. Perhaps it was a natural effect of South Africa being out of the official game. Supporting Australia against the Poms, against the Windies, against all the other Test-playing nations, I just settled into supporting them, period. What had started as a surrogate cricketing identity, active in the context of the Ashes only, evolved now into a permanent one. By the time South Africa came back into international cricket in the early 1990s I was 'lost' to them (though they remain the team I support against everyone else). Never let it be said, consequently, that the shift in loyalties resulted from an opportunistic search for cricketing triumph. The truth is demonstrably otherwise: this shift occurred when England were mostly getting the better of Australia; it was the reaffirmation of an old allegiance, forged with the drama of Ashes cricket as its backdrop, and extended now to cover the entire field.

And lo and behold, what should in due course happen but the dawning of a period of Australian cricketing ascendancy beyond my wildest dreams. From 1989 Australia began to appear truly mighty where the Ashes were concerned. They put together one success after another until those supporting England began to wonder whether their team would ever win again. *Theories* were spun as to why Australia were bound henceforth to enjoy a natural cricketing superiority over England, theories to do with everything from the differing climates of the two countries to the structure of the English domestic game.

It can be told in many ways, the Australian Supremacy of the next decade and a half. Look at the sequence of series scorelines before England would again win the Ashes (in 2005): 4–0, 3–0, 4–1, 3–1, 3–2, 3–1, 4–1, 4–1. One-sided? You bet. That's 28–7, a ratio for Australia of four victories to every defeat. Or look at Australia's largest totals: in 53 Ashes Tests between 1989 and 2007 they made more than 600 in an innings six times, more than 500 in an innings eight times, and more than 400 in an innings sixteen times. Thirty times, then. England's figure for the same thing in the same period is 10. The disparity for totals above 500 and above 600 was, in turn, 14 to 1 and 6 to 0. Fully six of England's meagre nine victories over Australia from 1989 to 2007 occurred when the contest for the Ashes was already settled and so didn't really matter. During this time Australia won the first Test of the series eight times to England's once, and the second Test of the series eight times to England's once. At Lord's, in Brisbane and in Perth, England won nothing while Australia won, respectively, four, four and five times. At none of the Test venues in either country, save only for the Oval, did England win more times than Australia. It was, in a word, magnificent.

Two of Australia's captains during this time – Allen Border and Steve Waugh – were my kind of Aussie cricketers. Both tough as they come, though in different ways: Border never too early on a declaration, keen for Australia to amass totals that would be unassailable; Waugh attacking, attacking and attacking, from the strength he knew he commanded. And each of the two only conceding his own wicket as if it were welded to his very being. Other cricketers I watched during this period and the like of whom you will see only once in a lifetime: Shane Warne, probably the greatest spin bowler ever and always offering a dramatic performance to enjoy – every grimace, every expostulation; Glenn McGrath, whose lethal accuracy during the most relentless of his spells was breathtaking to watch; Adam Gilchrist, on his day a terrifying proposition, coming in at number seven with a bat full of quick, devastating runs.

I lived, ate, breathed and dreamed these years of Australian cricket. I watched three full Ashes series – in 1997, 2001 and 2006–7 – and wrote accounts of the first two of them. When I say I watched the three series in full, I mean at the ground, every day, and from the first ball of each Test to the last. If I missed a few deliveries here or there to go and attend to my bodily needs, I scarcely missed two consecutive overs. In addition to that, in 1989 I saw the whole of the Test at Old Trafford and a couple of days at Lord's, and in 1993 I saw three days at Lord's and the whole of the Test at Old Trafford. And when I wasn't watching at the ground I'd be watching – plenty – on TV or listening on the radio.

I have seen not only Allen Border and Steve Waugh (in the latter case, including his two hundreds in the same Test at Old Trafford in 1997); not only – all at the ground – Warnie's 'Ball of the Century' in 1993, and his 400th Test wicket at the Oval in 2001, and his 700th wicket at the MCG [Melbourne Cricket Ground] in 2006; not only Gilchrist's 152 in 143 balls at Edgbaston in 2001 and his century in 59 balls at the WACA [Western Australia Cricket Association] in 2006. I have seen, as well, Terry Alderman bowling himself towards a tally of 41 wickets in 1989, how many of them LBW; and Mark Taylor, David Boon and Michael Slater making hundreds in the same innings at Lord's in 1993; and Ian Healy stumping Mark Butcher at Old Trafford in 1997, so quick that many around me in the stand didn't know what had happened; and Jason Gillespie taking 7 for 37 at Headingly in the same year; and hundreds by Ricky Ponting at Headingley in 1997 and 2001 – the second of these 'wasted', as it happens, because of a complacent declaration by stand-in captain Adam Gilchrist that seemed to infuriate no one else but me – and, again, at Old Trafford in 2005, this one not at all wasted but saving the day; and Mark Waugh *passim*, in his case, not just batting, elegant, relaxed, but also taking catches at second slip with the same apparent nonchalance and ease.

In 1989 I watched David Boon hit the winning runs at Old Trafford to regain the Ashes. In 1993, late on during an opening stand of 260 between Mark Taylor and Michael Slater, I heard the crowd at Lord's applauding ironically when one of the two (I don't remember which) played at a ball and missed; it had been the first England 'success' for a while. In 2001 I had a second close encounter with Richie Benaud, this time at Headingley. He came down from the TV commentary box, on his way out to the middle of the ground to present Simon Katich with his Australian cap, and walked along the row of seats in which I was standing with a friend. 'How're you doing?' he said as we made way for him. Doing fine, I was. Gilchrist's irresponsible declaration still lay in the future of the game about to begin.

It had to happen, finally, that I should travel to Australia, distant place of this passionate cricketing allegiance; and it did. I went in 2006–7 with Ian Holliday, the friend with whom I had also followed the series in 1997. Call it mere coincidence, or call it nothing at all, but *exactly* in the summer I chose to be there, Australia beat England in all five Tests for the first time in 86 years, to achieve a 5–0 clean sweep. How could I, for my part, not see Fate as having taken a hand?

It was, in any event, the holiday of a lifetime. Part of this was directly because of the cricket and matters related. Flying from Brisbane to Adelaide, I found myself in the seat next to Ian Healy, who was kind enough to talk to me about cricket for some of the journey. This was a double coincidence. It wasn't just me, Australia supporter in Australia for the first time and for the Ashes, finding myself in the seat next to ... *Heals*. More than that: I'd already come across him inside the airport, where he happened to be on the phone in the next booth as I checked my emails. I'd obtained his signature, together with good luck wishes, on my 3 Mobile series brochure! Next thing, not an hour afterwards, he strolls on to the plane and takes the adjacent seat, saying 'Hello Norm, small world.' Imagine my surprise when, talking later, he referred to the 1989 series as 'the one we stole'. Stole? At 4–0? But he reminded me of what the expectations had been at the beginning of that series. Then, once I was *in* Adelaide, Australia's victory there on the last afternoon was one of the most satisfying I have ever watched, a victory scarcely foreseeable at lunch on that final day and due as much as anything to English folly, but seized on by an Australian side with aggression and confidence to spare. The win at the SCG [Sydney Cricket Ground] to clinch the 5–0 result, and the 'party' afterwards to mark the simultaneous retirements of Warne, McGrath and Justin Langer, are still fresh in my memory. And visiting the five Test venues for the first time, places I'd been reading about for more than 50 years, meant a great deal to me in itself.

Beyond the boundary, aside from the cricket, it was the holiday of a lifetime for other reasons too. Here I was in the beautiful country of Australia at last, and though following the Test series didn't leave me much time for going about, I went about enough to get some feel for each of the five cities I spent time in, and to see – especially in Sydney, thanks to the immense hospitality of a friend – some of the natural splendours. Everywhere I went in Australia I received such kindness, hospitality and friendship, including help with obtaining tickets for the five Tests. The land only of a cricketing affiliation heretofore, and of my researches and imaginings in that department, Australia between November 2006 and January 2007 treated me like a returning son. Rather an old son, at 63; but what the hell – the time for it was then, and I wouldn't have had it in any other year by preference.

Now, as I write this [in January 2011], it is four years, give or take only a few days, since I returned from that unique holiday. Four short years, and the might of Australian cricket has all but disappeared. Ponting's side has lately been blown away by Andrew Strauss and his men. In 2010–11 Australia somehow managed a victory at Perth, but otherwise suffered three defeats by an innings. They went through days full of pain for them and their supporters, as their bowling looked all but threadbare and their batting not a whole lot better. Fragility is hardly the word for it: they were humiliated.

And it dawns on me, finally, that those twin but opposite images from my boyhood, of this great cricketing country, are no more than particularistic and exaggerated versions of a much more general experience we all have in following sport. You win some and you lose some. True, there are victories less crushing than those Australia enjoyed over England for much of the period 1989 to 2007; and there are defeats less one-sided and demoralizing than the ones Australia have just suffered. But when all is said and done, in victory and defeat in sport both the players and their followers partake to an extent of universal, atavistic experiences, willingly or unwillingly inflating the results in both directions so that these results often feel much better and worse, respectively, than they are. 'Crushed', after all, is only a metaphor and happens to nobody on a cricket field; players and supporters walk away and resume their lives. No one dies. The joy of victory, equally, though it can make a person's day or even their week or month, subsides; it gives way to more pressing, or just more continuous, preoccupations. Mighty and fragile in this domain, tough and feeble, are in their way symbols of life outside the cricketing arena: of how, for example, small disappointments, reverses, obstacles can turn a day into a bad day, and small welcome occurrences, or compliments, or pleasant surprises, can put a person, as the saying is, on top of the world. In cricket we live – as well as its beauties, its skills and its dramas – the ups and downs of life, and must know how to take them both, in order to appreciate the game's inner verities, its true stature.

And that other duality from my youth, the one that made the young South Africa supporter I was an Australia loyalist when the Ashes were in contention – this too points outwards into the world beyond the cricket field. Returning in January 2007 from that wonderful Australian holiday into the dark morning of the Manchester winter, where was I returning but home? I was returning to England, which had been to that point my home for 44 years, and one I would not, at my age, exchange for any other. Yet in cricket I have supported

Australia *against* England. It is the way of the world. There is something of the contingent and accidental in sporting allegiance. This is true even where the allegiance is based on national identity, or regional or local connection. Many times, the supporter just latches on to a team that is, in some way for him or her, 'to hand' – close by, in the news, winning something, boasting a great or attractive player or what have you. And the allegiance then both sticks and grows. Yet it matters – in the way and to the extent that it does matter – despite the adventitious nature of this origin. Of how much else in life is the same thing true. We are beings, we humans, with needs we have in common with others, with the shared abilities and concerns that make us, precisely, human, and with universal rights on account of these common traits. But we each have our own particularities and attachments, and these matter as much as anything does: our specific purposes, families, loves and loyalties. Accepting and respecting that combination of the general and particular, and getting it in a proper balance, is the art of just moral and political order.

In the years of my maturity Australia at cricket has been for me a continuous and special passion. It has been the very heart of my love for the greatest of all games.

Why does football matter?

I prefer short to long titles on blogposts. That's why I've posed the question like that. But, fully spelled out, it would be: why does football matter to those to whom it does matter, even if it also doesn't matter? The question is prompted by a column of Simon Kuper's ['Why I've Fallen out of Love with Football', *Financial Times Magazine*, 8 February 2013].

There are several strands to Simon's explanation, and most of them I find quite understandable: he's 'got too close to the adored object and seen what it's really like'; a lot of football is boring; there's too much repetition (including in watching Lionel Messi); the anger over refereeing decisions; and the hatred directed by rival fans at one another.

One strand, however, consists of football's not mattering. This is what Simon reports a friend of his as having realized, and it's how he's come to feel too. The same point is reflected in his comment on the vast critical apparatus attached to football when 'the media lack resources to cover actual news'.

Despite all that, here is why football matters. It matters because it isn't a reasonable expectation on anyone that they should devote all their time to paying attention to and trying to do something about things in the world that *really* matter, on account of affecting people adversely. Even if one thinks – as I do – that we have obligations as human beings to others in grave need, difficulty or danger, to demand of people that they give *all* of their time and attention to such things amounts to demanding of them that they sacrifice the whole part of their lives which might otherwise be given to pursuing their own enjoyments and their own happiness. That would be an exorbitant expectation.

Football matters to those to whom it does matter just in the way that, for others, ballet, music, walking in the countryside, literature, movies and gardening matter – in the way, indeed, that life, liberty and the pursuit of happiness matter. And those other things that, so to say, *really* matter often matter because they are about situations where life and liberty and the pursuit of happiness are being denied to others. If we care about that sort of denial, we should have no problem with the pursuit of happiness when it takes forms that do not happen to interest us.

That's how and why football matters.

Fiction like green vegetables?

You are an avid reader of fiction. Yes, you are – don't argue. You've always got a novel on the go. Soon after finishing one, you start another. (If you're absolutely determined that this isn't true of you, please either imagine that it is or look away now.) So, will you be pleased to be told that reading fiction is good for you? You can inform yourself of some research published in the July–August 2011 edition of the *Literary Review of Canada* purporting to show that 'people who read mainly fiction [have] substantially greater empathy than those who read mainly non-fiction'. They are better at identifying with others and understanding human relations:

> Fiction is not best thought of as something that is just made up. It is best thought of as narrative with the subject matter of selves in the social world. It is a simulation that is useful because negotiating the social world effectively is extremely tricky, requiring us to weigh up myriad interacting causes and effects. Just as computer simulations can help people negotiate complex tasks such as flying a plane, so novels, stories and dramas can help us understand the complexities of social life.

OK, now suppose that you got nothing overtly rewarding out of reading fiction but you knew it did you good, this sort of good above-described. Would you still read as much of it as you do? I doubt it. It's not that it does you good by making you a better person – assuming it really does do this – that attracts people to reading fiction; it's that it *gives* you something you don't otherwise get – alternative inner worlds or some such.

And if reading fiction is indeed good for you in the empathy-generating way, then it's excellent that we also enjoy it. So many enjoyable things turn out to be bad for us.

Jane Austen's kick

In the final chapter of *Mansfield Park*, Jane Austen allows the authorial 'I' to put in an appearance. This is her opening paragraph:
Let other pens dwell on guilt and misery. I quit such odious subjects as soon as I can, impatient to restore every body, not greatly in fault themselves, to tolerable comfort, and to have done with all the rest.

Quite a postmodern passage you might think, forcing it upon the attention of her readers that she is the creator of these people, Fanny Price, Edmund, Henry and Mary Crawford, and all the others in her cast of characters. She can restore them forthwith (or, at any rate, some of them) to tolerable comfort. Just like that. Shrewd as ever, though, Austen doesn't allow that thought to settle before following up, immediately, with this one:

> My Fanny, indeed, at this very time, I have the satisfaction of knowing, must have been happy in spite of everything. She must have been a happy creature in spite of all that she felt, or thought she felt, for the distress of those around her. She had sources of delight that must force their way. She was returned to Mansfield Park, she was useful, she was beloved; she was safe from Mr. Crawford …

Fanny *must* have been happy, she had compelling sources of delight – and this Jane Austen has the satisfaction of (factively) knowing, rather than simply determining. No sooner than it has been put in question, the *reality* of the world of Mansfield Park is reaffirmed. What is to be made of this swift one-two?

She's reminding us that her story is mere fiction and, the reminder once delivered, returning *inside* the fiction that Fanny and the others are real people. Alternatively, no – they *are* real people, those whose story she tells; but, as the teller, she has her rights and so may 'restore' some of them to tolerable comfort by a quicker rather than a slower telling.

A few pages later, look:

> I purposely abstain from dates on this occasion, that every one may be at liberty to fix their own, aware that the cure of unconquerable passions, and the transfer of unchanging attachments, must vary much as to time in different people. I only entreat every body to believe that exactly at the time when it was quite natural that it should be so, and not a week earlier, Edmund did cease to care about Miss Crawford, and became as anxious to marry Fanny as Fanny herself could desire.

She's done it again! We're all at liberty, seemingly, to decide on our own date for Edmund to be over his attachment to Mary Crawford, as if the whole thing were just made up. But – the author then says (and you better believe it) – his getting over her happened at the time that it 'naturally' would and 'not a week earlier'.

Only one conclusion is possible. Jane Austen anticipated the folly that goes under the name of postmodernism and delivered it a sound kick. She tempts her readers with the suggestion that this is all mere play of the mind, then corrects them by her insistence that there's a reality out there that constrains even the novelist, even the creator of fictions – in its way.

February 07, 2012

It's his party, you can cry if you want to

If a lot of people are celebrating and generally making a hoo-ha about something or somebody, you can bet your finest silk garment that someone will in due course pop up and start throwing cold water. Just so, with respect to Dickens today on his bicentenary – and John Sutherland, who says 'Enough with the Charles Dickens hero-worship' (*The Guardian* February 6, 2012]. I don't get it. Nobody is obliged to read Dickens, much less to like his books, and nobody has to join the party. So keep out of it if that's your preference. But the cold water? Let those who want to enjoy the man's books do so, why don't you.

I mean it's only *Charles Dickens*. Once you go beyond expressing your own lack of enthusiasm to mount a general case against the size of the party, you're bound to perpetrate some folly or other. And so Sutherland does. Thus, by a reference to Julian Barnes's winning of the Booker for *The Sense of an Ending*, he (Sutherland) has a pop at 'elevating [Dickens] above all the others as "the champ"'. This reflects, so he says, an 'ethos of competition' in which if some win, others lose – like all the superb novels that didn't win the Booker and so became 'certified losers'; and, by implication, like all the other Victorian novelists who weren't Dickens. Come on, already! You can think – as I do – that *The Sense of an Ending* was a worthy winner without devaluing any other recent book. It's a literary prize (and everyone knows, or should do, how that works), not some golden ranking in the Hall of Eternity.

Similarly, it is Dickens's bicentenary year. It might therefore be OK for those who want to mark it to mark it, and without buying a fat pig. This doesn't, not in any way, entail disrespect for other English novelists. Me, I'm celebrating Dickens's birthday, even though I wouldn't rank him above Jane Austen. I'll celebrate her birthday too. Sutherland, by listing 10 Victorian novels, 'as good as, or better than, anything Dickens wrote', cautions us against forgetting the others: Eliot, *Middlemarch*; Hardy, *The Mayor of Casterbridge*; Brontë, *Jane Eyre*; other Brontë, *Wuthering Heights* ... My goodness, who knew? But let me point out one relevant consideration if you're talking comparisons, as Sutherland plainly is here. Set Charles Dickens against Emily Brontë, just for example, and he enjoys a certain advantage over her. No, it's not that he's male; and it's not that *Wuthering Heights* can't compete against many of the Dickens books and come out a winner. Through no fault of her own, Emily Brontë completed only one novel. Dickens created a fictional world so large, so abundant and so perceptive about the human predicament that he still speaks across the generations and in every language. The cold water just splashes back at those who throw it.

Ordinary women

In the years during which I taught a course on the Holocaust at Manchester, one of the topics I covered concerned gender aspects of that historical experience. We looked at women as victims and the ways in which their sufferings were similar to those of men and the ways in which they were different; at specific aspects to do with sexuality, pregnancy and the care of children; at the role of women in the resistance to Nazi brutality; and, inevitably also, at women as bystanders to and perpetrators of genocide. At the time I didn't know of any systematic study on women as perpetrators, but what was scattered across the Holocaust literature was pretty much the same range of behaviour as was to be found for men – from extreme cruelty, through 'run-of-the-mill' harshness, to the occasional example of a more humane woman camp guard who would try to mitigate the treatment being meted out as a matter of routine. In general the judgement of historians and other observers was that the behaviour of women perpetrators matched in cruelty that of male guards.

This may come as a surprise to some, but to me it never was. Women are people and while there are undoubtedly gender differences relevant to the role they can come to play in brutal episodes, as members of our species enough women will share those attributes of human nature that undermine, corrupt and provoke individuals to behave shockingly for there to be an adequate complement of them filling whatever spaces for brutality happen to be available at any given time.

A new book by Wendy Lower – *Hitler's Furies: German Women in the Nazi Killing Fields* – is reviewed by Roger Moorhouse in *The New Statesman*, October 3, 2013. It should throw some light on this unhappy topic:

> Distilling many years of research into the Holocaust, Lower focuses her account on the experiences of a dozen or so subjects ... ranging from provincial schoolteachers and Red Cross nurses to army secretaries and SS officers' molls. Despite coming from all regions of Germany and all walks of life, what they had in common was that they ended up in the Nazi-occupied east, where they became witnesses, accessories or even perpetrators in the Holocaust.
>
> Lower is scrupulously fair to her subjects, providing a potted biography of each, explaining their social and political background and examining the various motives – ambition, love, a lust for adventure – that propelled them to the 'killing fields'. This objectivity is admirable, particularly as most of the women swiftly conformed to Nazi norms of behaviour, at least in turning a blind eye to the suffering around them. One woman, a Red Cross nurse, organised 'shopping trips' to hunt for bargains in the local Jewish ghetto, while another, a secretary, calmly typed up lists of Jews to be 'liquidated', then witnessed their subsequent deportation.
>
> Most shocking of all are the accounts of the women who killed. One of Lower's subjects, a secretary-turned-SS-mistress, had the 'nasty habit', as one eyewit-

ness put it, of killing Jewish children in the ghetto, whom she would lure with the promise of sweets before shooting them in the mouth with a pistol. Lower presents another chilling example: that of an SS officer's wife in occupied Poland who discovered a group of six Jewish children who had escaped from a death-camp transport. A mother, she took them home, fed and cared for them, then led them out into the forest and shot each one in the back of the head.

Despite these horrors, Lower's book resists the temptation to wallow in emotive rhetoric; nor is it drily academic. She writes engagingly, wears her considerable erudition lightly and has opted to stick with a broad narrative account, comparing and contrasting but never allowing her analysis to outweigh the fundamental humanity of the stories. The book's power lies in its restraint.

Neither can *Hitler's Furies* be imagined as some sort of Woman's Hour rereading of the Holocaust. There is no special pleading for the subjects and the gender studies aspect of the book is kept well within bounds. Indeed, in analysing the women's progress from nurses and secretaries to accomplices and perpetrators, Lower is at times eager to emphasise that the forces that drove and shaped them were in some ways the same forces experienced by Germany's men – the seductive appeal of Nazism, the heady lawlessness of the occupied eastern territories and the 'new morality' of the SS.

It's worth remembering here that many of those women who committed crimes could not resort to the time-worn excuse that they were 'following orders'. They were not. They were merely reacting and adapting to their surroundings.

Heady lawlessness – never forget that.

Primo Levi and Jean Améry 4: shame

Having shown the clear difference of emphasis in the responses of Levi and Améry to their experiences at the hands of the Nazis, I now want to look beyond it, and explain why I think there is a deeper affinity between the two men than that contrast would suggest, and why it is of critical importance. For all that the category of hope plays its part in Levi's writing, he was not the sponsor of any redemptive vision in which hope or other humane qualities might make good the evils done across Nazi-occupied Europe, or might, as it were, 'level out' the human propensity for evil. For him, too, what had been done was not to be got over; it was an irredeemable atrocity. In this regard he and Améry are closer than they may at first appear. For Levi not only adverts repeatedly, both directly and indirectly, to the theme of hope, he also registers why social hope must be permanently qualified by the consciousness of the grave wrongs human beings have done and are ever capable of.

I go on in the rest of the present series of posts to enlarge upon this thesis. Between hope and resentment there is a middle term, and that term is 'shame'.

In Levi's Auschwitz story and reflections, shame figures in more than one way. There is a personal shame he confesses to having felt in certain situations, and having continued to feel subsequently. After being forced to witness a hanging, he and his friend Alberto are 'oppressed by shame'. Why? Because they stood by and did nothing to protest or intervene? Yes. That is a common response reported amongst survivors, even though to have done anything of the kind in such circumstances would have meant certain death. Later, having survived and returned, Levi had the worry that perhaps he and his fellow survivors had not sufficiently resisted, despite the fact that there was not much rational basis for such a regret. He had the worry, also, of 'having failed in terms of human solidarity'. He tells of himself and Alberto – who shared everything they managed to come by – not having included Daniele in the benefit of a small amount of extra water he found once, and being later, after they were liberated, chided about it by Daniele. Should Levi have been, belatedly, ashamed? He didn't know. But he was.

In any case, in connection with the horrors they had to witness at Auschwitz, Levi also wrote, in *The Truce*, of a shame more impersonal and far-reaching in scope:

> the shame which the just man experiences when confronted by a crime committed by another, and he feels remorse because of its existence, because of its having been irrevocably introduced into the world of existing things, and because his will has proven nonexistent or feeble, and was incapable of putting up a good defence.

He returned to this theme in *The Drowned and the Saved*, speaking now of a 'vaster shame, the shame of the world'. Levi described it thus:

> [T]he just among us, neither more nor less numerous than in any other human group, felt remorse, shame and pain for the misdeeds that others and not they had committed, and in which they felt involved, because they sensed that what had happened around them in their presence, and in them, was irrevocable. It would never again be able to be cleansed ...

In these two passages he connects – notwithstanding his own emphases on hope and its cognates – to the rational kernel in Améryan resentment. Note how the second passage repeats the thought present in the first: the crime is, the misdeeds are, *irrevocable*. It is a thought that threads its way through his writings about Auschwitz.

There is a scene described in *If This Is A Man* where, after a selection for the gas chamber, the prisoner Kuhn is praying, thanking God for not being one of those selected; and Levi writes:

> Kuhn is out of his senses. Does he not see Beppo the Greek in the bunk next to him, Beppo who is twenty years old and is going to the gas chamber the day after tomorrow and knows it ...? Does Kuhn not understand that what has happened today is an abomination, which no propitiatory prayer, no pardon, no expiation by the guilty, which nothing at all in the power of man can ever clean again?/

Nothing at all can ever clean again – the same thing is said in the passage I quoted just before from *The Drowned and the Saved*: 'it would never again be able to be cleansed'.

On the way back from Auschwitz to Turin, and passing through Vienna, Levi wrote of the anguish he and his comrades felt in that city, of 'the heavy threatening sensation of an irreparable and definitive evil which was present everywhere, nestling like gangrene in the guts of Europe and the world, the seed of future harm'. And in connection with other crimes – in Algeria, Vietnam, the Soviet Union, Chile, Argentina, Cambodia, and South Africa – he would say, in the same vein, 'I know no human act that can erase a crime'.

Let me interject here that by this insistence he did not mean to imply that forgiveness of the perpetrators was never appropriate. Any too easy forgiveness he was indeed not inclined towards. He withheld forgiveness *unless* the guilty had made a serious attempt to acknowledge the error of their ways; but if they did that, then they ceased to be enemies, and could be forgiven.

(Améry's view seems to have been similar, though expressed more sharply. He spoke disparagingly of Jews who, soon after the Holocaust, were 'trembling with the pathos of forgiveness'. They were 'distasteful' to him. He thought that forgiveness, when lazy and cheap, was immoral. But he seems also to have allowed the possibility of a form of moral resolution – though he judged it unlikely to occur – in which there would be a thoroughgoing German acknowledgement of the country's criminal past and a disowning of it.)

Whatever the circumstances in which forgiveness was or was not appropriate, however, Levi's treatment of shame meets Améry's holding on to the feeling of resentment, in the language which they use in common of the 'irreparable' and the 'irrevocable'. The crime that was the Nazi genocide taints the world; it ruins the moral universe. In a poem of 1985, Levi lets the millions who have died in vain threaten the world's political leaders so: 'If the havoc and the shame continue / We'll drown you in our putrefaction.'

'Drown' is the operative word. He applies it in this case to 'putrefaction', but it evokes another image used by him more than once: of the 'ocean of pain' that surrounded him and his fellow prisoners at Auschwitz, and nearly submerged them; of the 'sea of grief [that] has no shores, no bottom; no one can sound its depths'.

Like the torture suffered by Améry, for Levi the crime is never over and its scope is unmeasurable.

September 21, 2003

15 great jazz albums

If you're a regular reader of normblog and a thoughtful and discriminating one – refuse the characterization who will – then you'll know this had to happen. And you were right, so well done. In fact I have some political stuff on my mind, but nothing that can't wait. I've been wanting to compile this list for a while now, and what better time than on a quiet Sunday morning? Two constraints, both of them artificial but helping to keep the task manageable: (a) to get on the list the album has to be in my collection; and (b) nobody gets on the list twice (unless as a sideman on someone else's session).

Under these assumptions, here's my list of 15 great jazz albums. They aren't ranked, just in alphabetical order (by musician).

Cannonball Adderley, Somethin' Else (1958). In a way Cannonball is lucky to get on this list, given some of those who didn't make it. But this album is way out ahead of everything else of his that I know and it has to go on.

Louis Armstrong, The Complete Hot Five and Seven Recordings (1925–9). Ideally, I'd want to have some later Louis as well, say the The Complete Town Hall Concert (1947), but 'Hey, you made the rules, so handle it.' Apart from Armstrong himself, just listen to Johnny Dodds's clarinet solo on 'Struttin' with Some Barbecue'. And play 'Once in a While', or play it again. If it doesn't make you want to do whatever is the jazz equivalent of 'Yeeeehah', you need a talking to.

Art Blakey, Moanin' (1958). I've owned a copy of Moanin' since 1959, when I was just acquainting myself with the music, and my sister Sue sent a copy for me back from Johannesburg to Bulawayo with my Mom. It was my first Blue Note album, with the marvellous picture of Blakey taking up nearly the whole cover – and with that opening riff by Bobby Timmons.

Dave Brubeck, Jazz Goes to College (1954). There are some as turn up their noses at Brubeck. Too bad. And Paul Desmond was somethin' else.

John Coltrane, Giant Steps (1959). The title says it.

Miles Davis, Kind of Blue (1959). How I first came upon Kind of Blue was: I was in a record shop one day browsing for new stuff and it's playing over the shop's sound system. 'What **is** this?', I ask one of the guys, and he tells me, slightly surprised I wouldn't know what is possibly the greatest of all jazz albums. It's a problem for me that my rules forbid Miles's Complete Live at the Plugged Nickel (1965), but this point's already been dealt with.

Coleman Hawkins Encounters Ben Webster (1957). I'd want both these blokes on, so no better way to do it than to combine them. Money track: 'Shine On Harvest Moon'. Listen to it and then tell me you wouldn't rather have been able to play tenor sax like that than do just about anything which you **can** do.

Keith Jarrett (no, not the bloody Köln Concert, but) **At the Blue Note: The Complete Recordings** (1994). Like the book says: '[T]wo sets from each of three consecutive nights at the New York club. It might be considered warts-and-all but for the fact that there are no warts.'

Brad Mehldau, The Art of the Trio 3: Songs (1998). I don't have the musical expertise to be able to describe this adequately, but put on the opening track, 'Song-Song', and listen to what happens. Long slow dawdling intro, you're wondering where it's going, indeed **if** it's ever going, and then – oh, man – you're suddenly hit by the loveliest melodic passage and set of variations.

Modern Jazz Quartet, Pyramid (1959–60). There are some as turn up their noses at the MJQ, but see above, the response on Brubeck. I loved John Lewis's playing when I was 16 and I still do. To say nothing of Milt Jackson.

Thelonious Monk, Brilliant Corners (1956). To be honest, this is a bit like Bunuel on a list of great movies. He's got to be on it, but which movie? Same with Monk here. I can't leave him out. Any of a number of his albums would do, though.

Lee Morgan, The Sidewinder (1963). His greatest – with the marvellous Joe Henderson on tenor sax.

Oliver Nelson, Blues and the Abstract Truth (1961). Freddy Hubbard playing his socks off on the best track, 'Stolen Moments', and Eric Dolphy, like-wise, on flute.

Art Pepper Meets the Rhythm Section (1957). What to say about Art Pepper? Dunno. I just love his stuff, and it's like with Monk: this one will do; it'll more than do.

Jimmy Smith, The Sermon (1957–8). It reminds me of when I was a grad-uate student, and Wife of the Norm and I first started going out; and of friends then, Chris and Marion, Murat, Franny. Oh yes, and it really rocks.

Oy, the things I've had to omit. I hope JDC isn't a jazz fan and getting ready to pounce on me for missing out, well, Duke Ellington. But I'm willing to venture this. If you have a jazz collection of, say, 75 or more albums and don't have at least half – therefore eight – of these, your collection is ... less good than it might be.

And now: the thoughtful and discriminating reader aforesaid will have anticipated the following as well. I'm inviting entries for the normblog top 15 jazz albums poll. Please send me your nominations, any number up to, but no more than, 15. Closing date Sunday 5 October, 11.59 PM normblog time. Come on, have a go, enter. You know it'll be fun.

Thinking about war

Writing as a guest blogger on Steven Levenson's blog at the *Washington Post* [on 26 October 2010] Richard Rubenstein claims that there have been five major justifications used for the US going to war. They are: self-defence, evil enemy, humanitarian duty, patriotism, and last resort. Rubenstein goes on to say that because these justifications have been invoked in support of unnecessary and unjust wars, 'each one should trigger a series of skeptical questions'. He's right, each one should. Never mind that the justifications have been misused in the past; they should trigger the questions anyway. War, to state the obvious, is a deadly business, and its deadliness can run into huge numbers. So every justification for a particular war must be critically scrutinized.

Yet when one looks at Rubenstein's own suggestions for what the sceptical questions ought to be, you could get the idea that he's not really giving these justifications a run for their money. Take the example of what he says about humanitarian duty:

> Humanitarian duty is often invoked to convince us to intervene to save oppressed peoples. But if we assume that America alone is capable of liberating the oppressed without becoming a new oppressor, we make the fatal assumption of our unique virtue and fruitlessly deny our own 'dark side'.

This is just a series of logically arbitrary assertions. To think that America has a humanitarian duty in a given instance one need not believe that that country *alone* is capable of fulfilling the duty; one might think merely that it is best-placed in the circumstances, or that it shares this duty with others but should not wait on these others in any case since the matter is pressing, or that it should take a lead. By the same token, to assume a duty needs no supposition of *unique* virtue. The duty may be general and one or other of those on whom it putatively falls feel that they for their part shouldn't shirk it, whatever others may do. Nor does anyone – a person or a country – have to deny their own 'dark side' in trying to act well. Indeed, it may be an awareness of this dark side that partly motivates a sense of humanitarian duty in certain circumstances. The words 'never again' come to mind, as applied to genocide.

Or take this:

> Claims of self-defense should make us ask who, exactly, is threatening us and what the threat consists of. If U.S. troops occupying another nation are attacked by local insurgents, is a war of counter-insurgency needed to defend our nation or merely to secure some imperial outpost?

Well, yes. But what if those aren't the circumstances? What if US troops aren't occupying Afghanistan, say, and there's an attack on New York and Washington orchestrated by a terrorist organization being hosted there?

All of Rubenstein's sceptical questions work in the same way: to suggest easy put-downs of the possibility that on some occasions war may be justified. But his approach doesn't encourage serious reflection about the issue of war and its difficulties. The first premise of such reflection is the simultaneous recognition that war is a calamity, bringing with it multiple horrors, *and* that sometimes wars are necessary to avert or defeat other great evils.

I just finished re-reading *Johnny Got His Gun* by Dalton Trumbo. I first read it at the age of sixteen and I have remembered it as one of the most powerful anti-war novels I've ever come across. I wanted to see if it held up as being this. It does. Not only that, but it's an ingenious piece of fiction in the unique and terrifying inner world of its protagonist that it imaginatively creates for the reader. *Johnny Got His Gun* was inspired by the experience of World War I and was first published, in 1939, on the eve of World War II. In an introduction written last year for the Penguin Modern Classics edition, E.L. Doctorow says: 'During World War Two Trumbo withdrew his novel from publication as an inappropriate pacifist tract championed by American fascists who wanted the United States to stay out of the war against Hitler'.

To keep on keepin' on

As he turns 70 today, those of us who have been following Bob Dylan's music from the off are reminded of how old we are. In my 21st year I went home to Bulawayo for the Oxford summer vacation and in my suitcase, along with a bunch of philosophy books and some texts of classical Marxism, I carried a copy of *The Freewheelin' Bob Dylan*. I wanted to introduce him to my family. One of my more vivid early Dylan memories is of sitting around one evening in the house at 6 Birchenough Road, playing 'Don't Think Twice, It's All Right', 'Talkin' World War III Blues' and the rest of those wonderful songs to a company that included one or two first-time-up sceptics. Never mind the songs, was the gist of their scepticism, but could the guy even sing, with that thin, not-quite-tuneful voice of his?

My, but could he sing. And could he write songs. For what this anniversary also brings home is how Dylan's albums and his lyrics have punctuated the lives of all those of us who have never stopped listening. Two years and a few months younger than he is, I can trace a line through times and events – from Oxford and Bulawayo to Manchester and, now, Cambridge – and associate them with the songs of Bob Dylan. Just over a year on from that Bulawayo gathering, in late 1965 I'm back in Oxford, in my first postgraduate year, Adèle and I have just started going out together, and the Dylan songs of that period are from *Bringing It All Back Home*. To this day it remains a usage of ours in appropriate circumstances – when one of us is on the point of leaving the house, for example – to ask, 'Do I have everything I need, am I an artist, do I not look back?' Those words of his, on each succeeding album. Those lines that would stick and never leave you. From the greatest song on *Bringing It All Back Home*, not only (most famously) 'But even the president of the United States / Sometimes must have to stand naked', but also 'he not busy being born is busy dying'. And *also* 'You discover that you'd just be one more / Person crying'.

How, before he's passed his first quarter century, can he know what some people need a lifetime to learn and others never learn at all? There's a song on *Freewheelin'* that I wouldn't till now have picked out as being among the best on that album; it's 'Bob Dylan's Dream'. Listening to it again a few days ago, I was taken aback to see that it makes more sense to a person who's passed 50 than it would to most people in their early 20s.

And so it has continued. Married, and living in a flat on Barlow Moor Road after we'd moved to Manchester, in 1967 we listened a lot, me and Adèle, to *John Wesley Harding*. That big fat moon sure was gonna shine like a spoon. Then, in the 1970s, a succession of further albums grabbed somewhere at one's imagination, each of them imprinting itself with a song or three – with a melody, a line, a way of phrasing: *Planet Waves* and *Blood on the Tracks* and *Desire*. Like all genius, it leaves you in a state of semi-shock. To do all this in so short a time. In our first house, in Mayville Drive, I listened to the two unforgettable love songs that close off *Planet Waves*. From 'Never Say Goodbye':

> *My dreams are made of iron and steel*
> *With a big bouquet*
> *Of roses hanging down*
> *From the heavens to the ground.*

A gem in its own right, this track serves merely as a prelude to the one that follows – 'Wedding Song' – which is a magnificent testimony to the infinity of love, whatever the future should hold. With *Blood on the Tracks* I was riveted by 'Idiot Wind', blowing 'like a circle around my skull / From the Grand Coulee Dam to the Capitol'; and after *Desire* how could you not want that 'one more cup of coffee before I go'? In the 1980s, in our second house, although by now I thought the best of Bob was behind him, I could still be bowled over by a track here or there. On *Infidels* 'Man of Peace' was Dylan at the top of his game again: 'You know sometimes Satan comes as a man of peace' – and that remains a fact. 'I and I', likewise, I could listen to without ever exhausting it. I *have* listened and listened to it, more times than I know the number of. On each occasion I have a different thought about possible meanings.

In that second house, in Danesmoor Road where we lived for 27 years, both our daughters grew into adults. In due course they too started listening to the man and they drew my attention to things in his songs which I hadn't noticed. So much is there in them that each listener will tell you something new. That Dylan's music wasn't just of its time but would continue to captivate new generations my children soon made clear to me.

Can he do any wrong musically? Yes, he can, of course. Just over five years ago, I saw him live in Manchester and it wasn't the best musical experience I've had, not by far. It wasn't even the best Bob Dylan experience. The original songs are better than he sometimes sings them live. But relative to what he has done over the last five decades, this is a quibble.

Out walking the other day in Cambridge, I listened again to *The Freewheelin' Bob Dylan*. Those songs aren't merely wonderful; as a *set* of songs they are breathtaking.

Epilogue:
reflections on the work of Norman Geras

Terry Glavin

I cannot place exactly when it was that I first encountered the work of Norm Geras, except that it was early in the first decade of the twenty-first century, at the height of the disorientation and mass lunacy brought about by the events of 11 September 2001. I was living on a small island off Canada's west coast, where I'd retreated from the daily newspaper racket to write books and raise my kids, and it was as though the entire Anglosphere was undergoing a kind of collective psychotic episode. There were times when I was reminded of old stories from the darker days on the coast. In the late 1930s, fishermen in the isolated cannery towns up the rainforest inlets had no idea whether the outside world had gone mad entirely, so they'd turn the dials of their shortwave radios to find some reassuring news: *This is the BBC World Service ...*

It's not that I'd dropped out of society or something. I was as engaged with the world as I'd ever been. A book I was writing at the time was taking me to the Russian Far East, Central America, the Himalayas, the arctic coast of Norway and other such places. I'd return to my island for long stretches, to sort out my notes and to write, and off I'd go again. I was still contributing regularly and occasionally to various magazines and newspapers. It wasn't the physical isolation that put me in these straits. It was more like an abiding sensation of estrangement from the mood of the times, from the consensus of all the intellectual, activist and literary circles in which I'd always moved.

It was mainly for some sort of reassurance, then, that I found myself increasingly tuning in to Norm's web log. Here was a genial Marxist professor of eclectic interests, from Manchester, around whom a constellation of writers, academics, artists, activists and eccentrics moved in conversation and friendly contention. Everyone spoke in a lexicon with which I was at least familiar. Their concerns were among my own. It was a kind of meeting place where intellectuals from a wide variety of backgrounds and genres and disciplines were introduced and sometimes profiled and interviewed. Reading Normblog always meant learning something, and it was what I imagined it must have been like, hearing the reassuring sound of far-off voices from a wireless in a fishboat galley, with news and analyses of the most momentous events of the day. Normblog was an unapologetically left-wing place, of at the very least a liberal milieu, and yet neither the host nor any of the contributors had lost their damn minds. There was even the occasional digression into cricket, and film, and country music.

By the time Norm's conversations evolved into the Euston Manifesto, Norm's helpfulness and the significance of his work was made plain in the way the modest document was greeted with such livid fury from so many on the left. A mere re-articulation of bedrock liberal and left-wing principles, and it was enough to set shrill voices to screaming. The manifesto became the central document in what Keith Kahn-Harris described, not unreasonably, in the *Guardian* as 'the most serious split within the left since the Soviet invasion of Hungary in 1956'. After writing favourably about the manifesto in an essay for the *Toronto Globe and Mail*, I went on to experience firsthand the enduring rage that lingered as a commonplace response to the Eustonards' impudence. But more than that, I came to know several of the Canadian signatories, and I'd go on to join with them in a variety of collaborations. A criticism one hears is that the Euston Manifesto failed to result in some sort of formalized political movement, but perhaps its greatest purpose was best expressed by the University of Toronto philosopher Paul Franks, who told me: 'It's just good to know there are some kindred spirits out there'.

After all these years it is remarkable how well Norm's works hold up, how immediately relevant his observations still appear, and how obviously necessary it was for the Euston Manifesto to set out a principled dissent from the orthodoxies of the left's hegemonic 'narrative' at the time. That is something that must be remembered.

It should also be well remembered that the plunging of those two airliners into the World Trade Center in New York on September 11, 2001 had caused something very much like a blunt trauma wound to the Anglosphere's cerebral membrane. It was such a shock to the mass-media system that it set off a sort of collective psychotic episode. The collapse of the twin towers coincided almost exactly with the emergence of ubiquitous digital technology and the Age of YouTube, allowing the instantaneous transmission of easily manipulable imagery that only the largest news organizations had been capable of producing. The 11 September atrocities were recorded by scores of cell-phone cameras. The clips were posted online in grotesque, round-the-clock re-enactments from almost every conceivable angle. Amateurs could easily patch together scenes and script to produce a nominally persuasive 'false flag' conspiracy-theory documentary with all the production values of a CBS *60 Minutes*' special report. And that's exactly what the amateurs behind the wildly popular 'Loose Change' accomplished. The celebrity filmmaker Michael Moore produced something similar but more sophisticated with *Fahrenheit 911*, earning unprecedented industry profits for a documentary film.

It didn't help that the events of 11 September 2001 occurred at a time when the dominant forms of criticism across the post-Cold War intellectual milieu were rapidly trending away from the traditions of empiricism and evidence-based inquiry and argument. The very notion of objective reality was giving way to a primacy of 'narrative', to postmodernist subjectivity and relativism. The 'Truthiness' that American satirists Stephen Colbert and Jon Stewart would later employ to amusingly critique the Republican right in 2005 had an embarrassment of 'left' antecedents. What happened on 11 September was like an Armageddon out of Hollywood, except it was all very real, and we all witnessed it live in real time and reconfigured later in countless iterations; freed from the burdens of evidence we were all capable of divining whatever 'truth' and meaning we wanted from it. How, then, to make sense of it all?

The otherwise firmly isolationist George W. Bush, elected only nine months earlier, had brought into his administration a small coterie of neoconservatives, so there were clear explanations and analyses and remedies at hand on the Right. There were ways to comprehend it all. The road forward required the projection of hard American power to unilaterally enforce an unforgiving and long overdue global-capitalist order upon the chaos that flowed from the collapse of the Cold War and the malingering of the Bill Clinton years. A lot of people migrated rightward as a result, sometimes directly as a kind of recoil response from what was on offer from the left. I didn't.

It was never going to be easy to articulate a coherent meaning from 9/11 and to situate the magnitude of the horror in ways that could be made to conform with the left's prevailing paradigmatic narratives. The Taliban were not exactly the Tupamaros. Al Qaida was not the Viet Cong. Saddam Hussein was not Daniel Ortega. But by the time the twentieth century came to a close, in the main currents on the left, in the humanities and social sciences, and in nearly all the places where the left used to be, progressive internationalism had been supplanted by crude forms of anti-globalisation – almost exclusively anti-Americanism, anti-Zionism and Third Worldism. Left-wing politics had been largely uprooted from conventional class politics. Postmodernist theory and the tropes of the counter-culture had come to stand in for socialism. Radical analysis had given way to the radical-chic. And suddenly, here was a big-screen spectacle, a vividly horrific mass atrocity carried out in Manhattan, ground zero of global capitalism, in plain view of the Statue of Liberty across the Hudson River. What was to be done?

If there is a single point when it can be said that the left's hegemonic narrative for the coming years was inaugurated, that the die was fatally cast and the primary expression of left-wing activism for more than a decade was set in motion, there is no better marker than 18 October 2001. At the Massachusetts Institute of Technology, the famous linguist and critic Noam Chomsky presented his seminal speech, 'The New War on Terror'.

While Norm Geras's writings and commentary retain a surprisingly vivid and prescient sense about them all these years later, what is astonishing about Chomsky's definitive assessment of the state of affairs in late 2001 is how lazy, sophomoric and downright crazy it appears now. It is useful to recall that, at the time, Chomsky was one of the top ten most-cited authorities in the humanities, and even his nemesis the *New York Times* considered him 'arguably the most important intellectual alive today'.

To Chomsky, the ongoing events of the real world in 2011 didn't even matter. Evidence didn't matter. Besides, 'the US doesn't want to present evidence', and in any case it didn't even matter to Chomsky who the perpetrators of the 9/11 atrocities were. Chomsky was willing to go so far as to concede that it 'looked obvious' that Islamists of the sort Osama bin Laden commanded were probably involved. But so what? 'Whether they were involved or not nobody knows. It doesn't really matter much.'

What mattered was that it was the fault of the CIA and other intelligence agencies for having incubated Islamists in the first place, and in the second place 9/11 was a 'small crime' compared to American outrages over the years, which Chomsky enumerated in a rambling and predictable run-through of horrors in Haiti, Costa Rica, Nicaragua, the Philippines, Hawaii, Mexico and so on. Chomsky disgraced himself by accusing the Bush administration of planning a 'genocide' in Afghanistan by an intent to 'impose massive starvation on millions of people' (Chomsky was later obliged to revisit this crackpot utterance – which he did by simply denying he'd said it, even though his words had been videotaped and transcribed). But what was Chomsky's way forward? What was to be done?

The thing to do was to take advantage of the mood of 'increased openness' that the 11 September atrocities had created in order to exploit the uncertainties of the time, Chomsky counselled. As an example, he favourably cited an article that had appeared in *USA Today* on 'life in the Gaza Strip'. And that was it. That was all that was required to close one's eyes to the world. Just retreat into a comforting counter-culture narrative. 'It doesn't really matter much' what is happening in the real world outside.

It would not be fair to single out Chomsky as the sole culprit for the indecencies that would characterise the so-called 'anti-war' movement in the years that followed: its open alliances with Khomeinist thugs, its Gaza flotilla escapades, its fundraising for Hamas, its serial betrayal of Afghan secularists and feminists and its rousing chorus of 'we had it coming' every time a psychopath shouted Allahu Akbar and went on a killing spree in London or Ottawa or Paris. But it is fair to notice that Chomsky would end up getting exactly what he wanted.

Geras and the Eustonards did not. There was no significant realignment that reached out 'beyond the socialist Left towards egalitarian liberals and others of unambiguous democratic commitment', as the Euston Manifesto counselled. There was a flowering of minor initiatives, such as the work of Britain's Labour Friends of Iraq. I like to think of the Canada–Afghanistan Solidarity Committee, of which I was a co-founder, as another small example. But in the main, the Chomksyite left prevailed.

It stopped no war, and with its Israel Apartheid Weeks and its Troops Out extravaganzas, it sucked the life out of all the spaces where a genuine international peace movement might have flourished. It smothered in the cradle every opportunity to build effective solidarity between what could have been a robust and well-resourced Euro-American left and its natural allies everywhere else in the world. Wherever the Chomskyite left did not prove itself wholly useless to anti-authoritarian struggle, it served as an active collaborator on the side of the tyrants.

This is a bitter pill to expect anyone within what one might call the 'actually-existing left' to swallow, so its leaders simply refuse to do so by ignoring the surfeit of incriminating evidence against them and fabricating evidence in their favour when the going gets tough. In the end, 'the most serious split within the left since the Soviet invasion of Hungary in 1956' did not pit the Stop the War Coalition and its satellites on one side against Norm Geras and the Eustonards and the American leftists around Michael Walzer's *Dissent Magazine* on the other. There was a split all right. But as the twenty-first century wore on, the most 'serious' split within the left since 1956 set the main bodies of the Euro-American left against millions of leftists, liberals, secularists, feminists, democrats, reformists and democratic revolutionaries engaged in clandestine agitation, open freedom struggles and desperate revolutions across the Maghreb, the Levant and Central Asia. When our comrades on these front lines needed us most, the left of the NATO capitals was either simply not there for them, or was actively campaigning against their demands and their interests, or was actively advocating for the positions of their worst tormentors.

I noticed this first and most vividly in Afghanistan, where I'd spent some time, mostly 'outside the wire', between 2008 and 2010. Back in Canada – as in Britain and the United States – the left-wing position was universally 'troops out'. In Canada, perhaps most absurdly, the mainline left-wing position was more elaborate: troops out, then send emissaries back to hector the Afghans on the virtues of a negotiated power-sharing and peace deal with Mullah Omar's Taliban. This was presented as an innovative, distinctly Canadian, honest-broker, anti-war position. To believe that, you'd have to ignore the fact that it was the long-held position of the crypto-fascist Afghan Mellat party, and had been more or less the unstable Afghan president Hamid Karzai's big idea as far back as 2003 as well. By 2010 it had become more or less the establishment position in Washington and London, too.

It should tell you something that this was the opposite of what our Afghan comrades wanted. Here is just one of several similar assertions that went routinely ignored by fashionable opinion in the world's more opulent neigh-bourhoods. In January 2010, delegates from more than two hundred Afghan women's rights and civil society organisations met at the Intercontinental Hotel in Kabul and crafted an eight-point consensus statement that began this way: 'Based on the persistent violation of the rights of women and men by the Taliban, whether when in power or after, objections were clearly and strongly expressed by all parties participating in this meeting regarding any negotia-tion with the Taliban.' The consensus statement was unambiguous: The Inter-national Declaration of Human Rights is 'non-negotiable'. No power-sharing with criminals. No to removing the names of Taliban leaders from UN terrorist lists. Yes to Taliban fighters who desert their ranks, but no to Taliban leaders lured into power-sharing with the promise of money and power. 'We strongly urge the international community to oppose the funding of any program that offers further support of terrorists and the Taliban.'

Washington and London proceeded anyway to do exactly what the Afghan democrats asked the 'international community' not to do. As expected, the peace-talks and power-sharing idea has failed utterly. The Taliban presses on with its campaigns of terror against the Afghan people, in the not unreasonable expectation that the 'anti-war' movement will solidify its gains before Afghan democracy fully takes root. At least Karzai's gone. At least there's that.

Another notable confluence of fervent left-wing opinion in the NATO capitals and the positions of the anti-democratic elites in the region was on the subject of drone strikes targeting Taliban positions in Pakistan's tribal areas. Among the soft-palmed of Rawalpindi and Islamabad, Los Angeles and London, US drone strikes are unpardonable violations of Pakistani sovereignty and imperialist war-making. The opposite view is taken by the left-wing polit-ical leadership of the Federally-Administered Tribal Areas and Khyber-Pakh-tunkwa, including the Talib-harried districts of Swat, Malakand and Buner. Here's what the local Awami National Party, the Pukhtunkhwa Mili Awami Party, the traditional Pashtun 'Red Shirt' secularist movement and the Amn Tehrik Peace Coalition had to say on the subject: 'NATO and ISAF are sent to Afghanistan under UN mandate. NATO and ISAF should stay in Afghani-stan until terrorism is uprooted, foreign interference in Afghanistan must be stopped and the institutions of army and police are established on solid foot-ings.' As for what the locals think about peace deals with Talibs: 'These people do not support any peace deals with the militants ... it is the [US] drone attacks which they support the most.'

This bizarre contradiction between what might be indelicately described as the leftish postures of rich white people and the poor people on the front lines of freedom struggles has been observed most astutely by the British-Ira-nian feminist Maryam Namazie. She describes the 'anti-war' movement of the NATO capitals as an anti-colonial movement animated by perspectives that coincide with those of the ruling classes in the so-called Third World. Its analysis is 'Eurocentric, patronising and even racist'. Its politics deny the existence of universal values and imagine the concept of human rights as 'Western', thereby imposing on the vast majority of the subject people 'the most reactionary elements of culture and religion, which is that of the ruling class'.

Far greater than the abandonment of Iraqi trade unionists and democrats and by orders of magnitude more disgraceful than its routinely toxic interventions in the Israeli–Palestinian agony was the Euro-American left's abdication of any effective duty of solidarity to the Middle East's young democrats during the tectonic eruptions of the Arab Spring. Perhaps most disgraceful is the case of Syria, where the 'anti-war movement' has had its way at every turn, and the death toll at the time of this writing has been estimated at 470,000, killed mostly by Bashar Assad and his allies in the Iranian Qods Force and its militias, Hezbollah and lately, Russian bombers.

Like Maryam Namazie, Yassin Al Haj Saleh, a leading intellectual among Syria's revolutionary democrats, holds no illusions about the 'progressive' role played by the Euro-American left. Its abstentionism, now triumphant among the cultural elites of the NATO countries, is 'better suited for the right and the ultra-right fascists', says Saleh. 'I am afraid that it is too late for the leftists in the West to express any solidarity with the Syrians in their extremely hard struggle … My impression about this curious situation is that they simply do not see us; it is not about us at all. Syria is only an additional occasion for their old anti-imperialist tirades … rank-and-file Syrians, refugees, women, students, intellectuals, human rights activists, political prisoners, do not exist.'

Norm Geras could have written that. We'd corresponded, but I'd never met him, and even so I came to feel as though I knew Norm Geras the way one knows a wise uncle, an old friend. Maybe Norm would have had some further insight into the bleak phenomenon Saleh describes, perhaps a way of looking at it that might at least make everything a bit more comprehensible, that might even notice something possibly redeeming and humane about our nature. More than anything I expect he'd have been able to discern at least something hopeful in all the despair. But he's gone, and I miss him terribly.

Norman Geras:
the complete bibliography

An online version of this bibliography is available at normblog.typepad.com.

1970

'Lévi Strauss and Philosophy', *Journal of the British Society for Phenomenology*, Vol. 1, No. 3, October 1970, pp. 50–60.

1971

'Essence and Appearance: Aspects of Fetishism in Marx's *Capital*', *New Left Review*, No. 65, January–February 1971, pp. 69–85.

'Essence et apparence: aspects du fétichisme dans *le Capital* de Marx', *Les Temps Modernes* (Paris), No. 304, November 1971, pp. 626–650.

1972

'Althusser's Marxism: An Account and Assessment', *New Left Review*, No. 71, January–February 1972, pp. 57–86.

'Marx and the Critique of Political Economy', in Robin Blackburn (ed.), *Ideology in Social Science*, Fontana, London, 1972, pp. 284–305.

'Marx and the Critique of Political Economy', in Robin Blackburn (ed.), *Ideology in Social Science*, Fontana, London 1972, pp. 284–305.

'Political Participation in the Revolutionary Thought of Leon Trotsky', in Geraint Parry (ed.), *Participation in Politics*, Manchester University Press, Manchester, 1972, pp. 151–168.

1973

'Marxism and Proletarian Self-Emancipation', *Radical Philosophy*, No. 6, Winter 1973, pp. 20–22.

'Rosa Luxemburg: Barbarism and the Collapse of Capitalism', *New Left Review*, No. 82, November–December 1973, pp. 17–37.

1975

'Rosa Luxemburg After 1905', *New Left Review*, No. 89, January–February 1975, pp. 3–46.

1976

'La teoria del crollo e il significato della formula "socialismo o barbarie"', in *Rosa*

Luxemburg e lo sviluppo del pensiero marxista (Annali della fondazione Lelio e Lisli Basso, Vol. 2), Gabriele Mazzotta, Milan, 1976, pp. 143–162.

Review of Lelio Basso: *Rosa Luxemburg – A Reappraisal, Political Studies*, Vol. xxiv, No. 1, March 1976, pp. 96–98.

The Legacy of Rosa Luxemburg, NLB, London, 1976 (paperback edition, Verso, 1983; second printing 1985), 210 pp.

1977

'Althusser's Marxism: An Assessment', in New Left Review (eds), *Western Marxism – A Critical Reader*, NLB, London, 1977, pp. 232–272.

'Über die Massentätigkeit im revolutionären Denken Leo Trotzkis', *Kritik* (Berlin), No. 14, 1977, pp. 25–44.

'Luxemburg and Trotsky on the Contradictions of Bourgeois Democracy', in Robin Blackburn (ed.), *Revolution and Class Struggle: A Reader in Marxist Politics*, Fontana, Glasgow, 1977, pp. 302–313

'Lenin, Trotsky and the Party', *International*, Vol. 4, No. 2, Winter 1977, pp. 3–8.

1978

Japanese translation in Japanese edition of Lelio Basso et al., *Rosa Luxemburg e lo sviluppo del pensiero marxista*, Biblioteca sine titulo, Tokyo, 1978, pp. 114–151.

'Rosa Luxemburg: la huelga de masas', in 'Rosa Luxemburg Hoy', special number of *Materiales* (Barcelona), 1978, pp. 115–129.

A Actualidade de Rosa Luxemburgo, Edicoes Antidoto, Lisbon, 1978, 235 pp.

1979

Rosa Luxemburg: Kämpferin für einen emanzipatorischen Sozialismus, Verlag Olle & Wolter, Berlin, 1979, 189 pp.

'Literature of Revolution', *New Left Review*, Nos 113–114, January–April 1979, pp. 3–41.

1980

Actualidad del pensamiento de Rosa Luxemburgo, Ediciones Era, Mexico, 1980, 172 pp.

Masas, Partido y Revolucion, Editorial Fontamara, Barcelona, 1980, 122 pp.

'Sensibilità letteraria e cultura politica nel giovane Trockij', in 'Trockij nel movimento operaio del xx secolo', special number of *Il Ponte* (Florence), November–December 1980, pp. 1132–1180.

1981

'Classical Marxism and Proletarian Representation', *New Left Review*, No. 125, January–February 1981, pp. 75–89.

'Leon Trotsky', in Justin Wintle (ed.), *Makers of Modern Culture*, Routledge & Kegan Paul, London, 1981, pp. 525–527.

1982

'Trotsky and Rosa Luxemburg: On the Political Representation of the Proletariat', in Francesca Gori (ed.), *Pensiero e azione politica di Lev Trockij*, Leo S. Olschki, Florence, 1982, pp. 165–183.

1983

'Rosa Luxemburg', in Tom Bottomore (ed.), *A Dictionary of Marxist Thought*, Basil Blackwell, Oxford, 1983, pp. 293–294.

'Fetishism', in Tom Bottomore (ed.), *A Dictionary of Marxist Thought*, Basil Blackwell, Oxford, 1983, pp. 165–166. (Second edition: 1991, pp. 190–191.)

'Louis Althusser', in Tom Bottomore (ed.), *A Dictionary of Marxist Thought*, Basil Blackwell, Oxford, 1983, pp. 15–18.

Marx and Human Nature: Refutation of a Legend, Verso/NLB, London, 1983 (Reprinted 1985, 1994), 127 pp.

'For Human Nature', *International*, Vol. 8, Nos 1–2, January–April 1983, pp. 20–21. (Excerpt)

The Legacy of Rosa Luxemburg, NLB, London, 1976 (paperback edition, Verso, 1983; second printing 1985), 210 pp.

'Den klassiska marxismen och proletariatets representation', *Rådsmakt* (Stockholm), No. 15, March 1983, pp. 14–22.

1984

'The Controversy About Marx and Justice', in 'A Marxian Approach to the Problem of Justice', *Philosophica* (Ghent), Vol. 33 (1), 1984, pp. 33–86.

1985

The Legacy of Rosa Luxemburg, NLB, London, 1976 (paperback edition, Verso, 1983; second printing 1985), 210 pp.

1986

Literature of Revolution: Essays on Marxism, Verso, London, 1986, 271 pp.

1987

'Rosa Luxemburg', in David Miller (ed.), *The Blackwell Encyclopaedia of Political Thought*, Basil Blackwell, Oxford, 1987, pp. 299–301.

'Louis Althusser', in David Miller (ed.), *The Blackwell Encyclopaedia of Political Thought*, Basil Blackwell, Oxford, 1987, pp. 9–10.

'Socialism and Democracy', *Africa Perspective* (Johannesburg), New Series, Vol. 1, Nos 3 & 4, June 1987, pp. 117–123.

'Post-Marxism?', *New Left Review*, No. 163, May–June 1987, pp. 40–82.

'Marxism and Moral Advocacy', *Manchester Papers in Politics* (Department of Government, University of Manchester), Manchester, 1987, 18 pp.

Review of Elzbieta Ettinger, *Rosa Luxemburg: A Life*, *New Statesman*, Vol. 113, No. 2929, 15 May 1987, pp. 27–28.

1988

'The Controversy About Marx and Justice', in Eric Corijn, Alain Meynen, Peter Scholliers and Luk Van Langenhove (eds), *Veelzijdig Marxisme*, Instituut Voor Marxistische Studies, Brussels, 1988, Vol. 2, pp. 355–431.

'Socialism and Democracy', *Manchester Left*, No. 1, December 1987–January 1988, pp. 27–29.

'Marxisme en het pleidooi voor de moraal', in L.W. Nauta and J.P. Koenis (eds), *Een toekomst voor het socialisme?*, Van Gennep, Amsterdam, 1988, pp. 185–201.
'Ex-Marxism Without Substance: Being A Real Reply to Laclau and Mouffe', *New Left Review*, No. 169, May–June 1988, pp. 34–61.

1989
'The Controversy About Marx and Justice', in Alex Callinicos (ed.), *Marxist Theory*, Oxford University Press, Oxford, 1989, pp. 211–267.
'Our Morals: The Ethics of Revolution', in Ralph Miliband, Leo Panitch and John Saville (eds), *Revolution Today: Socialist Register 1989*, The Merlin Press, London, 1989, pp. 185–211.
'La nostra morale', *Teoria Politica* (Milan), Vol. V, Nos 2–3, 1989, pp. 261–292.

1990
'Essence and Appearance: Aspects of Fetishism in Marx's *Capital*', in Bob Jessop with Charlie Malcolm Brown (eds), *Karl Marx's Social and Political Thought. Critical Assessments*, Routledge, London, 1990, Vol. 4, pp. 207–225.
'Lénine, Trotsky et le parti', in Norman Geras and Paul Le Blanc, 'Marxisme et Parti 1903–1917', *Cahiers d'Etude et de Recherche* (Amsterdam), No. 14, 1990, pp. 27–33.
'La représentation du prolétariat dans le marxisme classique', in Norman Geras and Paul Le Blanc, 'Marxisme et Parti 1903–1917', *Cahiers d'Etude et de Recherche* (Amsterdam), No. 14, 1990, pp. 35–43.
'Marxism and Moral Advocacy', in David McLellan and Sean Sayers (eds), *Socialism and Morality*, Macmillan, London, 1990, pp. 5–20.
'La nostra morale', in Norberto Bobbio e altri, *Sulla rivoluzione*, Franco Angeli, Milan, 1990, pp. 261–292.
Discourses of Extremity. Radical Ethics and Post Marxist Extravagances, Verso, London, 1990, 171 pp.
'Seven Types of Obloquy: Travesties of Marxism', in Ralph Miliband and Leo Panitch (eds), *The Retreat of the Intellectuals: Socialist Register 1990*, The Merlin Press, London, 1990, pp. 1–34.

1991
'Rosa Luxemburg', in Tom Bottomore (ed.), *A Dictionary of Marxist Thought*, Basil Blackwell, Oxford, 1983, pp. 293–294. (Second edition: 1991, pp. 327–329.)
'Fetishism', in Tom Bottomore (ed.), *A Dictionary of Marxist Thought*, Basil Blackwell, Oxford 1983, pp. 165–166. (Second edition: 1991, pp. 190–191.)
'Louis Althusser', in Tom Bottomore (ed.), *A Dictionary of Marxist Thought*, Basil Blackwell, Oxford, 1983, pp. 15–18. (Second edition: 1991, pp. 16–19.)
'Seven Types of Obloquy: Travesties of Marxism', *Graduate Faculty Philosophy Journal* (New School for Social Research, New York), Vol. 14, No. 1, 1991, pp. 77–115.
'"The Fruits of Labour" – Private Property and Moral Equality', in Michael Moran and Maurice Wright (eds), *The Market and the State: Studies in Interdependence*, Macmillan, London, 1991, pp. 59–80.
Review of Steven Lukes, *Moral Conflict and Politics*, *New Statesman and Society*, Vol. 4, No. 154, 7 June 1991, pp. 43–44.

1992

'Leon Trotsky: 1879–1940', in Robert Benewick and Philip Green (eds), *The Routledge Dictionary of Twentieth-Century Political Thinkers*, Routledge, London, 1992, pp. 221–224. (Second edition: 1998, pp. 242–245.)

'"De vruchten van de arbeid." Privé-eigendom en morele gelijkheid', *Vlaams Marxistisch Tijdschrift* (Brussels), Vol. 2, June 1992, pp. 69–91.

'Bringing Marx to Justice: An Addendum and Rejoinder', *New Left Review*, No. 195, September–October 1992, pp. 37–69.

'Democratie en de doelstellingen van het Marxisme', *Vlaams Marxistisch Tijdschrift* (Brussels), Vol. 4, December 1992, pp. 7–24.

1993

'Marxisme et approche éthique', *Quatrième Internationale* (Paris), No. 46, September–November 1993, pp. 73–84.

'Marxismo e approccio etico', *Bandiero Rossa* (Milan), No. 40, December 1993, pp. 30–35.

'Permanent Revolution', in William Outhwaite and Tom Bottomore (eds), *The Blackwell Dictionary of Twentieth-Century Social Thought*, Basil Blackwell, Oxford, 1993, pp. 456–458. (Second edition: Outhwaite, *The Blackwell Dictionary of Modern Social Thought*, 2003, pp. 469–471.)

'Trotskyism', in William Outhwaite and Tom Bottomore (eds.), *The Blackwell Dictionary of Twentieth-Century Social Thought*, Basil Blackwell, Oxford, 1993, pp. 677–678. (Second edition: Outhwaite, *The Blackwell Dictionary of Modern Social Thought*, 2003, pp. 702–703.)

'Leninism', in William Outhwaite and Tom Bottomore (eds), *The Blackwell Dictionary of Twentieth-Century Social Thought*, Basil Blackwell, Oxford, 1993, pp. 330–333. (Second edition: Outhwaite, *The Blackwell Dictionary of Modern Social Thought*, 2003, pp. 343–346.)

1994

'Democracy and the Ends of Marxism', in Geraint Parry and Michael Moran (eds), *Democracy and Democratization*, Routledge, London, 1994, pp. 69–87.

'Democracy and the Ends of Marxism', *New Left Review*, No. 203, January–February 1994, pp. 92–106.

'La democracia y los fines del marxismo', *Viento Sur* (Madrid), No. 14, March–April 1994, pp. 83–95.

'That Most Complex Being', in Patrick Dunleavy and Jeffrey Stanyer (eds), *Contemporary Political Studies 1994*, UK Political Studies Association, Belfast, 1994, Vol. 2, pp. 714–729.

'Richard Rorty and the Righteous', in Patrick Dunleavy and Jeffrey Stanyer (eds), *Contemporary Political Studies 1994*, UK Political Studies Association, Belfast, 1994, Vol. 2, pp. 651–662. (Abbreviated version.)

1995

'Marxisme en proletarische zelfbevrijding', *De Internationale* (Amsterdam and Brussels), No. 54, Summer 1995, pp. 16–19.

'Democracy and the Ends of Marxism', *Society and Change* (Calcutta), Vol. X, Nos 1 & 2, April–September 1995, pp. 13–31.

'Richard Rorty and the Righteous Among the Nations', *Journal of Applied Philosophy*, Vol. 12, No. 2, 1995, pp. 151–173.

Solidarity in the Conversation of Humankind: The Ungroundable Liberalism of Richard Rorty, Verso, London, 1995, 151 pp.

'Language, Truth and Justice', *New Left Review*, No. 209, January–February 1995, pp. 110–135.

'Human Nature and Progress', *New Left Review*, No. 213, September–October 1995, pp. 151–160.

1996

Rosa Luxemburg: Vorkämpferin für einen emanzipatorischen Sozialismus, ISP Verlag, Cologne, 1996, 190 pp.

'Socialist Hope in the Shadow of Catastrophe', in Leo Panitch (ed.), *Are There Alternatives? Socialist Register 1996*, Merlin Press, London, 1996, pp. 239–263.

'Progress Without Foundations?', *Res Publica*, Vol. 2, No. 2, 1996, pp. 115–128.

1997

Bengali translation of 'Essence and Appearance: Aspects of Fetishism in Marx's *Capital*', in Hasanuzzaman Chowdhury (translator), *Somaj Somikkha (Studies in Social Relations)*, Bangla Academy, Dhaka (Bangladesh) 1997, pp. 31–49.

'La esperanza socialista al borde del abismo', *Viento Sur* (Madrid), No. 33, July 1997, pp. 82–103.

'Marxists before the Holocaust', *New Left Review*, No. 224, July–August 1997, pp. 19–38.

'Marxists before the Holocaust', *MANCEPT Working Paper Series* (Manchester Centre for Political Thought, Department of Government, University of Manchester), Manchester 1997, 33 pp.

Ashes '97: Two Views from the Boundary, Baseline Books, Tisbury, 1997, 163 pp. (Co-authored with Ian Holliday.)

1998

'Post-Marxism?', in Stuart Sim (ed.), *Post-Marxism: A Reader*, Edinburgh University Press, Edinburgh, 1998, pp. 45–55. (Excerpt)

'Leon Trotsky: 1879–1940', in Robert Benewick and Philip Green (eds), *The Routledge Dictionary of Twentieth-Century Political Thinkers*, Routledge, London, 1992, pp. 221–224. (Second edition: 1998, pp. 242–245.)

'La speranza socialista all'ombra della catastrofe', *Lo Straniero* (Rome), No. 4, Autumn 1998, pp. 154–175.

'Marxists before the Holocaust: Trotsky, Deutscher, Mandel', Japanese translation in 'Ernest Mandel: The Man and His Thought', special number of *Trotsky Studies* (Tokyo), Nos 25–26, Spring 1998, pp. 224–261.

'Holocaust'tan Önce Marksistler: Troçki, Deutscher, Mandel', in Gilbert Achcar (ed.), *Ernest Mandel'in Marksizmi*, Yazin Yayincilik, Istanbul, 1998, pp. 209–236.

'Richard Rorty: 1931–', in Robert Benewick and Philip Green (eds), *The Routledge Dictionary of Twentieth-Century Political Thinkers*, Second Edition, Routledge, London, 1998, pp. 214–216.

The Contract of Mutual Indifference: Political Philosophy after the Holocaust, Verso, London, 1998 (paperback edition, Verso, 1999), 181 pp.

1999

'The Controversy About Marx and Justice', in Bob Jessop with Russell Wheatley (eds), *Karl Marx's Social and Political Thought. Critical Assessments – Second Series*, Routledge, London, 1999, Vol. 8, pp. 592–633.

'Les marxistes face à l'Holocauste: Trotsky, Deutscher, Mandel', French translation in Gilbert Achcar (ed.), *Le marxisme d'Ernest Mandel*, Presses Universitaires de France, Paris, 1999, pp. 171–193.

'Marxists Before the Holocaust: Trotsky, Deutscher, Mandel', in Gilbert Achcar (ed.), *The Legacy of Ernest Mandel*, Verso, London, 1999, pp. 191–213.

'A Different Kind of Contract', in Iain MacKenzie and Shane O'Neill (eds), *Reconstituting Social Criticism: Political Morality in an Age of Scepticism*, Macmillan, London, 1999, pp. 137–149. (Excerpt)

'The View from Everywhere', *Review of International Studies*, Vol. 25, No. 1, January 1999, pp. 157–163.

'Old Trafford 1998', *The Journal of the Cricket Society*, Vol. 19, No. 2, Spring 1999, pp. 7–15. (Co-authored with Ian Holliday.)

'Minimum Utopia: Ten Theses', in Leo Panitch and Colin Leys (eds) *Necessary and Unnecessary Utopias: Socialist Register 2000*, Merlin Press, London, 1999, pp. 41–52.

2000

'Four Assumptions About Human Nature', in Norman Geras and Robert Wokler (eds), *The Enlightenment and Modernity*, Macmillan, London, 2000, pp. 135–160.

'Léon Trotski', in Élie Barnavi and Saul Friedländer (eds), *Les Juifs et le XXe Siècle*, Calmann-Lévy, Paris, 2000, pp. 707–712.

'Life Was Beautiful Even There', *Imprints*, Vol. 5, No. 1, Summer 2000, pp. 23–37.

2001

'Barbarzynstwo i upadek kapitalizmu w mysli Rozy Luksemburg', *Rewolucja* (Warsaw), No. 1, 2001, pp. 158–185.

'La democracia y los fines del marxismo', in Juan Trías and Manuel Monereo (eds), *Rosa Luxemburg: Actualidad y clasicismo*, El Viejo Topo, Spain, 2001, pp. 141–165.

'Progress without Foundations?', in Matthew Festenstein and Simon Thompson (eds), *Richard Rorty: Critical Dialogues*, Polity, Cambridge, 2001, pp. 158–170.

2002

Marx ve Insan Dogasi: Bir Efsanenin Reddi, Birikim Yayinlari, Istanbul, 2002, 131 pp.

'That Most Complex Being', in Alan Malachowski (ed.), *Richard Rorty*, Cambridge University Press, Cambridge, 2002, Volume 3, pp. 215–231.

'The True Wilkomirski', *Res Publica*, Vol. 8, No. 2, 2002, pp. 111–122.

'The Ideal of Multivious Care (Utopia and Inequality)', *Rethinking Marxism*, Vol. 14, No. 1, Spring 2002, pp. 1–7.

Men of Waugh: Ashes 2001, Norman Geras, Manchester, 2002, 122 pp.

'Marxism, the Holocaust and September 11: An Interview with Norman Geras', *Imprints*, Vol. 6, No. 3, 2002–3, pp. 194–214.

2003

'Permanent Revolution', in William Outhwaite and Tom Bottomore (eds), *The Blackwell Dictionary of Twentieth-Century Social Thought*, Basil Blackwell, Oxford, 1993, pp. 456–458. (Second edition: Outhwaite, *The Blackwell Dictionary of Modern Social Thought*, 2003, pp. 469–471.)

'Trotskyism', in William Outhwaite and Tom Bottomore (eds), *The Blackwell Dictionary of Twentieth-Century Social Thought*, Basil Blackwell, Oxford 1993, pp. 677–678. (Second edition: Outhwaite, *The Blackwell Dictionary of Modern Social Thought*, 2003, pp. 702–703.)

'Leninism', in William Outhwaite and Tom Bottomore (eds), *The Blackwell Dictionary of Twentieth-Century Social Thought*, Basil Blackwell, Oxford, 1993, pp. 330–333. (Second edition: Outhwaite, *The Blackwell Dictionary of Modern Social Thought*, 2003, pp. 343–346.)

'Marxisten angesichts des Holocaust: Trotzki, Deutscher, Mandel', in Gilbert Achcar (ed.), *Gerechtigkeit und Solidarität: Ernest Mandels Beitrag zum Marxismus*, ISP, Cologne, 2003, pp. 199–223.

'In a Class of Its Own?', in Eve Garrard and Geoffrey Scarre (eds), *Moral Philosophy and the Holocaust*, Ashgate, Aldershot, 2003, pp. 25–55.

'Redemptive and Other Meanings: Roman Polanski's *The Pianist*', *Imprints*, Vol. 7, No. 1, 2003, pp. 54–63.

2004

'How Free?', *The European Legacy*, Vol. 9, No. 5, October 2004, pp. 619–627.

2005

'Pages from a Daily Journal of Argument', in Thomas Cushman (ed.), *A Matter of Principle: Humanitarian Arguments for War in Iraq*, University of California Press, Berkeley and Los Angeles, 2005, pp. 191–206.

'The Reductions of the Left', *Dissent*, Winter 2005, pp. 55–60.

'Genocide and Crimes against Humanity', in John K. Roth (ed.), *Genocide and Human Rights: A Philosophical Guide*, Palgrave Macmillan, New York and Basingstoke, 2005, pp. 167–180.

'Just Association', *The Philosophers' Magazine*, Issue 32, 4th quarter 2005, pp. 55–58.

'Crimes Against Humanity: A Normative Account by Larry May' (review article), *Democratiya 3*, Winter 2005. Online publication.

'The Euston Manifesto' (principal author – with input from Damian Counsell, Alan Johnson and Shalom Lappin). Online publication: see http://eustonmanifesto.org/the-euston-manifesto/ and http://normblog.typepad.com/normblog/2006/04/the_euston_mani.html

2007

'Enforcing Human Rights', *Dissent*, Winter 2007, pp. 130–135. (Abbreviated version.)

'Beyond Human Nature', *Dissent*, Fall 2007, pp. 102–105.

2008

'The True Wilkomirski', *Contemporary Literary Criticism*, Vol. 252, 2008, pp. 210–216.

'Social Hope and State Lawlessness', *Critical Horizons*, Issue 1, 2008, pp. 90–98.

2009
Chinese translation of excerpt of 'The Controversy About Marx and Justice', *Journal of Marxism and Reality* (Beijing), No. 6, 2009, pp. 11–20.
'Games and Meanings', in Stephen de Wijze, Matthew H. Kramer and Ian Carter (eds), *Hillel Steiner and the Anatomy of Justice: Themes and Challenges*, New York and Abingdon, 2009, pp. 185–200.

2011
Crimes against humanity: Birth of a concept, Manchester University Press, Manchester, 2011, 162pp.
'My Australia'. Online publication: see http://normblog.typepad.com/normblog/2011/07/my-australia.html

2012
'Responses', in Stephen de Wijze and Eve Garrard (eds), *Thinking towards humanity: themes from Norman Geras*, Manchester University Press, Manchester, 2012, pp. 256–279.
'What Does It Mean to Be a Marxist?' in Matthew Johnson (ed.), *The Legacy of Marxism: Contemporary Challenges, Conflicts, and Developments*, Continuum, London and New York, 2012, pp. 13–23.
'A Convenient Alibi for the Trendy Left', *The Jewish Chronicle*, 17 August 2012, p. 26. (Abbreviated version.)
'Israel som alibi för antisemitism', *Nyhetsbrev* (Stockholm), October 2012, pp. 8–10. (Swedish translation of abbreviated version.)

2013
'Staying Home: G.A. Cohen and the Motivational Basis of Socialism', *Contemporary Politics*, Vol. 19, No. 2, June 2013, pp. 234–246.
'Alibi Antisemitism', *Fathom*, Issue 2, Spring 2013, pp. 17–24.
'Marx's Economy and Beyond' (Co-authored with Mark Harvey). Online publication: see http://normblog.typepad.com/files/meabpdf.pdf

Index